BRITAIN, FRANCE, AND THE NEW AFRICAN STATES

A Study of Post Independence Relationships

1960-1985

Charles O. Chikeka

Studies in African Economic and Social Development
Volume 3

The Edwin Mellen Press
Lewiston/Queenston/Lampeter

Library of Congress Cataloging-in-Publication Data

Chikeka, Charles Ohiri, 1931-
    Britain, France, and the new African states : a study of post
independence relationships, 1960-1985 / by Charles Chikeka.
        p.   cm. -- (Studies in African economic and social development
; vol. 3)
    Includes bibliographical references.
    ISBN 0-88946-516-9
    1. Africa--Foreign economic relations--Great Britain. 2. Great
Britain--Foreign economic relations--Africa. 3. Africa--Foreign
economic relations--France. 4. France-- Foreign economic relations-
-Africa. 5. Africa--Foreign relations--Great Britain. 6. Great
Britain--Foreign relations--Africa. 7. Africa--Foreign relations-
-France. 8. France--Foreign relations--Africa. 9. Africa-
-Dependency on foreign countries. I. Title. II. Series: Studies
in African economic and social development ; v. 3.
HF1611.Z4G73   1989
337.6041--dc20
                                                               89-13073
                                                                 CIP

This is volume 3 in the continuing series
Studies in African Economic and Social Development
Volume 3 ISBN 0-88946-516-9
SAESD Series ISBN 0-88946-514-2

A CIP catalog record for this book
is available from the British Library.

The Edwin Mellen Press   The Edwin Mellen Press
        Box 450   Box 67
Lewiston, New York   Queenston, Ontario
    USA 14092   CANADA L0S 1L0

                  The Edwin Mellen Press, Ltd.
                    Lampeter, Dyfed, Wales
                  UNITED KINGDOM SA48 7DY

              Printed in the United States of America

To Enyinna, and Chiedozi

CONTENTS

ACKNOWLEDGEMENT

For the inspiration, encouragement, and assistance that have contributed so much to this book the author's gratitude runs deep to the Morgan State University Faculty Research Committee whose financial support enabled this researcher to travel abroad for data gathering and who covered his typing expenses.

PREFACE

This study focuses mainly on the post-independence relationships between two former European imperial powers – Britain and France – and the new African states. There is probably no other topic more frequently or more fiercely debated in the literature on Africa than one involving the post-colonial ties between the former colonizers and their former African dependencies. The debate has generally involved those elements who support close ties between the former metropolitan powers and the new states and those who advocate the severance of the umbilical cord between the former colonizers and their former colonies.

When Britain and France relinquished political control by granting independence to the new African states in the late fifties and early sixties, they traded positions of political power with positions of influence. Institutions and traditions which were established during the colonial days have continued after the former dependencies achieved political independence. Thus, the patterns of trade, the flow of aid and capital investments established in colonial times have not been altered very drastically.

This study covers two decades of post-colonial relationships and demonstrates elements of continuity and change. These relationships have been characterized by increased economic, financial, and cultural dependence of African states on their former colonizers. Thus, Britain and France succeeded in converting their African colonial empires into a commonwealth and a community respectively. Both powers claimed that the old relationships of dominance had been replaced by special relationships of partnership or interdependence. Nevertheless, of the two ex – imperial powers, France has maintained very close ties with Francophone states and has very frequently been criticized by the ex – British dependencies of being neo-colonialist. These critics question the blending of African cultural nationalism with *La Mission Civilisatrice* of France.

The main thrust of this book is an objective examination, evaluation, and analysis of these complex post – colonial relationships within the 1960-1985 period. The author tries to explain what forms these relationships have taken; and what factors or forces have influenced or have conditioned them, such as the impact of colonial heritage and the role of the new elite groups who now make policies for their states. In the examination of these post-independence relationships this research concentrates on six vital areas; namely, a) trade, b) investments, c) foreign aid, d) cultural ties, e) diplomatic and political relations, and f) security arrangements. Each of these areas constitutes a chapter of this book. Finally, Chapter 8 contains the final analysis, observations and recommendations as to how African states' dependence on European powers could be reduced.

CHAPTER 1

INTRODUCTION

The subject of this study is the post-independence relationships between two European ex-imperial powers – Britain and France – and the new African states. These post-colonial relationships have generated heated discussion among African nationalists, statesmen, scholars and researchers. The debate has generally involved those elements who support close ties between the former metropolitan powers and their former dependencies and those who advocate the severance of the umbilical cord between the former colonizers and the new states.

Terms such as community, association, partnership, cooperative ventures, commonwealth, neo-colonialism, interdependence, and dominance-dependence have been used by various researchers and scholars in recent years to characterize these post-independence relationships between European powers and the new African states. However, while imperialists and their sympathizers have preferred to use such terms as association, commonwealth, community, interdependence, and partnership to explain these complex post-colonial relationships, African nationalist and socialist writers have used terms such as dominance, dependence, and neo-colonialism to characterize these relationships. Thus, while the former group has stressed the mutual benefits for all the parties involved in these relationships, the latter group has emphasized the fact that these continued ties between the former colonial masters and the new states have simply resulted in greater dependence and eventually greater exploitation of these new states by the former colonizers.

Britain and France traded positions of political power with positions of influence when they relinquished political control by granting independence to the new states in the late fifties and early sixties. Institutions and traditions which were established during the colonial days have continued after the former colonies achieved political independence. Thus, the patterns of trade, the flow of aid, and investments established during colonial times have not altered very drastically. It is quite obvious, however, that the leaders of Anglophone and Francophone Africa are making concerted efforts to reduce or lessen their dependence on the former colonial powers through the process of diversification of contacts within the world community at large.

The main thrust of this study is an objective examination, evaluation, and analysis of these complex relationships between European powers and the new African states within the 1960-1985 period. An attempt is made to explain what forms these relationships have taken; and what factors or forces have influenced or have conditioned them, such as the impact of colonial heritage and the role of the new African elite groups who succeeded the colonial authorities.

In the examination of these post-independence relationships this researcher focuses on six vital areas; namely, (a) trade, (b) investments, (c) foreign aid (economic and technical), (d) cultural ties, (e) diplomatic and political ties, and (f) security arrangements (undertakings). Each of these areas forms a chapter of this book.

The Imperial Past

In order to have a clearer understanding of the post-independence relationships between these two European powers and the new African states, one has to look into the remote past for answers. Thus, a brief account of the imperial past would shed some light on this discussion. It is the contention of this author that the colonial situation which included (a) the style of colonial policy adopted by the metropolitan power, and (b) the socialization and attitudes of the African elite groups who succeeded the colonial powers as policymakers, must be recognized as among the leading factors which influenced these post-independence relationships.

The period 1880-1914 witnessed what many historians have described as the classical or the golden age of European imperialism. This period was characterized by the European scramble to partition Africa. Britain and France were the leading scramblers in this competition for colonial empires on the African continent. By 1914 almost all of the continent of Africa had been carved up into colonies by Britain, Belgium, France, Germany, Portugal and Spain. However, Britain and France had the lion's share.

In the context of this discussion, imperialism is defined simply as the domination and exploitation of the weak states by the more powerful ones. One writer described it as a complex of economic, political and military relations by which the less economically developed lands are subjected to the more economically developed states. Imperialism, he notes, remains the best word for the general system of unequal world economic relations.[1] E. M. Winslow defines imperialism as an economic phenomenon, implying certain relationships in the international division of labor in trade and the movement of capital.[2]

David S. Landes notes that imperialism arises whenever there is an imbalance of power between two social groups in which the stronger one tries to exploit the weaker.[3]

In his work *Economics and Empire 1830-1914*, D. K. Fieldhouse advanced an explanation of imperialism. He theorized that imperialism was the consequence of instability generated on the frontiers of empire by advancing parties of traders, missionaries, and other Europeans coming into contact with indigenous societies. He claimed, therefore, that Europe was pulled into imperialism by the magnetic force of the periphery.[4]

The rights and wrongs, merits and demerits of imperialism are subjects which have generally aroused heated discussions between critics and defenders of the system. European imperialists and their sympathizers have always justified their dominance and exploitation of the non-European peoples largely through ideologies which clearly asserted the superiority of the colonizer and the inferiority of the colonial subject.[5] Europeans considered themselves as leaders of civilization and as pioneers of industry and progress. They justified imperial expansion as a fulfillment of the divine mission of the "superior" races right to rule the "inferior" peoples more or less permanently.[6] The French referred to this simply as their civilizing mission.[7]

Imperial expansion in all its forms, according to John Gallagher and Ronald Robinson, seemed not only natural and necessary, but inevitable; it was preordained and irreproachably right; it was simply the spontaneous expression of an inherently dynamic society in search of maximum opportunity.[8] According to J. F. A. Ajayi, Europeans believed that they were the harbingers of a new civilization and that they were destined to leave their mark on the physical and mental nature of man in Africa.[9] He argued that the promoters of the colonial enterprise saw the establishment of colonial rule as the beginning of a long process of educating Africans in the technologies of the new civilization.[10] This meant, therefore, a very prolonged process of tutelage to be measured in centuries.[11]

European businessmen, financiers, investors, merchants, manufacturers, missionaries, philanthropists, and statesmen were enthusiastic supporters of their countries' policies for the exploitation of other lands. These groups, according to Baumgart, were the pillars of the imperialist and colonial movement.[12] In Britain and France, imperialist associations flourished and pressured their governments to become actively involved in the race for colonial acquisitions.[13]

These European imperialists, according to William Clark, were really certain that they knew what was right not only for themselves but for others.[14] For example, the British were convinced their mission was to bring the colonial peoples forward into the mainstream of Western political thought and by education to prepare them for self-government.[15] By contrast, the French practiced assimilation and hoped to make Africans Frenchmen. Their self-confidence led them to believe that what they were doing was also right.[16]

The justification of the colonial system which the defenders presented to the world, and even to themselves, was that it was applied to infant peoples incapable and without personality.[17] It was generally believed by Europeans that all African cultural manifestations were puerile and barbaric.[18]

Technological advances or innovations of the eighteenth and nineteenth centuries did enhance the cause of imperial expansion in Africa and indeed stimulated that process. European states exploited their technological and military superiority to exercise economic and political control over unwilling Africans all over the continent. Improved communications and transportation systems such as railways, roads, steamship lines, and sub-marine telegraph cables led to the consolidation of economic and political exploitation of the African continent. Thus, Daniel R. Headrick has emphasized the part played by the technological revolution in European imperial drive overseas. He argued quite persuasively that the real triumph of European conquest of the so-called backward areas was simply a triumph of technology, not ideology.[19] He noted that European technology has transformed the world more than any leader, religion, revolution, or war could have done.[20] According to Headrick, these technological developments proved very useful to the imperialists in Africa. They made imperialism so cheap that it reached the threshold of acceptance among the peoples and governments of Europe and led nations to become empires.[21] In other words, these technological innovations helped to lower the cost in both financial and human terms of penetrating, conquering, and exploiting new territories.[22]

Winfried Baumgart expressed a similar opinion when he pointed out that the development of steam navigation was indeed responsible for revolutionizing the structure of overseas trade and that it drew the continents closer together.[23]

Military superiority on the part of European powers enhanced their expansionist ambitions. Superiority in terms of weapons systems as well as bureaucratic organization of the armies were important determinants of imperial expansion.

The disparity of fire power between the European intruders and the African defenders during the period of the new imperialism was very wide. Bows and arrows and *assegai*[24] were no match for rifles, or later, machine guns. Thus, it has been observed that the gap or differential in military power between the Africans and Europeans would never again be so great as it was between about 1880 and the 1920s.[25] Rifles, and later automatic rifles, were few indeed under African control.[26] Fieldhouse asserted that around 1880 there was a profound disequilibrium between Europe and most parts of the less-developed world. Never had one continent possessed so immense a power advantage over the others or been in such close contact with them.[27] The firepower of the imperialist forces made African-European confrontations lopsided, turning battles into massacres or routs, as Headrick explained.[28] Quite often the European forces faced indigenous armies larger than the invading forces, nevertheless, the European firepower made the difference in terms of outcomes. For example, in 1873-74, General Wolseley defeated the powerful Ashanti with a force of 6,500 men armed with rifles, gatling guns, and 7-pounder field artillery.[29] Similarly, B. Olantunji Oloruntimehin described how a French force of 1,400 men armed with Gras-Kropatcheks routed the army of the Senegalese ruler, Mahmadon Lamine, whose forces were simply armed with spears, dane guns, and poisoned arrows.[30]

It would be very misleading indeed to assume that the imperialist invaders always easily overcame African resistance through superior firepower. There were instances when African countries held back the imperialist invaders for many years. The case of Samori Touré, a Mandinka warrior who harassed the French troops in Western Sudan until his capture and exile in 1898, is a good example to illustrate this point. French officers who fought against this Mandinka warrior were greatly impressed by his abilities. One of them described him as an outstanding leader of men, possessing audacity, energy, the ability to follow up an advantage and plan an advance, and above all an irrepressible tenacity which could not be destroyed.[31] Another case which involved intense African resistance to imperialist pressures was Ethiopia. In 1896, Emperor Menelik's army routed an Italian army of 17,000 men which tried to conquer Ethiopia at the Battle of Adowa. These two examples of African resistance demonstrate that whenever Africans obtained modern weapons, they were able to match their foes in terms of tactics, strategy, and discipline.

The European states deliberately undermined African states' efforts to defend themselves by restricting the supply of weapons and ammunitions to Africans. They recognized the fact that the import of guns into Africa would affect pacification efforts on the continent.[32]

To stem the flow of arms, the Brussels Treaty of 1890[33] prohibited the sale of breechloaders to Africans between the twentieth parallel North and the twenty-second parallel South.

While superior technological and military power enabled the European states to dominate and exploit the African continent, the primary motives advanced by writers to explain this phenomenon included economic, cultural, political, and humanitarian considerations. The most important motive for imperial expansion, however, was economic. Critics such as J. A. Hobson and Karl Marx generally emphasized economic motives: the need for raw materials, secure markets, or investment opportunities.[34] Thus, European states made their colonial empires economically managed trading areas, such as through the institution of the franc and sterling zones in Africa by the French and the British, respectively.[35] The economics of colonialism in practice tied the countries of Africa more closely to the international system in general and the metropolitan in particular.[36]

As Sheldon explained, the colonial situation gave the metropole the power to monopolize economic policy and impose a system of enforced bilateralism. This meant, therefore, that trade was generally oriented toward the metropole, that nationals of the metropolitan power controlled the most important sectors of the colonial export economy and that colonial development policies reflected the interest of metropolitan banks, import-export companies, mining companies, and shipping firms.[37] These imperial nations asserted their right to exclude others from their turf and colonize areas appropriately on the map. "Thus the colonial system provided the metropole with outlets for its manufactured goods, raw materials for its industries, and tropical products for metropolitan consumers on terms which were advantageous to the colonizers."[38]

In areas of Africa with a large concentration of white settlers such as Algeria, the Rhodesias, and Kenya, economic exploitation was most pronounced. These white settlers regarded the African population as sources of cheap labor. During the colonial era the white settler population was primarily concerned with acquiring land and access to cheap labor in these territories.

According to Sheldon Gellar, "The subordinate position of Africans within the colonial economic system was maintained by discouraging African competitors in the modern capitalist sectors of the colonial economy."[39] Thus, European import-export companies and banks thwarted the development of a modern African entrepreneurial class in places like Kenya and Senegal by withholding credit to African traders and middlemen.[40]

European firms and the colonial administration further discouraged African competition in the modern sectors of the economy by using non-indigenous groups as middlemen (Syrians, Lebanese, Indians): for example, the Lebanese in West Africa and the Asians in East Africa.[41]

Colonial economic policies also made it difficult for Africans to compete with Europeans in agriculture. Thus, the British in Kenya did not permit African farmers to grow coffee and other cash crops produced by the white settlers, while the French administration in the Ivory Coast clearly discriminated against African cocoa producers by offering higher prices to French planters.[42]

However, in many West African territories and in Uganda, where there were very few European settlers, Africans enjoyed greater economic opportunities to participate in the colonial economy, although they were increasingly vulnerable to fluctuating world market conditions. They managed to produce cocoa, coffee, cotton, groundnuts (peanuts), and palm produce for European markets.

Many critics of the imperial system have indicated that a principal purpose of European colonialism was the material enrichment of the European colonizers, and that the welfare of the indigenous people was often irrelevant, or at best, secondary to the colonizers' aspirations and needs.[43] A leading British empire builder, Lord Lugard, justified colonialism in terms of a dual mandate. He explained:

> Civilized nations have at least recognized that, while on the one hand the abounding wealth of the tropical regions of the earth must be developed and used for the benefit of mankind, on the other hand an obligation rests on the controlling power

not only to safeguard the material rights of the natives, but to promote their moral and educational progress.[44]

Critics have questioned the genuineness or sincerity of the dual mandate since it was self-imposed and unilateral on the part of the colonizers whose main desires, according to Ibingira, were to make the colonies viable and profitable.[45]

In his critique of imperialism, Hobson[46] recognized the economic crises of the industrial states, which included overproduction, the decline of the rate of profit in capital investments in the home market, and unemployment. Thus, there was the need for the export of capital which could no longer find any profitable investment in the home market. As a consequence, the capital investor demanded not only government protection, but also the extension of political control over those areas where he invested his capital, simply to ensure its safety as the home market. Cairncross and Baumgart support this contention. Both writers confirmed that the rate of profit was more favorable in overseas investments than in home investments.[47] Thus, the metropolitan investors found it extremely lucrative to invest in the colonies.

Like their British couterparts, many French imperialists recognized the importance of acquiring colonies for the export of French capital. In his famous speech in the Chamber on July 28, 1885, Jules Ferry stated:

For wealthy countries colonies are places where capital can be invested on the most favorable terms.[48]

Addressing himself on the connection between capital export and colonial acquisiton, Pierre Paul Leroy-Beaulieu expressed a similar view. He noted that it was more advantageous to export capital to one's own colonies than to totally foreign countries.[49]

In their dealings with the non-European peoples of the world, these imperialists exhibited a sense of superiority and self-righteousness. They claimed that they were committed to lead the so-called backward races to civilization. Thus, the expression "the white man's burden" was frequently used to explain this humanitarian concern.

The European states placed heavy emphasis on the humanitarian motive as the primary drive that led to their presence in Africa. These Europeans claimed that they went to Africa to combat ignorance, disease, superstition, barbarism and savagery, and misery.[50] Colin Morris explained how returned missionaries, explorers, and administrators thrilled audiences in European capitals with their horrendous tales of the cruelty and misery they had encountered during their adventures (stay) and how these "worthy citizens" thanked God that their motherland was extending to these heathens the blessings of civilization and commerce.[51]

It is common knowledge that from early times Christian missionaries, doctors, nurses, and educators moved into the African interior and have ever since remained a powerful force and instrument for the spread of European culture throughout Africa and an important link between the colonial powers and their subjects.[52] In general, these missionary groups viewed colonial expansion simply as an engine of progress, and in many instances, the flag followed the Cross. The European missionaries usually sought and welcomed the protection offered by their home governments for themselves as well as for their converts. Many of them supported and identified with the policies of their home governments.

Political considerations such as prestige, national pride, and strategic interests were among the most compelling reasons for the acquisition of colonial empires overseas.

The desire for national pride and strategic interests had their effects in an era when nation states were judged by the size of their overseas dependencies.[53] To have overseas possessions was then considered the attainment of great power status, since these territories were sources of wealth and power for the possessors. The British and French policymakers were proud of the fact that most of the world was theirs and that they were certain they knew what was right not only for themselves but for others.[54] Britain was sure that her mission was to bring colonial peoples forward into the mainstream of Western political thought and, by education, to prepare them for self-government in the remote future.[55] The French, by contrast, practiced assimilation, which emphasized making Africans French. They too believed, in their self-confidence, that what they were doing was right.[56] This feeling of pride and superiority was indeed a very important psychological part of the imperial past. Even today, after the demise or dismantling of colonial empires overseas, there are still groups in both countries which cherish the glories of that past era.

African nationalism, which swept all over the African continent in the postwar period, shook the self-confidence of these two imperial powers. Britain, for example, became less certain of what her mission was or, to put it differently, she began to adjust to the new reality. She adopted political measures which permitted a rapid decolonization process. Like Britain, France adjusted to the new situation with wounded pride.

Strategic interests played an important part in the race for colonies. The obsession with national security influenced European drive for colonial acquisitions. Areas of strategic importance such as the Suez Canal region and the Cape in South Africa, to name only two, were considered crucial to control the sea lanes and protect markets overseas. Thus, the Suez Canal was viewed by British naval planners as the spinal cord of the empire, necessary for the control of the sea routes to India and other British possessions east of Suez. In their competition to control strategic regions, European states managed to bring large portions of the world under their control. They hoisted their flags around the world's oceans, and established bases and protectorates in many places on the grounds of strategic necessity.[57]

The Colonial Heritage

The colonial situation influenced quite considerably the post-independence relationships between Britain and France and their former African dependencies. The term "colonial situation" includes the colonizer's style of colonial administration and the socialization as well as the attitudes of the African elite groups.

Both Britain and France developed systems of colonial administration in Africa that differed quite considerably in their theoretical definitions which, as Robert July pointed out, were not always so easily distinguishable in practice.[58] There were differences in style, but the outcome was generally the same – European dominance and African subjugation. While the French placed heavy emphasis on assimilation and paternalism, the British adopted a policy of indirect rule in their colonial possessions. The policy of assimilation as practiced by the French colonial authorities meant that Africans could be made to become French in all respects. Those Africans who became assimilated enjoyed the rights and privileges of French citizens,[59] such as exercising voting rights, freedom to participate in party and union activities, as well as the right to criticize the colonial administration. Once they had become assimilated, no avenue of advancement was closed to them.[60] They could enter any of the professions or become senior civil servants. Such persons usually were recognized by French society as French citizens. The way the French treated their educated native Africans aroused the bitter envy of their counterparts in British colonies.[61]

The French assimilationist stance can be traced as far back as 1792 when a revolutionary decree in France declared that all men, without distinction of color, domiciled in the French colonies were French citizens and enjoyed all the rights guaranteed by the Constitution. The French assumed that the people of their colonies could become Frenchmen and therefore adopted policies to integrate them into a single Greater France revolving about Paris.[62] French policy of assimilation meant that all education had to be in French, since no other access to civilization was preferred. The French generally despised African institutions, including African languages.

The year 1848 was indeed a landmark in the relationship between France and Africa. In that year, French citizenship was formally granted to Africans[63] and, very shortly thereafter, they were welcomed in French parliaments and governments as deputies and ministers. Thus, French possessions in Africa were not referred to as "French colonies" but simply as "Overseas France". French colonial administration was more direct and centralized than its British counterpart.[64] The end result was that French culture managed to penetrate deeply wherever France has ruled – the outcome of her assimilationist policies in the colonies. The assumption which governed the attitude of French policymakers towards the Africans was that French civilization was essentially superior and needed only to be presented to the intelligent African for him to adopt it. Britain's principle of colonial administration which allowed the preservation and development of indigenous institutions was sharply criticized by the French who regarded it as nothing but a disguised form of "color-bar," that is, a means of perpetuating the gulf between the dominant European and the subject native.[65] The French were convinced that native institutions were doomed to disappear; hence, they embarked on a policy which called for the grooming of a privileged elite group – the *évolué* – who eventually would serve as a bridge linking the masses and the colonizers.[66]

France's policies of assimilation and paternalism in her African colonies led to their complete dependence on her for their survival. The French Parliament provided funds in colonial times to balance the budgets of colonial territories and provide social services. France continued to play this role after these former colonies had attained their political independence, thus deepening their dependence on the former metropole for support and even their survival. Thus, relationships which were established during the colonial era have contributed greatly to shaping or determining the post-independence relationships between France and Francophone Africa.

Britain's style of colonial administration in Africa differed very remarkably from the French system. Nevertheless, the British colonial administrators, like their French counterparts, shared almost without exception two prevailing assumptions; namely, that the colonized peoples were not capable of governing themselves and that the relationship between the interests of the colonized and the colonizer was basically reciprocal rather than an exploitative one.[67] The British colonial policy was prepared by its previous experience in the remote past. E. W. Evans asserted that it was based on precedent rather than on principle.[68] Britain's experiences in North America and elsewhere affected her thinking or attitude towards colonies. After the loss of her North American colonies, Britain began to look at colonies as apples which usually fall down when they get ripe. There was a realization on the part of British policymakers that Britain would not stay in the colonies forever. There comes a moment when the mother country and the colonies will have to end the relationship. With this attitude in mind, the British claimed they were committed to guiding dependent peoples step by step to independence. "Our goal in the administration of the dependencies," declared Leopold Amery, Under-Secretary of State for the Colonies in 1920, "was to enable every part of the Empire to obtain, in the fullness of time, and when conditions made it possible, full power of controlling its own affairs and developing its own destinies."[69] This policy goal, according to E. A. Brett, meant that the period of tutelage or guidance for the colonized peoples must stretch well beyond the foreseeable future.[70] Many British colonial administrators shared this view expressed by Leopold Amery in 1920, that the object of colonial administration was primarily educative.

To realize this policy objective, the British authorities, from early times, set up legislative assemblies in the colonies where African members had a limited opportunity to criticize and discuss proposals and policies of the colonial administration. As a consequence, the British colonial territories gained political experience of a kind which their French counterparts did not have until quite late in the 1950s. They gained practical experience in such matters as budgeting, trade and commerce, education, forestry, health, and transportation.

Some observers have generally noted that British colonial policy was empirical.[71] A British writer once observed, "...the British govern without benefit of theory. They claim a genius for empiricism. . .[and a] reluctance to conceive and much less define any end or ultimate goal."[72] According to this writer, British commitment to empiricism meant simply that decisions should be taken by those on the spot who have first-hand acquaintance with the facts.[73] Thomas Hodgkin elaborated when he explained that this policy was normally developed piecemeal in relation to specific situations or as a means of solving specific problems.[74] The empirical nature of Britain's colonial policies can be explained in terms of the manner in which the British handled the diverse political situations within the various African colonies. For example, it can be said that British colonial rule was a judicious mixture of the concepts of direct and indirect rule,[75] depending on the local situation. Thus, the British utilized the system of indirect rule in areas where traditional rulers operated from solid political foundations, while they ruled directly in Crown colonies or in decentralized societies.

Britain's fiscal policies in the colonies tended to foster or enhance the spirit of independence in British African possessions. Right from the outset of colonial administration, the British authorities insisted that all colonies balance their budgets. Britain justified the acquisition of a new colony largely on the basis of its economic return.[76] Thus, as Professor Wallerstein explained, British colonies were always self-financing, a fact which made it extremely difficult for the colonial administration to pay for basic public works and social services.[77] To run the colonies, Britain depended on funds raised by local taxation. Unlike France, she neither subsidized heavily nor allowed taxes to be overly burdensome, for fear of riots. In the long run, however, the British African dependencies learned from early times how to take good care of themselves by managing their meager resources. They were able to avoid relying too heavily on the metropolitan power for their survival. This was not the case of their counterparts in French territories, who relied very heavily on France for support. This dependence on France by former French colonies for their survival continued after they had achieved their political independence.

The African Elite

The attitudes and socialization of the African elite during the colonial period are important determining factors which shaped or influenced the post-independence relationships between these two ex-imperial powers and the new African states. The colonial policies of Britain and France led to the emergence of a new elite class in both Anglophone and Francophone Africa. The policy variations however, involved the colonial powers' attitudes towards education and missionary activity in general, and the opportunities provided for an African educated elite in the colonial administration. In the context of this discussion, the term "elite" refers to the Western-educated[78] groups, usually the products of colonial or metropolitan educational institutions, professional groups, bureaucrats, businessmen, and soldiers. These educated elements in the colonies, though very small, were vocal and well organized, particularly in the British areas. They wielded some influence toward the end of the colonial era as well as during the post-colonial period.

Both metropolitan powers utilized the services of African functionaries such as office clerks, court clerks, interpreters, postmasters, and administrative cadres. Nevertheless, opportunities for the educated Africans differed widely from one imperial system to the other. Thus, the sharp contrast between the two imperial systems can be said to lie in the extent to which the Westernized elements were brought within the cultural heritage of the metropolitan power. In this regard, one can say that the French were more successful at indoctrinating the Africans they educated in French ways of life and thought than their British counterparts.

French colonial administration aimed at creating a capable elite thoroughly groomed and indoctrinated in French culture. To attain this goal, France encouraged state aid to education in the colonies. Bright students were encouraged to pursue their education in such prestigious schools as Dakar Medical School, Lycée Faidherbe, the William Ponty Normal School, and the Lycée Van Vollenhoven. Others were admitted to French universities and technical schools. When they completed their course of study, the French authorities made provisions for their employment in the different branches of the colonial government. Thus, the French African elite developed a special emotional tie with France and with everything French. Paris, the metropolitan capital, became a second home to these assimilated gentlemen. They developed French manners and tastes. In the 1920s and early 1930s, for example, one Blaise Diagne,[79] a product of French assimilation, became the chief spokesman for the *évolués*. He believed quite strongly about the superiority of French civilization and the ultimate necessity for African absorption into the French way of life. He was thoroughly convinced that the only future for Africa lay in political if not cultural assimilation with France. According to Davidson, these educated few, the *lettres*, were converted to the general idea that Africa had no civilization, that civilization must come from outside, and that the colonial system was its necessary agent.[80] While the African elite in British colonies was pressing for constitutional reforms which should grant them political concessions towards territorial self-rule, the *évolués* in French Africa were demanding citizens' rights within the framework of a Greater France to which they were culturally and intellectually attached.

The manner in which leaders in French-speaking Africa have identified with France and have embraced French culture have been sources of irritation and embarrassment to African nationalists. President Felix

Houphouet-Boigny of the Ivory Coast, who served as a deputy to the French National Assembly in Paris from 1946-1948 and was a minister of state in President Charles de Gaulle's government from 1958 to 1959, embarrassed his African colleagues in an address before the United Nations when he praised France as the home of liberty, equality, and fraternity. He indicated that he was indeed proud as a member of the French Community.[81] At a meeting with Prime Minister Dr. Nkrumah in Abidjan shortly after Ghana had achieved its independence from Britain, Felix Houphouet-Boigny rejected for Africans of French culture the political solution which Dr. Nkrumah had won for the Gold Coast (Ghana), seeking instead, "a community of peoples, equal and fraternal."[82] He advocated a Franco-African partnership, with France as the senior partner.[83] President Léopold Senghor of Senegal, who, in his writings, has emphasized a greater sense of Africa's distinctive cultural heritage, has argued very strongly that a federal union with France could have real meaning only if each of the partners to it was strong and autonomous. He therefore demanded the maintenance and strengthening of the two federations of African colonies, namely, French West Africa and French Equatorial Africa, as a prior condition of Franco-African community.

It is not an overstatement to suggest that the elite in French-speaking Africa were more closely attached to France than their British counterparts were attached to Britain. This difference can be explained in terms of French colonial policy which encouraged assimilation and association. The African critics of the elite in Francophone Africa have charged that they played the role of collaborationists rather than the role of nationalists.

Like the French, the British recognized the need to develop an elite group to man the lower levels of the civil service. Thus, by the twenties, Britain had developed a unified colonial service which included both administrative and technical branches but seemed to have no consistent policy for an African educated class.[84] Some observers have noted that Britain produced the largest number of educated people in tropical Africa[85] but refused to employ the elite in the administration and professional services of her colonies.[86] Critics charged that Britain frowned upon an elite as an embarrassment to the "Indirect Rule" system.[87] Thus, indirect rule, which was considered the cornerstone of British colonial administration, provided no place for a Western-educated elite.[88]

Britain's attitude towards its educated Africans was characterized by racial arrogance; it was rather animated by an intense color-consciousness. As early as 1886, the head of the African Department of the Colonial Office expressed the opinion that "the educated native was the curse of the West Coast."[89] This expressed opinion by a British policymaker continued to influence the "official mind" of British Africa for many years. Similarly, Lord Hailey, an experienced British observer, stated that the preference for the uneducated over the educated native was much more conspicuous in British than in French territories.[90] Compared with their French counterparts, the elite in English-speaking Africa experienced more widely and more deeply felt grievances. They complained bitterly about their exclusion from the colonial administration at both the local and central levels. They demanded reforms in the colonial administration which would allow Africanization of the colonial service, adoption of measures to ensure fair competition between African and European businessmen, as well as increased representation on the legislative councils of the different colonial territories. The very few who entered the colonial civil service did not feel at home in British colonial administration. They were humiliated, ridiculed, and despised by their white colleagues, most of whom were their classmates at Oxford, Cambridge, and London Universities. They were segregated from their white colleagues, who assumed airs of superiority over them. They lived in separate quarters, dined separately, and were generally ignored by their white colleagues. Nevertheless, it was this class that spearheaded the nationalist drive in the forties and fifties to win complete independence for the colonies and eventual separation from the metropolitan power. This elite group claimed to be the natural leaders of the countries in a changing world and argued that they were best equipped to succeed the colonial power. Thus, that close emotional tie which characterized the relationships between France and the leaders of Francophone Africa was absent in relationships between Britain and her educated Africans. Because of their bitter experiences in the British colonial system, such men as Dr. Nnamdi Azikiwe of Nigeria, Dr. Kwame Nkrumah of Ghana, and Jomo Kenyatta, to name but a few, became the sharpest critics of Britain's colonial policies. They refused to identify with the metropolitan power and rationalized that they would be better off after the British imperialists had been ousted from Africa. This situation explains the lack of any warm or intimate relationships or emotional ties between Britain and leaders of Anglophone Africa.

In contrast to their French counterparts, the leaders of the English-speaking countries have not been seeking close ties with the former colonizer. For example, during the first five years of independence, they revised their British-imposed constitutions and moved toward republican status within the British Commonwealth. It was Ghana which initiated this trend in 1960 when Prime Minister Nkrumah was elected president under a republican constitution. The other countries followed in rapid succession Ghana's example and replaced the British monarch as head of state with popularly elected presidents under republican governments.

Decolonization Process

The manner in which independence was granted by the colonizer influenced these post-independence relationships. Thus, where decolonization was achieved without a bitter struggle, the relationships tended to be characterized by mutual respect and friendship between the former colonizer and the new state, whereas in areas independence was marked by bloodshed or sharp disagreements between mother country and colony, these relationships were characterized by mutual suspicions, tensions, distrust, fragile coexistence, and open hostility.

Decolonization, in the context of this discussion, is defined as the elimination of alien rule and the attempt by the indigenous elite to exercise their rights of self-determination and political independence. Thus, it means the formal transfer of political authority from a colonial state to indigenous leaders within the framework of state sovereignty.[91] Professor Wasserman used the term "consensual decolonization" to characterize that system or process of transferring political authority in which there was a large measure of agreement among the participants that the outcome of the process was to be independence.[92] As Professor Wasserman pointed out, this definition dealt only with the formal transfer of "authority," referring to the capacity to legitimate political decisions and not with political "power" which may be taken to mean the ability to influence those decisions. He distinguished "authority" and "power to influence decisions," stating that a state without power is a satellite to some other country, whereas a state with relatively autonomous power is independent.[93]

The term "transition" has been used to refer to the process whereby a colonial territory achieves political independence. Gwendolyn M. Carter used this concept to mean the evolution towards full political control of the instrument of government.[94] Thus, in this usage, transition is synonymous with decolonization.

Descriptive terms such as "effective," "geniune," "complete," "fictitious," and "real" have been used by analysts to characterize the different levels of independence which the new states have attained. For example, Professor Mittleman has drawn a distinction between "legal" and "effective" decolonization. He suggested that an effective decolonization would entail the adoption of autonomous self-defined independent development strategy, based on locally derived goals, a cohesive national economy, and a dynamism freed from subordination to external force.[95] Commenting on Frantz Fanon's claim that independence in Africa can be regarded as a deal between the colonialists and the bureaucratic bourgeoisie, he recognized that the "independence bargain" preempted effective decolonization. He noted that, although legal decolonization may prove to be a charade whereby indigenous peoples do not gain control over their own affairs, "flag independence" can be regarded as an indispensable first step for moving from relationship of dependence to independence.[96]

In their struggle to achieve independence from colonial powers, the African nationalists utilized two main strategies during the postwar period. The first strategy involved the achievement of nationalist objectives through the Gandhian nonviolent means. This approach emphasized peaceful negotiations for independence between the colonial powers and the elite in the colonial territories. Such agreements were reached in either a constitutional conference or by a referendum. In many instances, an "Independence Act" regulated the modes of this transfer of power from the colonial authority to the new African elite, and contained, if necessary, the constitution of the new state. Important questions of state succession, such as continuity of existing laws, acquisition of nationality, particularly in areas with a large number of white settlers, or the safeguard of private rights, were usually regulated in devolution agreements. In short, these agreements provided for the new state's succession to international obligations and rights of its predecessor. In recent years, however, some new African states have refused to sign devolution agreements with the colonial powers; rather, preferring to pick and choose international agreements to which they wanted to be bound.[97]

A variation of the nonviolent strategy was President Kwame Nkrumah's strategy of "positive action," which he adopted to achieve independence for Ghana, a former British dependency. Dr. Nkrumah's positive action was simply a combination of nonviolent methods with effective and disciplined political action. It included political agitation, newspaper and educational campaigns, strikes, boycotts, and other forms of noncooperation. This strategy was adopted in 1950, when the British Government rejected Dr. Nkrumah's demands for a general election and a referendum to allow the people of Ghana, then the Gold Coast, to decide whether to accept the British recommendations for constitutional reform. Dr. Nkrumah's imprisonment ended quite abruptly in 1951 when a direct election gave his party, the Convention People's Party (CPP), a majority of legislative assembly seats and paved the way for his rise to power.

The second approach involved the use of violence to effect political change. It called for "wars of national liberation" against the colonial powers or supremacist regimes which bluntly rejected the political aspirations and demands of African nationalist groups for independence. The violent strategy was justified by Africans as a viable means to achieve decolonization when peaceful methods failed. In the view of the practitioners of this strategy, violence did not originate with the Africans. Violence by Africans was frequently a direct reaction to forceful provocation by the regimes in power. Violence was therefore necessary if the colonial power in charge of a territory refused to transfer power peacefully.

The colonial problem was further compounded by the presence of European settlers in territories such as Algeria, Kenya, and the Rhodesias

(Zambia and Zimbabwe). The settlers' insistence on predominance, and even for a self-determination of their own, slowed down the process of decolonization in these territories. The conflicting claims and demands of Africans and settlers were hotly debated in the metropolitan countries. For example, in Britain and France, politicians and the general public were sharply divided over the question of granting independence to these countries. The parties of the Right and other imperialist forces in the metropole usually endorsed settlers' demands for superiority and dominance, and they opposed independence on the grounds that it would bring about a complete domination of the white minority by the African majority. On the other hand, the Liberals and parties of the the Left, in general, were more sympathetic toward the nationalist aspirations for independence, provided there were adequate safeguards to protect the "legitimate rights and interests" of the European settlers. In the end, such situations were resolved either in an open violent rebellion, as in Algeria and Zimbabwe, or by special agreements between the colonial power and the colony, in which Africans were granted independence while guarantees were instituted to protect the so-called legitimate interests of the settlers.

The dismantling of European colonial empires in Africa was indeed a process of prime historic importance in the postwar period. The decade that began in 1957 has been described as the "decade of African independence" or sometimes referred to as the "classical period of decolonization." This period witnessed the determination of Africans to liberate their countries from the yoke of colonial bondage after more than six decades of colonialism.[98] For example, between 1957 and 1977, over thirty-eight African countries achieved independence from their colonial rulers. By late 1977, only two decades after Ghanaian independence, all but two countries in sub-Saharan Africa had achieved their political independence. The two exceptions were Namibia and Zimbabwe. The colonial powers, according to Richard Hull, reasoned that these colonies could be granted formal "political" or "flag" independence without drastically disrupting or changing their economic relationships with them.[99]

Post-war developments were contributing factors that influenced the decisions of European imperial powers to dismantle their colonial empires in

Africa. The war discredited the racist ideologies which had served as the original rationale for European colonial enterprise overseas. It heightened the nationalistic aspirations of African peoples for independence; it also weakened the capability[100] as well as the will of Britain and France to maintain their overseas empires and thus set the stage for the era of political decolonization.[101] Although they were members of the winning coalition in that war, Britain and France, nevertheless, experienced vast devastation and war-weariness. They did appreciate their dependencies' wartime loyalty and contributions to Allied victory, and counted on continued loyalty as well as on African resources, despite the fact that colonialism was becoming increasingly unpopular in the international community.[102] The process of decolonization moved on smoothly with the exception of small pockets of resistance where supremacist white minority regimes vowed not to yield power and opposed internal and external pressures to decolonize Africa.

Both Britain and France adopted similar decolonization policies in Africa. For example, the two powers utilized the process of constitutional conferences and referendum to ascertain the colonial people's input in deciding how or when the colonizer would grant independence to its dependencies. In white settler regions both colonial powers adopted almost identical policies. Thus, French policy in Algeria resembled British policy in Kenya. Both colonial powers, in the 1950s, responded pragmatically to the various political, economic and cultural realities in different parts of Africa.[103]

With a few exceptions, African countries under British and French rule achieved independence with relative ease and without resorting to armed rebellion. Thus, independence was achieved by African nationalists not out of the barrel of the gun, but, as Richard Hull indicated, through well-organized political demonstrations, strikes, boycotts, and positive action, as well as diplomatic bargainings.[104]

It was the British Colonial Secretary Malcolm MacDonald who in 1938 proclaimed Britain's commitment to self-government for British colonies. He said:

> The great purpose of the British Empire is the gradual spread of freedom among His Majesty's subjects in whatever part of the world they live. That spread of freedom is a slow evolutionary process. In some countries it is more rapid than in others....But, it is a major part of our policy even among the most backward peoples of Africa, to teach them and to encourage them always to be able to stand a little more on their own feet.[105]

In 1948, another British policymaker, Arthur Creech Jones, reiterated that the central purpose of British colonial policy was simple; it was to guide the colonial territories to responsible government within the Commonwealth in conditions that would ensure to the people concerned both a *fair* standard of living and freedom from oppression from any quarter.[106]

The admirers of the British colonial tradition have generally asserted that Britain was more committed to decolonization as an ideal than any other colonial power.[107] In British territories, Richard Hull pointed out that the decolonization process was gradual and that the devolution of power to Africans was in a series of stages.[108] Britain believed that independence for the colonies was not to be achieved by a sudden revolutionary thrust, but by a gradually increasing degree of participation in the political decision-making process set up by the colonial regimes.[109] From these observations one can conclude that Britain's policy was aimed at leading colonial peoples to self-rule within the British Commonwealth. However, critics of Britain's colonial policy have asserted that in no place was it considered in the founding and consolidation of these overseas colonies that the indigenous people were to be systematically trained and educated in the art of governing themselves, or that they were destined to be independent in some new state structure after a long and purposeful training in self-government.[110] Other critics noted that the idea of preparation was simply an afterthought.[111]

After researching this question, this author concluded that British decolonization in Africa was indeed an evolutionary process. Britain became committed quite early to preparing its dependencies for independence, though this proved to be easier in those areas where European settlement was minimal than regions where there were large numbers of expatriate white colonialists.[112] British policymakers responded favorably to African nationalist demands for independence. Reforms were instituted to increase African representation in both the Legislative and Executive Councils in the late forties and fifties. By the mid-1950s, Executive Councils were developing into cabinets headed by African prime ministers. In 1956 Ghana emerged as the first black African country to achieve its independence from Britain. Then, in rapid succession, Nigeria, Sierra Leone, Somalia, Tanzania, Uganda, Kenya, Botswana, Lesotho, and Swaziland achieved their political independence.

In the French territories a similar process of decolonization was taking place, although before 1958 full independence was not contemplated. French-speaking African countries watched the constitutional developments in neighboring English-speaking areas with interest. Under pressure of the rising African nationalism, France began to copy the British style of colonial administration which called for a gradual devolution or transfer of power to the African elite. The first step was taken in 1944 at the Brazzaville Conference. At this conference General de Gaulle was determined to transform the French Empire into the French Union. The second step involved the 1956 constitution which granted to each of the territories an elected local assembly with budgetary powers and the right to send deputies to the French Parliament. The *loi-cadre* introduced universal suffrage for the elections of local assembly members and an African government directed by a French governor. This body became responsible for internal affairs in each territory. Thus, after the *loi-cadre*, the French government devolved greater power and authority on the legislative and executive bodies in these newly created territories.

The most ambitious decolonization scheme occurred in 1958 when President de Gaulle assumed power in France. In a referendum he proposed the French Community, which was to replace the French Union. Each territory would become a republic. Questions such as defense, currency, external affairs, and international economic policy would be handled by an Executive Council made up of the prime ministers of each African republic and presided over by the President of France. The colonies were offered an opportunity to opt for complete independence and secession from the *Communauté* or remain in it. A referendum on the new constitution which was held in September 1958 was a great victory for France, because only Guinea decided to be fully independent. France cancelled all financial aid to Guinea and ordered all French colonial civil servants and teachers to leave Guinea immediately. French medical personnel stripped hospitals and clinics of supplies. All these measures were aimed at demonstrating to other colonies the consequences of a display of disloyalty to France or a show of ingratitude on the part of any one of them toward France.[113] The fact that Guinea managed to survive despite these drastic measures helped to convince others that they, too, could make it without the French Community. Thus, the *Communauté* lost its original meaning and virtually ceased to exist as an institution.[114]

Continued Dependence

The post-independence relationships between former colonialists and the new African states have generally been characterized by dependence, though some writers have preferred the term interdependence in their examination of these relationships. Theories of dependency have varied. The thrust of this study will emphasize dependence rather than interdependence. The reason for this emphasis is simply that interdependence connotes the relationships between equals. Dependence, as a concept, has been defined as a situation that the history of colonialism has left and that contemporary imperialism creates in underdevelopment countries.[115] Johnson concluded that dependence is imperialism seen from the prespective of underdevelopment.[116] Professor Joan Edelman Spero has noted that dependency exists when *one* country is influenced by actors or events in another country.[117] Dependence, Professor Spero explains, usually takes one or more forms, such as trade, monetary, investment, aid, and security dependence;[118] she elaborates by asserting that these economic dependencies – trade, investment, money, aid – are usually reinforced by other types of relationships, such as cultural ties, alliances and treaties, informal political ties, and military links ranging from military aid to military intervention.[119] Dependency means then that the alternatives open to the dependent nation are defined and limited by its integration into the institutions of the dominant party.[120] As Susanne Bodenheimer explained, the distinguishing feature of dependent as contrasted with interdependent development is that growth in dependent states occurs as a reflex of the expansion of the dominant states and is geared toward the needs of the dominant economies. Thus, attention is paid to foreign rather than the national needs.[121] Professor J. Edelman Spero argued that interdependence is irrelevant in any discussions involving the interactions between the rich and the poor countries, noting that whereas interdependence involves a high level of mutual economic, political, and military interaction or partnership, dependence suggests unequal interactions in these fields.[122] Thus, the association of unequal partners always works against the interests of the weaker number.

Many years after the new African states achieved political independence there is still evidence to support the contention that imperialism has remained alive and well. The manner of dominance, however, has become more subtle. The new states have continued to depend on the former metropolitan powers that once colonized them. Thus, political independence did not by any means indicate, for example, economic independence[123] as was earlier expected. William Clark asserted that the end of colonialism did not denote the end of colonies.[124] In a detailed analysis of these post-independence relationships between European powers and their former African dependencies, William Clark stated that the question before European imperial powers was what their new relationships with these new states should be. How differently would their motives be mixed in the post-imperial era from the mixture that constituted imperialism?[125] He reminded his readers that, in the recent past, Europe plunged into the colonial enterprise for reasons which included economic, strategic, philanthropic, and prestige motives, and that in the future these will continue to be determining factors in these relationships, though in a different mixture,[126] because, he claimed, history is a continuum without sudden breaks; the end of colonial power removes only one strand in a complex relationship.[127]

The dependency of the new African states on their former colonizers can be traced to the colonial era when European colonists dominated the cultural, political, economic, and social life of African peoples. It can be argued that these post-independence relationships developed out of the colonial heritage. As Professor Spero explained, colonies were usually integrated into the metropolitan economic system which was designed to serve the interests of the metropole. The colonial powers controlled trade and investment and regulated currency and production, and this established structure of economic dependency in the various colonies which would endure for longer than their actual political authority.[128] Both Britain and France introduced in their colonies economic systems based on export-oriented economy with a limited range of products, limited capital, and markets. As a direct consequence, African countries remained for years mere exporters of primary raw materials and agricultural products such as cocoa, cotton, coffee, peanutes, and palm produce. Thus, from early times these countries' economies were subject to fluctuations in world markets.[129] After independence, the economies of the new states still retained their colonial character. Attempts at industrialization by African countries since independence have not yet altered the fundamentally complementary character of these economies. All over Africa, foreign control of the major industrial sectors is evident through direct ownership and control over production, control of marketing and distribution, as well as control of patents and licenses.

The new states have also depended on the former colonizers as sources of their technological know-how, aid, and investment. They secure their supply of arms and in some instances have agreements with the former colonizer to intervene militarily and put down internal revolts.[130]

In economic, political, and cultural matters, for example, the African states have resented their former status as mere appendages to former metropolitan countries and the exploitations of past years; nevertheless, they have continued to maintain many links with their former colonizers.[131] The critics of these post-colonial ties have simply characterized them as nothing but neo-colonialism, thus implying that the former rulers had not really left, but were still pulling the strings from behind the scenes. Neo-colonialism is indeed a sensitive subject to African nationalists whose preoccupation has been how to break away from dependency so that their recently achieved flag independence can become a reality. B. T. G. Chidzero has argued that a simultaneous process of breaking up of the colonial umbilical cord must be a necessary condition for genuine independence.[132] The advocates of this strategy of disengagement point out that the old political and economic ties with the ex-colonial powers should be cut off.[133] They have criticized quite sharply the division of Africa into monetary zones such as franc and sterling zones as well as foreign-controlled trade zones roughly corresponding to the monetary zones.[134]

When the African colonies became independent, the two ex-imperial powers recognized an obligation to assist the new states. Both powers instituted aid programs without much public debate.[135] However, it must be pointed out that the French showed greater concern and as such, made more elaborate plans than their British counterparts to handle what observers have called "the crisis of independence."

It has been suggested by analysts that France's post-colonial policies toward Francophone Africa were motivated by the desire to cope quite effectively with the aftermath of colonialism as well as creating a new image and source of influence in Africa.[136] Edward A. Kolodzieg noted that the goals served by colonialism still largely were honored – grandeur, security, economic gain, cultural radiation, a sense of universal mission, and moral vindication.[137] The French seemed to appreciate the fact that political independence did not relieve the chronic economic and cultural dependence of the new states on France.[138] Thus, France expressed genuine concern about the depressed conditions in these territories and decided to do something about it following her tradition of paternalism. Since achieving independence in the early 1960s, Francophone African states have continued to maintain intimate relations with France. Kaye Whiteman asserted that there has, since independence, been a form of "special relationship" between the black Francophone countries and the Elysée palace.[139] This special relationship has been reinforced by the close economic, financial, educational and cultural links between French-speaking Africa and Paris.[140] These close attachments have caused critics to charge that these states are victims of the "dependency syndrome."[141] These critics point out that many years after independence, France continued to provide personnel to staff the army in the former dependencies, run the banks, and provide administrative assistance to these new states.[142]

Martin and O'Meara note that the dependency syndrome is manifest by the simple fact that there were several times as many French technicians, businessmen, and teachers in Francophone Africa during the post-colonial period as there were prior to 1960.[143] They also note that France has remained the source of investment capital and market for these new states with the exception of Guinea and Mali. France's membership in the European Common Market has also meant that these states benefited from their association with the EEC. The Rome Treaty (1957) and the Yaoundé Conventions (1975, 1980), provided trade, aid, and investment benefits for these associate members.[144] Their participation in the EEC has opened what was once considered a closed French market to France's EEC partners.

Leaders of Francophone Africa have sharply disagreed with critics who have charged that the special ties between France and French-speaking Africa would be detrimental to the interests of the latter in the long run.

Relationships between Britain and Anglophone Africa are not as close as those between France and Francophone Africa. Anglophone African states, unlike their Francophone counterparts, with the exception of Guinea and Mali, have pursued active programs of diversification in their contacts in terms of trade partners as well as sources of aid, investment capital, and arms. Generally, these states have relied less heavily on Britain for survival than their French-speaking neighbors have relied on Paris; hence one can argue that dependency is more concentrated in former French colonies.

Unlike their French counterparts, the ex-British territories, since becoming independent, have adopted programs of disengagement, that is, loosening the ties between them and the former metropolitan power. Although these states are members of the British Commonwealth, they have not hesitated to embarrass or criticize Britain at international conferences over British decolonization policies, particularly in southern Africa where entrenched supremacist white minority groups refused to share political and economic power with the African majority. Some of them have even challenged Britain's leadership of that international association. The character of the Commonwealth has changed quite drastically since these states were admitted to its membership. As Martin and O'Meara have pointed out, membership to this international association does provide the African members with a forum for voicing their opinions on international problems.[145] They are also beneficiaries of aid programs organized by the developed members of this body. Such aid has usually included economic, financial, technical, and education assistance. These states also enjoy the privileges of Commonwealth preference in matters of trade among Commonwealth members.[146] These privileges did not deter them from creating their own heads of state and thus refusing to recognize the British sovereign as their head of state. They did this by becoming republics within the Commonwealth itself.

Anglophone African states refused security arrangements proposed by Britain for their defense. For example, Nigerian Military Understanding, which Nigeria signed at the time of independence, caused such an uproar in Nigeria that it nearly brought down Sir Abubakar's Government. Its immediate repeal restored normalcy in the country.

The concern to reduce their economic dependence on the former colonial powers led to the pursuit, by some African states, of joint cooperative ventures such as the Niger River Basin Commission[147] composed of nine riparian states. The main reason for creating this commission was simply to develop the Niger river basin. Thus, there is the realization or awareness among African states that the achievement of economic independence would definitely involve all African states pooling their resources together and cooperating closely in the overall interest of all countries.[148]

The late fifties and early sixties witnessed a dramatic increase in the number of new African states. The dismantling of European colonial empires which characterized the postwar period indeed stimulated the spirit of liberation everywhere on the African continent. By the late sixties a large majority of African countries had attained the status of independent states. But, sadly enough, independent Africa has not been a success story but just the exact opposite as some observers or analysts see it.[149] Thus, according to these critics independent Africa has become a byword for incompetent government; political corruption and instability; and finally, economic problems of great magnitude. The end result has been that the enthusiasms of independence turned sour. Earlier expectations, for example, that African states could modernize their economies with assistance coming from foreign aid donors in the form of loans, investments and commercial concessions failed to materialize. Their hopes were dashed to pieces when these expectations died quietly. Since independence, foreign aid has rather been very meager indeed, resulting in the accumulations of large foreign debts. The advanced industrial powers have deliberately ignored the pleas of the developing states for the liberalization of trade relations between the rich and the poor states.

In addition to the errors of miscalculation on the part of African states, other economic forces have joined to make the economic situation much worse. For example, economic problems which were partly inherited from the remote colonial past have been worsened by African mismanagement or other forces upon which the finances and trade of African states depend.

Endnotes Chapter 1

[1] John S. Galbraith, "The Turbulent Frontier as a Factor in British Expansionism," *Comparative Studies in Society and History* 2, No. 2 (January 1960): 150-60.

[2] See E. M. Winslow, *The Pattern of Imperialism* (New York: Columbia University Press, 1948), pp. 77-91.

[3] David S. Landes, "Some Thoughts on the Nature of Economic Imperialism," *Journal of Economic History* 21 (1961): 510-11.

[4] D. K. Fieldhouse, *Economics and Empire 1830-1914* (London: OUP, 1973), pp. 81 and 463.

[5] See Phyllis M. Martin and Patrick O'Meara, eds., *Africa* (Bloomington: Indiana University Press, 1977), p. 137.

[6] See J. F. A. Ajayi and J. B. Webster, "The Emergence of a New Elite in Africa," in *Africa in the Nineteenth and Twentieth-Centuries*, eds. Joseph C. Anene and Geofrey N. Brown (London: Ibadan University Press, 1966), p. 152.

[7] Martin and O'Meara, *Africa*, p. 133.

[8] Ronald Robinson and John Gallagher, *Africa and the Victorians: The Climax of Imperialism* (Garden City, NY: Doubleday and Company, Inc., 1968), p. 3.

[9] See J. F. A. Ajayi, "Colonialism: An Episode in African History," in *Colonialism in Africa 1870-1960*, eds. L. H. Gann and Peter Duignan, vol. 1, *The History and Politics of Colonialism 1870-1974* (London: Cambridge University Press, 1969), p. 497.

[10] *Ibid.*, p. 498.

[11] *Ibid.* See also Leonard Thompson, *France and Britain in Africa: Imperial Rivalry and Colonial Rule* (London: Yale University Press, 1971), p. 778.

[12] See Winfried Baumgart, Imperialism: *The Idea and Reality of British and French Colonial Expansion 1880-1914* (Oxford: Oxford University Press, 1982), p. 778.

[13] In Britain, for example, the following were the pressure groups – Primrose League, The Imperial Federation League, The United Empire Trade League, and the Imperial Defense Committee; in France there were the *Comité de l'Afrique française*, founded in 1890; the *Union coloniale française*, established in 1893, and the *Groupe Colonial*. See John E. Kendle, *The Colonial and Imperial Conferences 1887-1911, A Study in Imperial Organization* (London: Oxford University Press, 1967), pp. 5-18;

Henri Brunschwig, *French Colonialism 1871-1914* (London: Oxford University Press, 1966), pp. 105-134.

14 William Clark, "New Europe and the New Nations," *Daedelus, Journal of the American Academy of Arts and Sciences* 93, No. 1 (Winter 1964): 137.

15 *Ibid.*

16 *Ibid.*

17 See Jean Suret-Canale, *French Colonialism in Tropical Africa 1900-1945*, trans. Till Gottheiner (New York: Pica Press, 1971), p. 369.

18 *Ibid.*

19 See Daniel R. Headrick, *The Tools of Empire: Technology and European Imperialism in the Nineteenth-Century* (New York: Oxford University Press, 1981), p. 4.

20 *Ibid.*

21 *Ibid.*, p. 206.

22 *Ibid.*

23 Baumgart, *Imperialism*, p. 21.

24 Short stabbing spears used by Zulu warriors under King Shaka.

25 Philip Curtin, Steven Feieman, Leonard Thompson, and Jan Vansina, *African History* (Boston: Little Brown and Co., 1978), p. 448.

26 *Ibid.*

27 Fieldhouse, *Economics and Empire 1830-1914*, pp. 460-461.

28 See Headrick, *The Tools of Empire*, p. 117.

29 John Keegan, "The Ashanti Campaign 1873-1874," in *Victorian Military Campaigns*, ed. Brian Bond (London: Oxford University Press, 1967), p. 186; see also J. K. Flynn, "Ghana-Asante" (Ashanti), in *West African Resistance: The Military Response to Colonial Occupation*, ed. Michael Crowder (London: Oxford University Press, 1971), p. 40.

30 B. Olantunji Oloruntimehin, "Senegambia-Mahmadou Lamine," in *West African Resistance*, ed. Michael Crowder (Evanston, IL: Northwestern University Press, 1968), pp. 93-105.

31 See Colonel Baratier, *A travers l'Afrique* (Paris: University of Paris, 1912), quoted in Michael Crowder, *West Africa Under Colonial Rule*

(London: Oxford University Press, 1968), p. 87; see also Robin Hallett, *Africa Since 1875, A Modern History* (Ann Arbor: The University of Michigan Press, 1974), p. 271.

32   R. W. Beachey, "The Arms Trade in East Africa," *Journal of African History* 3, no. 3 (1962): 453.

33   *Ibid.*, pp. 455-457.

34   J. A. Hobson, *Imperialism: A Study* (London: Oxford University Press, 1902).

35   See Clark, "New Europe and the New Nations," pp. 134-154.

36   See Sheldon Gellar, "The Colonial Era," in *Africa*, eds. Phyllis M. Martin and Patrick O'Meara, p. 146.

37   *Ibid.*

38   *Ibid.*

39   *Ibid.*, p. 147.

40   *Ibid.*

41   *Ibid.*

42   *Ibid.*

43   See Grade Stuart Ibingira, *African Upheavals Since Independence* (Boulder, Colorado: Westview Press Inc., 1980), p. 3.

44   F. J. D. Lugard, *The Dual Mandate in British Tropical Africa* (London: Blackwood and Sons, 1922), p. 18.

45   Ibingira, *African Upheavals Since Independence*, p. 3.

46   See Hobson, *Imperialism: A Study.*

47   See Baumgart, *Imperialism*, p. 125; Alexander K. Cairncross, *Home and Foreign Investment 1870-1913, Studies in Capital Accumulation* (Cambridge: Cambridge University Press, 1953), Repr. Clifton, NJ, 1972, pp. 226-227

48   See Brunschwig, *French Colonialism 1871-1914*, p. 76.

49   Pierre Paul Leroy-Beaulieu, *De la colonisation chez les peuples modernes*, 2nd ed. (Paris: Presses Universitaires de France, 1882), p. 642.

50   See Colin Morris, *Nationalism in Africa* (London: Edinburgh House Press, 1963), p. 7.

51 *Ibid.*

52 See Clark, "New Europe and the New Nations," p. 136.

53 See Morris, *Nationalism in Africa*, p. 6.

54 Clark, "New Europe and the New Nations," p. 137.

55 *Ibid.*

56 *Ibid.*

57 *Ibid.*

58 See Robert W. July, *A History of the African People*, 2nd. ed. (New York: Charles Scribner's Sons, 1974), p. 499.

59 *Ibid.*

60 See E. A. Boateng, *A Political Geography of Africa* (London: Cambridge University Press, 1978), p. 63.

61 See L. P. Mair, *Native Policies in Africa* (New York: Negro Universities Press, 1960), p. 189.

62 See Rupert Emerson, *From Empire to Nation: The Rise to Self-Assertion of Asians and Africans* (Boston: Beacon Press, 1960), p. 69.

63 The four Senegalese Communes – St. Louis, Dakar, Gorée, and Rufisque enjoyed political and civil rights as French citizens. They were later joined by others.

64 B. W. Hodder, *Africa Today: A Short Introduction to African Affairs* (New York: Africana Publishing Co., 1978), p. 16.

65 See Mair, *Native Policies in Africa*, p. 189.

66 *Ibid.*

67 See E. A. Brett, *Colonialism and Underdevelopment in East Africa: The Politics of Economic Change 1919-1939* (New York: NOK Publishers Ltd., 1973), p. 41.

68 E. W. Evans.

69 House of Commons, Debates ii viii 20, V. 133, C. 490.

70 Brett, *Colonialism and Underdevelopment*, p. 42; see also Charles Jeffries, *The Colonial Empire and its Civil Service* (Cambridge: Cambridge University Press, 1938), p. 134.

71   See Thomas Hodgkin, *Nationalism in Colonial Africa* (New York: New York University Press, 1957), p. 40.

72   W. G. M. Ormsby-Gore (later Lord Harlech), *Developments and Opportunities in the Colonial Empire* (London: n.p., 1929), p.xi.

73   Report of the Commisson on Closer Union of the Dependencies in Eastern and Central Africa, Cmd. 3234 g 1929, p. 87.

74   Thomas Hodgkin, *Nationalism in Colonial Africa*, p. 40.

75   The idea of "indirect rule" was innovated by Britain's leading empire-builder, Lord Lugard. In theory, indirect rule was the exact opposite of French colonial administration. It emphasized the maximum use of traditional custom and governmental machinery, encouraging the people to continue in their traditional patterns of government. In practice, however, it was indeed a system whose ultimate authority clearly lay beyond the control of Africans themselves. It proved to be an economical system in that it allowed large areas to be administered by relatively few officials. See B. W. Hodder, *Africa Today: A Short Introduction to African Affairs* (New York: Africana Publishing Co., 1977), p. 15.

76   See Immanuel Wallerstein, *Africa: The Politics of Independence* (New York: Random House, 1971), p. 64.

77   *Ibid.*

78   J. F. A. Ajayi and J. B. Webster, "The Emergence of a New Elite in Africa," in *Africa in the Nineteenth and Twentieth-Centuries: A Handbook for Teachers and Students*, eds. Joseph C. Anene and Geofrey N. Brown (London: Ibadan University Press, 1966), p. 149.

79   See Raymond Leslie Bruell, *The Native Problem in Africa*, vol. 11 (New York: Macmillan, 1928), p. 81.

80   Basil Davidson, *Let Freedom Com: Africa in Modern History* (Boston: Little Brown & Co., 1978), p. 186.

81   Address on Togoland and Black Africa, Speeches and Press Conferences No. 85 (New York: Ambassade de France, Service de Presse et d'Information, January 1957), pp. 3, 7.

82   Felix Houphouet-Boigny, "Black Africa and the French Union," *Foreign Affairs* 35, no. 4 (July 1957): 597.

83   Victor C. Ferkiss, *Africa's Search for Identity* (New York: George Braiziller, 1966), p. 241.

84   See Ajayi and Webster, "The Emergence of a New Elite in Africa," p. 155.

38

85   *Ibid.*

86   *Ibid.*

87   *Ibid.*

88   *Ibid.*

89   See R. Symonds, *The British and Their Successors* (London: Oxford University Press, 1966), p. 125.

90   Lord Hailey, *An African Survey* (London: Oxford University Press, 1938), p. 258.

91   See Gary Wasserman, *Politics of Decolonization: Kenya, Europeans and the Land Issue* (London: Cambridge University Press, 1976), p. 4.

92   *Ibid.*, p. 5.

93   *Ibid.*, p. 4.

94   Gwendolyn M. Carter, *Transition in Africa: Studies in Political Adaptation* (Boston: Boston University Press, 1958,) p. 9.

95   James H. Mittleman, "Collective Decolonization and the UN Committee of 24," *Journal of Modern African Studies* 14 (1976): 42.

96   *Ibid.*, p. 43.

97   The "Nyerere Formula," as it is known, has been adopted by Kenya, Malawi, Tanzania, and Uganda.

98   Richard N. Hull, *Modern Africa: Change and Continuity* (Englewood Cliffs, NJ: Prentice-Hall, 1980), p. 169.

99   *Ibid.*, p. 172.

100   See Gellar, "The Colonial Era," p. 149.

101   Hull, *Modern Africa*, p. 172.

102   See Curtin et al., *African History*, p. 585.

103   See Martin and O'Meara, *Africa*, p. 140.

104   Hull, *Modern Africa*, p. 172.

[105]   Hansard, 342:   1246, December 7, 1928, cited in Rudolf von Albertini, *Decolonization: The Administration and Future of the Colonies, 1919-1960* (New York: Doubleday, 1971), p. 85.

[106]   See Sir Charles J. Jeffries, *Transfer of Power: The Problem of the Passage to Self-Government* (London: Oxford University Press, 1960), p. 15.

[107]   Russell Warren Howe, *The African Revolution* (New York: Barnes and Nobles, Inc., 1969), p. 243.

[108]   Hull, *Modern Africa*, p. 169.

[109]   See Irving Leonard Markovitz, *Power and Class in Africa: An Introduction to Change and Conflict in African Politics* (Englewood Cliffs, NJ: Prentice Hall, Inc., 1972), p. 60.

[110]   Ibingira, *African Upheavals Since Independence*, p. 4.

[111]   Semakula Kiwanuka, *From Colonialism to Independence* (Nairobi: East African Literature Bureau, 1973), pp. 84-88.

[112]   B. W. Hodder and D. R. Harris, eds., *Africa in Transition: Geographical Essays* (London: Methuen and Co. Ltd., 1967), pp. 7-8. See also Colin Legum,ed., *Africa: A Handbook to the Continent* (New York: Frederick A. Praeger, Inc., 1962), p. 409.

[113]   Albertini, *Decolonization*, p. 450.

[114]   Colin Legum, *Africa: A Handbook to the Continent*, p. 407.

[115]   See Dale L. Johnson, "Dependence and the International System," in *Dependence and Underdevelopment: Latin American Political Economy*, eds. James D. Cockcroft, André Gunder Frank, and Dale L. Johnson (New York: Doubleday & Co., Inc., 1972), p. 71.

[116]   *Ibid.*

[117]   Joan Edelman Spero, *The Politics of International Economic Relations* (New York: St. Martin's Press, 1977), p. 14.

[118]   *Ibid.*, pp. 14-15.

[119]   *Ibid.*, p. 15.

[120]   See Susanne Bodenheimer, "Dependency and Imperialism: The Roots of Latin American Underdevelopment," in *Readings in U.S. Imperialism*, eds. K. T. Fann and Donald C. Hodges (Boston: Porter Sargent, 1971), p. 158.

[121]   *Ibid.*

122   Spero, *The Politics of International Economic Relations*, p. 14.

123   See Markovitz, *Power and Class in Africa*, p. 72.

124   Clark, "New Europe and the New Nations," p. 134.

125   *Ibid.*

126   *Ibid.*

127   *Ibid.*

128   See Spero, *The Politics of International Economic Relations*, p. 7.

129   Hodder, *Africa Today*, p. 21.

130   Robert K. A. Gardiner, "Africa and the World," in *Africa and the World*, p. 14.

131   *Ibid.*

132   B. T. G. Chidzero, "Constructive Disengagement," in *Africa and the World*, eds. Robert K. A. Gardiner, M. J. Anstee, and C. L. Patterson (Addis Abaga: Oxford University Press, 1970), p. 29.

133   *Ibid.*, p. 32.

134   *Ibid.*, p. 29.

135   Clark, "New Europe and the New Nations," p. 151.

136   Edward A. Kolodzieg, *French International Policy under de Gaulle and Pompidou: The Politics of Grandeur* (Ithaca, NY: Cornell University Press, 1974), p. 448.

137   *Ibid.*

138   See *La Documentation Française, La Politique de Coopération avec les pays en voie de developpement*, (Paris: November 1964).

139   See Kaye Whiteman, "Pompidou and Africa: Gaullism and de Gaulle," *The World Today* (June 1970): 243.

140   *Ibid.*

141   See Martin and O'Meara, *Africa*, p. 405.

142   *Ibid.*

143   *Ibid.*

144 *Ibid.*, p. 406.

145 Martin and O'Meara, *Africa*, p. 405.

146 *Ibid.*

147 The membership, which includes Anglophone and Francophone states, is as follows: Cameroun, Chad, Benin, Guinea, Ivory Coast, Mali, Niger, Nigeria, and Upper Volta. The Commission was established in 1964.

148 This view was expressed by Dr. Abedalyo Adedeji, a former Nigerian Federal Commissioner for Economic Development and Reconstruction.

149 See Peter Calvocoressi, *Independent Africa and the World* (New York: Longmen Group Ltd. 1985), p. 1.

CHAPTER 2

TRADE RELATIONSHIPS

Trade is one major area where the two ex-colonial powers exercised dominance over the new African states. This dominance was firmly established during the colonial period. In colonial days, the metropolitan powers controlled quite effectively the external trade in their respective colonial possessions. In order to have a clearer understanding of the post-colonial trade relationships between Britain and France on the one hand and the new African states on the other, one has to examine the patterns of trade in colonial times which helped to shape these post-independence trade relations.

The trade policies of Britain and France in colonial Africa were based on two different theoretical foundations. The former emphasized "free trade" or the "open door" policy, while the latter adopted a rigid protectionist stance in regulating trade relations between the metropole and the dependencies. Britain exercised greater flexibility in the control of colonial trade. Nevertheless, in practice, both imperial powers dominated the external trade of their African dependencies.

From the very beginning of the colonial enterprise, statesmen, policymakers, and publicists in Britain and France realized the economic usefulness of colonies – particularly colonies which had economic potential. It was generally assumed at that time that colonies were necessary to safeguard markets, provide raw materials and food items, and absorb capital looking for profitable investment openings.[1] Thus, in these terms, colonies looking for profitable investment openings.[1] Thus, in these terms, colonies were expected to provide, as David Fieldhouse put it, economic returns.[2] The imperialist groups in both countries viewed the colonial and metropolitan economies as complementary parts of a single system. Thus, colonial prosperity depended directly upon the prosperity of metropolitan industry while the colonies were able to find markets for their products.[3] These imperialist groups actively supported the general idea that colonies should be acquired to ensure for their states a complete dominance or monopoly of trade in these colonial territories. This situation was uniquely more true with France, which was indeed protectionist, than with Britain, which practiced free trade. France quite deliberately organized her African colonial empire to conform to the concepts of national economy.[4] French colonies enjoyed close trade integration within the highly protected franc zone and eventually depended quite heavily on their trade with the metropole. For example, in colonial times, most Francophone countries imported over 70 percent of their manufactured goods from France, and about the same proportion of their exports were sold in the French market.[5] This was in tune with the French imperial philosophy based on the concept of a mutually interdependent trade-oriented economic system.[6]

The determination of the imperial powers to maintain complete control of the external trade of the dependencies led to their imposition of monetary or currency controls. Thus, two monetary systems, namely the franc and the pound sterling, were established in colonial Africa. Through these monetary systems the imperial powers exercised control over the colonial economy. They linked their African dependencies with European currencies and so tied them to the metropolitan economy. As a result, currency alignment encouraged trade with the other parts of the same monetary system.[7] Exchange restrictions made it possible for the imperial powers virtually to force the dependencies to buy within their own currency area and surrender the bullion and foreign currency they earned as support for the metropolitan currency as a whole.[8] As David Fieldhouse explained, these monetary controls were meant to isolate the colonies within an economic enclosure.[9]

Trade in French Africa during the colonial period was dominated by import-export companies. These limited-liability companies monopolized trade, banking business, and transport systems, which included roads and railways. Tariff protection made it possible for these French companies to set the prices for most African exports and even imports. They opposed the establishment in African colonies of export items which would in effect compete with metropolitan products.[10] The trade which they controlled centered around forced production of tropical products such as peanuts, coffee, cocoa, bananas, and cotton for the French market. The introduction of these cash crops in the colonial territories resulted in African producers becoming vulnerable to world market conditions and also forced them to depend very heavily on France.[11]

France utilized many different methods to maintain full control of the colonial economy. These methods included the use of tariff barriers, imperial preference, and currency restrictions. The establishment of the franc zone bound the colonial territories very closely to France in trading relations. Currency control was a major instrument of French trade monopoly in her colonies. By limiting the amount of hard currency available to them for the purchase of goods outside the franc zone, France made sure that she would be the principal source of the colonies' imports. Thus, currency restrictions ensured that specific African exports would be sold only to France and that French manufactured products would dominate the African market.[12] The mere fact that restrictions on purchases in non-franc areas were imposed meant that Francophone countries in Africa were forced to pay higher than world prices for the primary products they imported from France.

To compensate the colonies for purchasing French goods at prices higher than the world prices, France instituted price-support funds for African producers of cocoa, cotton, and coffee, and paid prices higher than those prevailing in the world market for African exports of peanuts, sugar, vegetable oils, and bananas. It is estimated, for example, that, in the post-war period, African producers of peanuts sold at 15 to 20 percent above world prices; coffee growers enjoyed the benefits of a 20 percent French tariff on coffee from non-franc zone countries; and the food processing industry was able to sell its products in France at prices substantially above the prices of comparable imports from other sources.[13]

The controversial question of who overpaid more as a result of these trade relations – the French consumers of tropical products or the African buyers of French manufactured goods – has been a subject of great concern and debate. Teresa Hayter has argued that it cost the African dependencies greater monetary losses than it did the French.[14] However, Thompson and Adloff have pointed out that these monetary losses were compensated by the multiple loans, grants, subsidies, and other contributions that France made to its African colonies which, in effect, resulted in their achieving a favorable balance of payments.[15] Some observations are in order in this connection. First, in terms of total French overseas trade, French Africa was always more significant as a market for French exports than as a source of her imports; secondly, in terms of African overseas trade, the relative importance of the French market increased quite considerably with the system of *surprix* for colonial products entering France. Thus, David Fieldhouse argued that this situation represented what he termed "the ultimate victory of the French protectionist ideal and the concept of economic interdependence."

Unlike France, Britain was less rigid in the regulation or control of trade in her African dependencies. However, she was rather very inconsistent in her commercial policy as it affected the colonies. Britain's commercial policy in Africa was theoretically based on the concept of free trade or the open door, but she did not hesitate to adopt a policy of strict imperial control when economic needs demanded it. For example, the economic hardships resulting from the first World War, such as wartime controls, raw material shortages, and production needs, forced Britain to adopt necessary control measures. Thus, in the late twenties and thirties, Britain began to advocate a policy of protectionism which involved the application of quotas and high tariffs. Her commercial policy resembled that of France. This situation prompted David Fieldhouse to observe that it was indeed difficult to see much difference between British and French commercial policies in dependent Africa.[16] He noted that the only difference was in matter of degree rather than of kind.[17]

The African market was important to British trade since Anglophone Africa was a relatively important consumer of British manufactured products. Britain remained the largest single market for each of the British African territories and, by the late fifties, accounted for more than a third of their overseas trade. As decolonization became imminent, Britain's policy of close imperial commercial control was loosened up as colonial economies emerged from the wartime controls By the sixties, British Africa was moving away from imperial control. After independence, the once-British dependencies were, in commercial terms, far less tied to Britain than their Francophone counterparts were tied to France. When the colonies achieved their political independence, both imperial powers were determined to preserve special commercial relationships with the new states, Britain within the British Commonwealth preferences and France within the Community arrangements and later through the EEC.

The achievement of political independence did not alter drastically the trade relationship between the new African states and the former colonizers in terms of its direction and flow, since many of the African states were still bound to the monetary systems, trading zones, and fiscal institutions they had inherited from the colonial period.[18] Thus, long after the colonies had become independent states, the ex-imperial powers were still able to preserve substantial commercial and monetary control over the new states. However, there have been determined efforts on the part of the African states to move gradually towards greater economic autonomy. The ex-British colonies are moving toward this direction. French control in Francophone Africa has remained firm, and analysts have concluded that, for the foreseeable future, these states would remain within the economic orbit of France.[19]

The economic interactions between the rich, developed countries and the poor, underdeveloped ones have generally been explained in terms of "north-south" relationships. Thus, the term "north" is used in this context to characterize the ex-imperial powers, Britain and France, while the term "south" represents the new African states. Professor Spero has observed that the north-south system is one of disparity and inequality and that a major problem of this unequal relationship is dependence.[20] Despite the fact that

African countries have now achieved the status of independent states, their economies have retained the colonial character. Their economies have continued to depend quite heavily on their trade with the former metropolitan powers and other industrial giants such as the members of the EEC, the United States, and Japan. The prosperity of these new states is excessively dependent on the export of a few primary mineral and agricultural products such as copper, petroleum, cocoa, cotton, groundnuts (peanuts), and palm produce, and they are forced to import most of their manufactured goods from abroad.[21] The experience of the past twenty years has demonstrated that colonial rule is not necessary to maintain good trade relations, as was earlier assumed. William Clark has asserted that the pattern of trade between the ex-imperial powers and their former dependencies which was established over many years has, in general, been maintained; traditional suppliers have retained their markets because of habit, he claimed, rather than political control or pressure.[22] Similarly, the flow of manufactured goods to former colonial markets has not been drastically interrupted by the ending of political control.[23]

The terms of trade have generally favored the developed, rich states because of their immense economic power. The producers of raw materials lack the power to influence the world market prices in their favor. The prices of their primary products have generally remained low, especially when compared with the constant rise in prices of industrial products that the new states must import.[24] Belai Abbai suggests that the reason why the exports of the developing countries lag behind the growth of their imports is due to the slow growth of primary exports, combined with the high income elasticity of import demand for manufactures on the part of the developing countries themselves.[25] This observer then concluded that a major problem which has confronted the developing countries has involved the fact that the bulk of their exportable items has consisted of primary products, namely food and raw materials, whose growth have been impeded partly by the low income elasticity for food and, partly, by the continuous application of modern technology in the advanced countries, resulting in cost-reducing innovations such as cheaper synthetic substitutes.[26] He noted also that policy impediments, such as protective tariffs and internal taxes, have also been invoked to account for the slow growth of primary exports.[27]

Both Anglophone and Francophone African states have made some efforts to achieve trade diversification and thus avoid putting all their eggs into one basket. This is a way of asserting their political independence. Nevertheless, these attempts at trade diversification have not altered in a dramatic fashion the pattern of colonial trade. It must be pointed out that both the moderates and radicals among the African states have maintained good trading relationships with the former colonial power with only a few exceptions. However, the radical states have been more aggressive in diversifying their trade contacts than their more moderate neighbors. These states professed neutralism and non-alignment as the cornerstones of their foreign policy. In Francophone Africa, for example, Guinea and Mali led all others in trade diversification. Guinea particularly presented the most striking reorientation of its trade relations with France. In 1958, France controlled over 70 percent of Guinea's trade; three years after Guinea had left the French Community, that trade had dropped to less than 20 percent. The Soviet Union had emerged as Guinea's major trading partner. In the case of Mali, France still remained her major trading partner, although that trade was declining. In Senegal, by contrast, the process of trade diversification proceeded much more gradually. For example, in 1961, France absorbed approximately 70 percent of Senegal's trade. By 1968, this figure had dropped to 55 percent. France's EEC partners, such as the Federal Republic of Germany, Holland, and Italy, are now beginning to establish their own commercial bridgeheads in an area once considered an exclusive French market.[28]

Similarly, Britain has remained the biggest single trading partner of Anglophone African states. These members of the British Commonwealth conduct a large portion of their commercial business in the pound sterling area. Since the post-colonial period, however, Britain's share of trade in Anglophone Africa started to fall steadily as she was challenged by more efficient producers such as the Federal Republic of Germany and Japan. Britain now began to turn to other developed markets that she considered much more profitable. The proportionate decline in British trade with ideological blocs. Despite Nigeria's efforts to diversify her trade relations, Britain has remained one of her most significant trading partners. Britain showed her displeasure in the 1960's over Nigeria's bid to seek a special relationship with the EEC. In the "Association Agreement" with the Common Market countries, Nigeria offered some minimal tariff concessions for twenty-six manufactured goods from EEC countries in return for exporting all her products (excepting cocoa beans, groundnut oil, palm oil, and plywood) duty-free into the EEC countries.

These 26 commodities on which Nigeria granted small customs concessions are as follows: "butter, sardines, canned fish, spaghetti, noodles, tomatoes, purée, sparkling wines, vermouth, beer, cognac, bitters and liqueurs, silk fabrics, stones, small glassware, metal household goods, motors, automatic distributors, various machine parts and fittings, radios, floating equipment, hats, watches, musical instruments, jewelry, and pipes."[29]

Duties ranging from 2 to 5 percent were imposed on these 26 items of non-EEC origin. This was calculated not to hurt Nigeria's world trade because the concessions were indeed minimal. For example, the exports of these 26 products from the U. K., Nigeria's leading trade customer, amounted to £108,000 in 1963, while Common Market exports of these 26 items amounted to £3.5 million. The practical effect of these concessions could not in any way damage Nigeria's trade with Britain and the rest of the world very seriously.

Britain threatened to re-examine her trade relationships with Nigeria because of the trade concessions which Nigeria had offered the EEC members. Britain was disturbed because she believed that these trade concessions would mean a diversion of Nigeria's trade from Britain to the Common Market countries. The British Government argued that a developing country like Nigeria should not offer trade concessions to industrialized countries. In her letter of protest, Britain pointed out that it was unwise for Nigeria to change quite abruptly her open-door trade policy adopted in the colonial period.

Like Nigeria, Britain has remained Ghana's best trade customer. For example, over 40 percent of the trade of Ghana is carried on with the sterling zone, with Britain taking the lion's share of it. Ghana, under the late was unwise for Nigeria to change quite abruptly her open-door trade policy adopted in the colonial period.

Like Nigeria, Britain has remained Ghana's best trade customer. For example, over 40 percent of the trade of Ghana is carried on with the sterling zone, with Britain taking the lion's share of it. Ghana, under the late President Kwame Nkrumah, pursued an active program of trade diversification. Under his leadership, Ghana's trade with the Soviet Union and other communist countries rose considerably. Ghana-USSR trade was conducted on the basis of a long-term five-year Trade Payments Agreement concluded in November, 1961. This trade agreement provided for the mutual grant of the "most favored nation" treatment by the parties in all matters pertaining to trade. On the basis of this agreement, the Soviet Union and Ghana annually concluded protocols on mutual deliveries of goods which determined the range and quantities of goods to be exchanged in the course of the corresponding year. The Soviet market did provide an outlet for Ghana's surplus cocoa. This trade arrangement suffered a setback when the military ousted Dr. Nkrumah and eventually ended his friendly policies towards the Soviet bloc nations.

Nevertheless, despite Ghana's attempts to diversify her trade, Britain has remained her best single trade partner, over 40 percent of her trade was conducted within the sterling zone.

The Treaty of Rome (1957), which provided Francophone countries preferential entry for their primary agricultural products into the European Common Market, made it possible for them to reduce somewhat their dependence on France. Following her usual policy of paternalism in dealings with French-speaking African countries, France made the admission of her African dependencies as associate members a condition for her participation in the EEC. France's enthusiasm to admit the African countries as associate members was not shared by the other founding members, especially the Federal Republic of Germany and the Netherlands. However, the fact that these French-speaking countries became members of the EEC and also remained in the franc zone after they had achieved independence reflected their dependence on the French market. The provisions of the Treaty of Rome led to greater and more diversified trade and investment in products eventually found unimpeded access to each others' markets. France's European partners benefited quite considerably because the Treaty of Rome assured them of supplies of raw materials from a region in which France had earlier exercised exclusive control. The association of these African countries with the EEC was, as Arnold Rivkin put it, the first multilateral institutionalization of a significant part of the African relationship with Europe.[31] The end result was a gradual transformation of a special economic relationship between France and Francophone Africa into one between Francophone Africa and the European Economic Community.[32] Thus, what used to be various forms of bilateral metropolitan influence gradually was being replaced with multilateral relations.[33]

The Treaty of Rome provided protection for economic interests of the associated members of the EEC. For example, they were permitted to levy taxes which were necessary for their development needs and fiscal policy.[34] The EEC member states applied to these associated countries the same rules and regulations for the removal of tariffs and quotas which applied to themselves.[35] Similarly, the Francophone African countries gave France's EEC partners the same tariff preferences which France had earlier enjoyed in the region. At the initial stages of their membership, their imports to France were exempted from the external tariff of the EEC.[36] At this early stage, France maintained her dominance in this area through her willingness to buy French-African products at prices higher than the world market value.[37]

The EEC faced a crisis in 1962 after the associated states had achieved their political independence and the provisions of the Treaty of Rome were about to end. The association provided for under the Treaty of Rome was for an initial five-year period, 1958-1962, after which the terms were to be reviewed. The accession of fourteen French dependencies to political sovereignty in 1960 brought about a re-examination of their association with the European Economic Community. Their achievement of independence raised the question of the legal status of the association as well as the terms of association that had been formulated at a time when they were still colonies. The main concern was whether the associated territories which derived their status in the EEC as dependencies of the EEC member association with the European Economic Community. Their achievement of independence raised the question of the legal status of the association as well as the terms of association that had been formulated at a time when they were still colonies. The main concern was whether the associated territories which derived their status in the EEC as dependencies of the EEC member states could retain that status even after they had become independent states. Two legal interpretations were expressed about this issue. According to one interpretation of the Treaty of Rome, independence invalidated the limited non-voting associate status of overseas dependencies, and negotiations for membership under Article 238 of the Treaty would have to take place just as in the case of any independent state seeking membership in the European Common Market. The other interpretation asserted that the achievement of independent status did not necessarily disrupt the associate status of former dependent territories provided they confirmed this status after becoming sovereign states. This latter interpretation of the treaty prevailed over the former when the Council of Ministers of the EEC unanimously adopted it. Thus, all the new states, with the exception of Guinea, which had denounced its associate status shortly after it had achieved its independence from France, declared their intention to retain their associate status.

By declaring their desire to continue association with the EEC, the new Francophone states ignored the criticisms of Pan-Africanists and Commonwealth countries particularly, who charged that the whole association plan was a grand design of European imperialists to perpetuate their economic domination of the African continent. The main point of criticism was that the associated African states had no part in the negotiations that led to the founding of the Common Market and that they had simply been brought into the scheme because of the existing relationships between them and the metropolitan powers. The decision of these Francophone African states to continue their association with the EEC seemed at the time a setback to these critics.

In the Yaoundé and Lomé Conventions, the African associate members continued to derive benefits from their association relations with the EEC. These Conventions continued in a progressive manner to liberalize trade between the European members of the Common Market and their

African partners. The Yaoundé Convention, which was signed in 1963, established a formal association between the EEC and eighteen individual French-speaking African states. Article 1 of the Convention of Association stated that the goal of the association was to strengthen the economic ties and the economic independence of the associated countries and eventually contribute to the development of international trade.[38] It provided that "goods originating in the associated states shall, when imported into member states, benefit from the progressive abolition of the customs duties."[39] In return for this trade concession, each associated country accorded identical tariff treatment to goods originating in any of the European states.[40] However, Article 3 provided that member states might retain or introduce customs duties and charges having an effect equivalent to such duties which corresponded to their development needs or their industrialization requirements or which were intended to contribute to their budget.[41] This was the so-called "Protective Clause." This article further provided that these duties "may not give rise to any direct or indirect discrimination between member states."[42] Article 6 provided that the associated states "shall not later than four years after the entry into force of the Convention, abolish progressively all quantitative restrictions on imports of goods originating in member states."[43] The same protective clause applied here. The African associated states were permitted to apply quantitative restrictions on imports of goods originating in member states only for the following purposes: to meet their development needs and industrialization requirements, to overcome difficulties in their balance of payments, or to satisfy the development needs of their agriculture.[44] Articles 8 and 9 provided that the Convention should not prevent the maintenance or the establishment of customs unions or free trade areas between one or more associated states and one or more third countries insofar as they neither were nor proved to be incompatible with the principles and provisions of the said Convention. These provisions were meant to remove the fears of the associated countries that the EEC might attempt to stop them from becoming members of regional economic organizations.

The Lomé Convention of 1975 marked a further Liberalization of trade between African and European states. Euro-African trade links became rather more institutionalized as a result. The Lomé Convention involved trade and cooperation between the EEC and forty-six African, Caribbean, and Pacific states (ACP). It provided that a vast majority of ACP manufactured goods and processed agricultural products were permitted to enter the EEC markets free of tariff or quota barriers. Thus, the EEC demonstrated a new flexibility when it provided for preferential access for ACP products to EEC markets without demanding reciprocal advantages for EEC products.[45] The European members established a compensatory finance scheme, STABEX, for the purpose of stabilizing the export earnings of the associated states by ensuring that they did not suffer a drop in such earnings through either a price decline or natural disaster. As Richard Hull explained, STABEX received only half-hearted support from some EEC members who feared it would weaken the free play of the market forces of supply and demand.[46]

As a direct consequence of their association with the European Common Market, the Francophone African countries received many economic benefits. They succeeded in diversifying their trade and thus improved on their position as buyers by widening their choice of suppliers of manufactured goods. They no longer had to depend solely on France. At the same time, they were permitted to manipulate their own tariffs and quota restrictions on imports from third countries as their domestic interests dictated. Their duty-free access to the EEC provided them with an immense advantage in terms of such key primary products as cocoa, coffee, palm oil, palm kernels, and groundnuts. Thus, the economies of the associate African members, which are still mainly dependent on primary agricultural commodities for their export trade, have continued to rely for the marketing of these products on an international market concentrated in the European geographic area.

To these countries, exports have provided a very large proportion of the total money income available.[47] It is quite evident that African trade is by and large conducted with the Common Market countries, as Table II, below, indicates.

In terms of trade and even aid, the EEC has favored the associated members over the non-members. This discriminatory policy of the EEC has led to bitter criticism and resentment in the excluded countries. It is estimated that over $100 million annually which flows from the EEC Development Fund to Francophone African states represents an increase of some 50 percent in the level of aid they received directly from their former colonizer. This continued support has helped these French-speaking countries to improve their economic situation.

To these new states, this support system has been very crucial, since economic development is one of their leading priorities. Their European partners realized that the acceleration of economic growth in these associated African states would depend on the expansion and exploitation of their agricultural resources to the fullest potential in order to enhance their industrial advancement.[48] Major emphasis has been placed on marketing food and industrial raw materials for the international market. It is assumed that the prices which these commodities bring would be a crucial factor in determining the rate of economic development, since imports have to be paid for by exports.[49] Thus, the rise of productivity in the associated countries would obviously increase their earning power and enhance their efforts to achieve rapid economic development.

There are other major consequences resulting from trade relationships between European members of the EEC and their African partners. In the first place, there have been trade diversions following the removal of customs barriers among participating members of the Common Market. For example, countries such as Nigeria and Ghana lost a large portion of their trade with former customers, now members of the EEC, because of high tariffs and quota restrictions with which their exports were confronted. As Duri Mohammed pointed out, while the effect of tariffs on products such as cotton and crude oil might be minimal, tariffs on other major commodities such as coffee and cocoa imported from a third country faced nine percent import duty, while associate members enjoyed free entry.[50] This situation is hurting third parties which produce identical products as associate members. For example, Ghana and Nigeria are among the leading exporters of cocoa, but while their products faced high tariffs in the European Common Market, the Ivory Coast, another leading cocoa producer, sends her product duty-free to the same market, being an associate member. As a result, the Ivory Coast has embarked on a program of expanding her cocoa production, while Ghana and Nigeria have no other choices but to cut down the amount of cocoa they produce because of the restrictions imposed on their exports to the EEC.

The economic integration between the EEC and the associated African members has been a source of bitter criticism of the Community and has led to charges of neo-colonialism, particularly by those excluded from the system. These critics have pointed out that European powers were once again reasserting their lost power through continued and frequently hidden political and economic ties with their former dependencies.[51] Thus, they viewed the new economic association of the African countries in the EEC as colonialist, imperialist, and a latter-day example of European attempts to divide Africa and thereby obstruct Pan-African efforts to unite the continent economically and politically. According to these critics, the benefits to the associate members were not, after all, obvious. They pointed to studies on the effect of economic unions on the economic welfare of the constituent units in terms of their rates of growth and prospects of development to support their criticism, and concluded that economic integration between the underdeveloped countries with highly developed ones would not assist the former and might even hinder the more backward economies. Their point of contention is that economic integration will most benefit those participants which are at much the same level of development.[52] They frowned at economic integrations between unequal members, since such associations would inevitably place the underdeveloped members in positions where they served as producers of raw materials and eventually hurt their efforts to become industrialized states.

The sharpest critics of EEC's relationships with the associated Francophone states were the radical[53] Pan-Africanists and Commonwealth countries who charged that France was the brain behind this scheme, and that it was her major objective to divide French-speaking Africa from the rest of Africa. To counteract EEC's programs and escape economic domination by European industrial powers, the Pan-Africanists called for the creation of an African Common Market and the promotion of intra-African trade as an African substitute for the EEC. They hoped that the creation of an African

Common Market would enhance closer cooperation among African states and reduce foreign influence. Carried away by their new enthusiasm, the Casablanca bloc states drafted a formal agreement to create an African Common Market. But critics doubted from the very beginning the usefulness of uniting the commerce of states which traded very little with one another in the past. The agreement was, however, never ratified due to lack of commitment on the part of members of the group and, thus, never came into force. In Africa as a whole, the idea of an African Common Market did not receive wide support since most African economies were rather competitive instead of complementary. The producers of primary cash crops such as coffee, cocoa, peanuts and vegetable oils were more interested in preserving their traditional European markets and paid little or no attention to the general idea of an African Common Market.

When this strategy failed, the Pan-Africanists embarked on still another plan which would involve cooperation or integration of neighboring countries to cope with the problem of industrialization in Africa. They believed that the enlargement of domestic markets and the creation of an integrated transport and communications system would serve as necessary preconditions for economic viability of the new African states.

Finally, they sought assistance from specific commodity agreements which they considered beneficial to large producers of traditional export commodities on which they depended for a significant part of their export earnings. It was their firm belief that commodity agreements might stabilize export earnings of large producers and thereby sustain a reasonable rate of economic growth. Furthermore, to escape from the evils caused by the rise and fall of prices at the international market, they advised their colleagues to diversify their exports.

In spite of the criticisms of economic cooperation between Francophone African states and European countries, the leaders of French-speaking Africa, with the exception of Guinea and Mali, hailed the EEC as an institution through which the concept of "Eurafrica" would be fully realized. To these states a bilateral relationship has been transformed into a multilateral arrangement to meet the requirements of a new situation.

Unlike others, Guinea's attitude and policy toward the EEC remained one of suspicion and doctrinal opposition.[54]

In conclusion, some observations will be in order. Trade relationships between these two ex-colonial powers and the new African states have not altered much from what they used to be in colonial days. The colonial trade pattern has continued almost intact with minor exceptions. The new states have remained overwhelmingly oriented to and have depended on their trade with the former metropolitan powers. Thus, the bulk of African trade is still conducted with the former colonial powers, which means that, although slight shifts have taken place in the distribution of African exports and imports, the countries of Western Europe have continued to dominate trade in African countries.[55] African exports in general are usually agricultural products which account for the large bulk of the export trade, with the exception of such countries as Zaire, Ghana, Zambia, and Nigeria, which export minerals and petroleum.

The Anglophone African states have asserted their economic independence more than their Francophone counterparts. Britain's trade with the new states has been declining steadily since independence. For example, between 1958 and 1959, the EEC members gained some ground at the expense of the United Kingdom. In 1959, the EEC bought 38% of Ghana's total exports compared with 33 percent in 1958. A similar shift took place in the trade of Nigeria. The share of EEC in Nigeria's total exports increased from 31 percent in 1958 to 34 percent in 1959. To reverse this trend, Britain decided to do something about the situation. At a meeting of the Commonwealth Heads of Government in May 1975, in Jamaica, Prime Minister Harold Wilson promised what he termed a new deal in world economies involving trade, particularly between nations and the terms of that trade. His proposed new deal included a general international commodity agreement, specific commodity agreements, stabilization of export earnings, and consideration of indexing prices of raw materials and manufactured products.[56] To this date, Britain has not been able to implement this new deal.

One major area where the Anglophone African states have demonstrated their independence has involved the monetary policy. It is true that these states remained in the sterling area after independence, but they quickly dismantled the colonial monetary system. Each new state set up its own currency more or less closely tied to the pound sterling through credits held in London and through use of the London money market for purchasing foreign exchange. The immediate result was that Britain had no responsibility for the currency of her ex-colonies. Thus, when Britain devalued the pound in 1967, very few African states went along with Britain in this currency devaluation. Each new state, though in the sterling zone, created its own Central Bank with a reserve system allowing it to issue its own clearing arrangements.[57] As a consequence, in British Africa, monetary systems have been weaker and fragmented.

By contrast, almost all Francophone states have remained in the franc zone and have held on to a system based on a precise monetary relationship with France.[58] For example, in French West Africa, states such as Benin, the Ivory Coast, Niger, Upper Volta, and Togo are members of the West African Monetary Union (UMOA) and share a common central bank, the Banque Centrale des Etats de l'Afrique de l'Ouest.[59] Similarly, the states of French Equatorial Africa, which include Cameroun, Chad, Congo, Gabon, and Central African Empire, have grouped themselves around their own central bank, the Banque des Etats de l'Afrique Centrale. Both central banks maintain most of their foreign exchange reserves at the French Treasury in Paris.[60] Under this arrangement, the currencies of these states have parity with the French franc and can be converted into French francs as the need arises. As Richard Hull indicated, the French Treasury guarantees the foreign exchange commitments of states which experience external trade deficit by offering them low-interest loans. In return for that privilege, the Francophone states have allowed French firms and their expatriate employees to transfer their profits and salaries directly to France.[61]

This linkage to the French monetary system has provided what Richard Hull termed a "compelling incentive" for the Africans to continue their close ecomonic ties with the former colonizer and has permitted French businessmen and civil servants to retain a large physical presence in the region and thus has retarded the process of Africanization.[62] Analysts have pointed out that the relative stability and high value of the franc tend to entice producers in weaker monetary systems to smuggle their goods out of their own countries into the franc zones. Hull cited the case of Ghana in the early 1970's which smuggled its cocoa crop into markets in neighboring Ivory Coast and Togo where it could be exchanged for a more valuable currency.[63]

The franc zone has remained almost intact in French-speaking Africa with minor exceptions, although it has been suggested that the economic advantages of trade and financial relations with African states are no longer crucial to France as before. Two factors explain the decline of the importance of sub-Saharan trade for France. The first factor has involved the fact that France no longer possessed the legal framework for maintaining the total dominance of trade which characterized the colonial period. The second explanation has involved the fact that these new states are now associate members of the EEC of which France is also a member. Their membership has meant that the legal rights of France in the region have been drastically undermined. At the time of independence, the ex-colonies signed economic cooperation agreements with France which provided for a continuing preferential system. Thus, African exports to France were accorded exceptions from French customs duties. Agricultural exports from African countries were assisted by French quota restrictions on agricultural imports from third parties and by continued French price supports. Similarly, French exports to these African countries were exempted from duties and quantitative restrictions. The EEC, however, forced France and her former dependencies to open the somewhat closed franc zone to the other European members. For example, the Treaty of Rome and the Yaoundé Conventions did provide for the elimination of French price supports and for the gradual extension of French trade benefits to France's other European partner in the EEC.

Nevertheless, if France's commercial dominance in her former dependencies has been trimmed back since independence, most of the Francophone African states still import between 40-60 percent of their goods and services from the ex-metropolitan power.[64] Their membership in the EEC has not stopped them from having close economic relations with France. The African market has remained essential for certain French exports such as sugar, petroleum products, textiles, pharmaceutical products, and insecticides, particularly. These French industries are not very competitive on the world market. Their exports of these products to the African market allows them to survive from forced modernization. It is estimated that French industry depends heavily on exports to Africa and about 300,000 French jobs are directly attributable to France's links with the underdeveloped countries, most of which are located on the African continent.[65] Thus, the economic arrangements between France and the new states have continued to be beneficial to France as usual. The network of French businesses in Sub-Saharan Africa and the familiarity with these markets are perhaps the most important factors in maintaining the high level of French imports in the region. The exports of these new states to France have continued to be heavy, although the EEC has become a new market for their exports as well as a source of their imports.

From the structural point of view, the African countries in the franc zone have continued to be a precious "captive market" for the beleaguered French economy.[66] Thus, an analyst claimed that Africa has remained a major geographical region where France was able, in 1982, to chalk up a trade balance surplus.[67]

French influence seems now to be declining gradually in Francophone Africa. Under Presidents Charles de Gaulle and his immediate successor, Georges Pompidou, France continued to exert a powerful economic influence on its former colonies, especially Gabon, the Ivory Coast, and Senegal. With the death of President Pompidou and the end of the Gaullist era, those relations appear to have lost that degree of intimacy. Ever since, the links between France and Francophone Africa have become looser and more flexible,[68] although the Socialist Government of President Mitterand reassured the French-speaking African countries of continued French friendship and support.

Trade in general between the new African states and the Communist countries of Eastern Europe, has remained small. However, the number of Trade Agreements between Communist states and African countries is rising, indicating that these new states are viewing trade with Socialist countries as very important as they plan to diversify their trading zones. This policy is in tune with their professed policies of neutrality and non-alignment in a world divided into two hostile ideological blocs.

In terms of its structural pattern, the post-independence trade discussed in this chapter still displays the features of the classical colonial economy which depended almost completely on the metropolitan power as a source of imports and as an outlet for its exports. Today, after two decades of political independence, the former metropolitan power remains a dominant or at least an important factor in the trade of the new African states, although some of them have expressed their commitment to widen their trade relationships. This policy of diversification, as H. P. White and M. B. Gleave put it, has been pursued with greater or less vigor and with variable results, so that current trade patterns fall along a continuum from most to least colonial.[69] Economic relationships with the former colonizers are as strong as ever. Minor shifts in terms of volume and direction of trade away from the former metropolitan power have been due largely to other industrial powers of Western Europe, the United States, Japan and the Soviet bloc nations.

It is interesting to note that political independence has not meant economic independence for the new African states since the economies of these states are still heavily dependent in many respects on the former colonizers. Nevertheless, political independence has indeed provided African states with some opportunity to choose where to establish new trade relationships. There have occurred a few sharp breaks of existing economic ties. Where these breaks have taken place, has generally involved economic sacrifice or hardship. Guinea and Mali serve as good illustrations. When Guinea decided to break away from the French political orbit in 1958 and become fully independent, France responded furiously by adopting punitive measures against it by way of cutting off aid, investments and withdrawing French personnel stationed in Guinea. Similarly, in 1960 when Mali tried to emulate Guinea, the relationships between her and France became very strained, although France remained her major trading partner and source of aid.

Among the factors which have encouraged or compelled the maintenance of close economic ties inherited from the colonial period include: currencies based on the franc and the pound sterling; and the dominant positions of British and French firms in all forms of economic activity such as banking and wholesale trade. The French, particularly, used tariff preferences, quota systems and subsidized guaranteed markets for Francophone African states' products. These incentives are so attractive that they prevent the pursuit of trade diversification on the part of the recipients of these "short term" economic benefits.

Both Anglophone and Francophone African countries have realized the dangers they face resulting from a complete dependence on the former colonial power for markets. Thus, radical states, such as Guinea, Mali, Tanzania, Nigeria, and Ghana under the late President Kwame Nkrumah, professed a non-aligned stance in the ideological warfare between East and West and, as a result, have established at least token connections with the Communist powers. However, most of these states still maintain far closer connections with the West, such as, for example, membership in the Commonwealth or association within the European Economic Community.

Anglophone states have been more successful in their diversification programs. Their success can be attributed to Britain's liberal economic policy in her dependencies during the colonial days. For example, in the years before independence, Britain did not totally control the external trade of its colonies to the same extent as France, especially those in East Africa where no imperial preference operated. However, Britain enjoyed the lion's share of the colonial trade and after the status of independence was attained by these countries, she continued to be their leading trading partner. Nevertheless, Britain's share since independence has dropped, particularly in Nigeria, Ghana, and Tanzania. As members of the Commonwealth, Anglophone African states enjoy special preferences in those commodities on which the Government of the United Kingdom imposes tariffs. Nevertheless, there are no guaranteed prices nor are there quotas for most of the exports from British Africa.

These states have sought trade links with either the EEC or with Communist countries. Nigeria, for example, sought a special association with the EEC but in the end concentrated on bilateral trade agreements with individual members of the Common Market to protect her major exports.

In Ghana, Nkrumah's policy was reversed following the military coup which caused the fall of his regime. Ever since, the United States became the beneficiary of that situation and thus increased her share of import trade to roughly 25 percent in 1968. Similarly, the EEC countries together were buying more goods from Ghana than did the United Kingdom in 1968.

France and Francophone states, by contrast, have maintained very intimate post-independence relationships, which African critics have characterized as pure neo-colonialism. The benefits which these French-speaking states have enjoyed include a guaranteed market in France for their exports, general quotas, and guaranteed prices paid on their goods at rates generally higher than world prices. In return, they gave France considerable tariff preferences. All these arrangements made it possible for France to dominate their economies. French firms such as Societé Commerciale pour l'Ouest Africain (SCOA) and Compagnie Francaise d'Afrique Occidentale (CFAO) still dominate the commercial life of such states as the Ivory Coast, Senegal and Gabon.

The participation of Francophone African states in the EEC as associate members has reduced their dependence on France slightly. As associate members of the Common Market they have modified their trade tariffs in order to provide equal preference to all European Common Market members, including France. Thus, in theory, the guaranteed prices paid by France would be discontinued. But in practice, France continued to provide some measure of price support. Despite the fact that France's EEC partners have now penetrated the once closed French market, the bulk of this trade remained with France. The exception to this rule involved two radical states – Guinea and Mali – which decided to break away from the French economic orbit and turn for trade and aid to Communist countries. However, after very rapid post-independence growth, their trade with Communist states began to show signs of decline and both states once again sought closer trade relations with France in particular and the capitalist world in general.

In general, trade or economic links between African states and Communist powers during the post-colonial period have not been as impressive as those with countries of Western Europe and North America.

The reason for this phenomenon could be traced to the colonial days when trade relations between Communist countries and African countries were either very negligible or non-existent. Two factors changed all that. The first involved the attainment of independence on the part of African states. Political independence did provide these states with some opportunity to choose their trading partners, their sources of aid, their political associations and sources of investment capital. Some countries, however, have achieved a greater freedom of choice than others.

The second factor involved the concerted efforts of Communist countries to increase economic and political contacts in Third World countries. Thus, the Soviet Union and China competed very sharply in Africa for influence. Soviet delegations signed Agreements of Friendship and Trade with African Governments. These Trade Agreements were directly linked with economic assistance programs. For example, since the early sixties, trade figures with Communist states including China have generally risen remarkably for such countries as Guinea, Ghana, Mali, Nigeria and Tanzania.

In addition to diversification of trade, these new African states have sought other ways and means to reduce their dependence on former metropolitan powers. These have included the increase of production of primary commodities or cash crops such as palm produce, cocoa, cotton, coffee and tea; finding new materials for export; and elimination of competition among producers of similar products.[70]

It is indeed very discouraging to note that intra-African trade is rather very small and on the decline. The few states which conduct a substantial portion of their trade with their African neighbors are such countries as Mali, Niger, Upper Volta and Chad which are geographically land-locked. This trade includes imports and exports in transit to and from the ports of the coastal states such as the Ivory Coast, Senegal and Nigeria.

It is rather very difficult to measure accurately the volume of the intra-African trade. Published states' statistics are misleading and can best be characterized as undercounts. For one thing, it is only trade passing through customs posts that is recorded. In many instances, land frontiers are long and thus very difficult to police. Furthermore, the local inhabitants ignore these artificial state frontiers. In these borders, significant amounts of unrecorded trade do take place. Smuggling is a common occurrence along national frontiers. For example, cocoa from Ghana is usually smuggled to nearby Togo; diamonds from Sierra Leone to Liberia; bicycles and textiles from Nigeria to Benin.

Analysts have explained the low levels of intra-African trade in terms of similarities between African economies which are characterized simply as competitive and not complementary. These states produce similar primary commodities and therefore, there is little need for trade.

In recent years however, there are increasing numbers of bilateral trade agreements between African countries and there is talk about the necessity of free-trade and economic unions on a continental basis.

Endnotes Chapter 2

1   David K. Fieldhouse, "The Economic Exploitation of Africa: Some British and French Comparisons," in *France and Britain in Africa: Imperial Rivalry and Colonial Rule*, eds. Gifford Prosser and Roger Louis William (New Haven: Yale University Press, 1971), p. 594.

2   *Ibid.*, p. 595.

3   See E. A. Brett, *Colonialism and Underdevelopment in East Africa: The Politics of Economic Change, 1919-1939* (New York: NOK Publishers, Ltd., 1973), p. 115.

4   Fieldhouse, "The Economic Exploitation of Africa," p. 603.

5   For further discussion, see Elliot J. Berg, "The Economic Basis of Political Choice in French West Africa," in *Independent Black Africa: The Politics of Freedom*, ed. William John Hanna (Chicago: Rand McNally and Company, 1964).

6   See Stephen H. Roberts, *The History of French Colonial Policy, 1870 - 1925* (Hamden, Connecticut: Archon Books, 1963), pp. 34-63.

7   Fieldhouse, "The Economic Exploitation of Africa," p. 606.

8   *Ibid.*, p. 607.

9   *Ibid.*, p. 609.

10   Virginia Thompson and Richard Adloff, "French Economic Policy in Tropical Africa," in *Colonialism in Africa, 1870-1960 Vol. 4, The Economics of Colonialism*, eds. Peter Duignan and L. H. Gann (London: Cambridge University Press, 1975), p. 143; see also, Albert Sarraut, *La Mise en Valeur des Colonies Françaises* (Paris: Colin, 1923),, p. 114.

11   *Ibid.*, p. 144.

12   *Ibid.*

13   Berg, "The Economic Basis of Political Choice," p. 621.

14   Terese Hayter, *French Aid* (London: Overseas Development Institute, 1965), p. 73.

15   Thompson and Adloff, "French Economic Policy in Tropical Africa," p. 145.

16   Fieldhouse, "The Economic Exploitation of Africa," p. 599.

17   *Ibid.*, p. 605.

[18]   Richard W. Hull, *Modern Africa: Change and Continuity* (Englewood Cliffs, NJ: Prentice-Hall, Inc., 1980), p. 215. [19]   Fieldhouse, "The Economic Exploitation of Africa," p. 613.

[20]   Joan Edelman Spero, *The Politics of International Economic Relations* (New York: St. Martin's Press, 1977), p. 14.

[21]   See B. W. Hodder, *Africa Today: A Short Introduction to African Affairs* (New York: Africana Publishing Company, Inc., 1978), p. 88.

[22]   William Clark, "New Europe and the New Nations," *Daedalus, Journal of American Academy of Arts and Sciences* 93, no. 1 (Winter 1964): 145.

[23]   *Ibid.*

[24]   See Paul Alpert, *Partnership or Confrontation? Poor Lands and Rich States* (New York: The Free Press, 1973), p. 68.

[25]   Belai Abbai, "Some Aspects of Trade and Development," in *Africa and the World*, eds. Robert K. A. Gardiner, M. J. Anstee, and C. L. Patterson (Addis Ababa: Oxford University Press, 1970), pp. 79-80.

[26]   *Ibid.*

[27]   *Ibid.*

[28]   Clark, "New Europe and the New Nations," p. 146.

[29]   See, "Europe" *Common Market No. 2173* (July 10, 1965): 3.

[30]   Thompson and Adloff, "French Economic Policy in Tropical Africa," p. 145.

[31]   Arnold Rivkin, *Africa and the European Common Market: A Perspective* (Denver: The University of Denver Press, 1963), p. 36.

[32]   Fieldhouse, "The Economic Exploitation of Africa," p. 605.

[33]   Hull, *Modern Africa*, p. 212.

[34]   Duri Mohammed, "Notes on the Common Market and Africa," in *Africa and the World*, eds. Robert K. A. Gardiner, M. J. Anstee, and C. L. Patterson (Addis Ababa: Oxford University Press, 1970), p. 123.

[35]   *Ibid.*

[36]   Fieldhouse, "The Economic Exploitation of Africa," p. 605.

[37]   Gardiner et al., *Africa and the World*, p. 123.

38   The Yaoundé Convention, Article 1.

39   *Ibid.*, Article 2.

40   *Ibid.*, Article 3, paragraph 1.

41   *Ibid.*, Article 3, paragraph 3.

42   *Ibid.*, Article 4, paragraph 1.

43   *Ibid.*, Article 6.

44   *Ibid.*, Article 6, paragraph 3.

45   Spero, *Politics of International Economic Relations*, p. 181.

46   Hull, *Modern Africa*, p. 213.

47   *Ibid.*; see also Mohammed, "Notes on the Common Market and Africa," p. 124.

48   Gardiner et al., *Africa and the World*, p. 122.

49   *Ibid.*

50   *Ibid.*

51   Cowan L. Gray, *Imperialism, Colonialism and After* (New York: Columbia University Library, 1966), not published, p. 3.

52   Mohammed, "Notes on the Common Market and Africa," p. 125.

53   The radical states of the sixties included Ghana, Guinea, Mali, Morocco, and Nasser's UAR. They constituted the so-called "Casablanca Bloc" of African states.

54   Rivkin, *Africa and the European Common Market*, p. 33.

55   Colin Legum, ed., *Africa: A Handbook to the Continent* (New York: Frederick A. Praeger, Inc., 1962), p. 476.

56   Speech on World Trade in Commodities, delivered by Prime Minister Harold Wilson to the Commonwealth Heads of Government Meeting in Kingston, Jamaica, May 1, 1975. (British Information Service, Policy and Reference Division, 33/75), p. 1.

57   Hull, *Modern Africa*, p. 215.

58   *Ibid.*

59   *Ibid.*

60   *Ibid.*

61   *Ibid.*, p. 216.

62   *Ibid.*

63   *Ibid.*

64   *West Africa*, June 27, 1983, p. 1499.

65   *West Africa*, No. 3382, May 1, 1982, p. 1437.

66   *West Africa*, June 27, 1983, p. 1499.

67   *Ibid.*

68   Hull, *Modern Africa*, p. 213.

69   H. P. White and M. B. Gleave, *An Economic Geopgraphy of West Africa* (London: G. Bell and Sons Ltd., 1971), p. 218.

70   Cocoa Producers Alliance is one good example. In January 1962, Ghana, Nigeria, the Ivory Coast, Comeroun and Brazil formed the Cocoa Producers Alliance. Similarly, in June 1962, Senegal and Nigeria decided to set up an African Groundnut (Peanut) Council.

CHAPTER 3

INVESTMENTS

Investments featured prominently in these post-colonial relationships. The two ex-metropolitan powers, Britain and France, exercised dominance over the new African states. A remarkable feature which has characterized the economies of most African countries is the lack of domestic capital needed for development. This has resulted in heavy reliance on aid and investment from abroad. Through the manipulation of aid and investments in Africa, Britain and France maintained a large measure of control in these areas. The donors dominated the recipients of aid in many ways. British and French aid and investments in Africa had their origin in colonial times. Colonial governments invested in infrastructure projects, but the overall rate of investment and aid was rather low. The bulk of these investments was in minerals and mineral-associated subsidiary industries, agriculture, transportation, and communications systems, such as railroads, roads, ports, and airfields, considered useful for the exploitation and shipment of products. Throughout the colonial period, foreign investors, both private and public, invested heavily in the export sector simply to stimulate the production of viable cash crops or mineral production which were believed to give the investors quick returns on their money. Thus, governments placed their investments, or the investments of the nationals, so as to favor local production for either the local market or for the world market.

The attitudes and policies of the imperial powers toward colonial development were indeed conditioned by their needs as major manufacturing and capital-exporting countries.[1]   E. A. Brett has pointed out that the resulting demand for external markets and cheap sources of raw materials had always influenced the policymakers in the metropolitan countries.[2]

The economic ideology of the period, as Brett explained, required both that colonial development be confined to forms of production which would not compete with metropolitan manufacturers, and that colonial consumers prefer metropolitan commodities however uncompetitive.[3] Therefore, metropolitan policymakers supported policies based upon the assumption that colonial economic development meant that evolution of primary export production was complementary to metropolitan manufacturing production.[4]   This view assumed a natural harmony of economic interests between the metropole and the dependency.   Thus, metropolitan capital invested in colonial infrastructure would facilitate rapid increases in the production of colonial primary products; their sales, preferably to metropolitan manufacturers, would in turn create the markets for manufactured exports.[5] A type of symbiosis resulted. It appeared as though the interests of both parties were reciprocal instead of being competitive. It seemed both parties benefited from the exchange and colonial welfare depended on and made possible the success of metropolitan industry.[6]

The goal of the colonial enterprise involved exploitation of the resources of the dependencies. The fact that the colonies in general lacked infrastructure projects to begin with, and private investors were reluctant to invest in the colonies due to lack of commercial viability of these infrastructures, it became evident that government assistance was inevitable for colonial development. Government support took the form of grants and loans which were provided on non-commercial terms and which, as a result, imposed some burden on metropolitan taxpayers.   Public investments constituted 47.7 percent in all British Africa, and about 61.2 percent in French tropical Africa.[7] In sheer volume, French public investment was by far greater than comparable British public investment in Africa. All capital invested in Africa came either from colonial public loans raised in Europe with or without metropolitan guarantees, or from direct private investment.[8] Soon after World War II, an increasing proportion of new capital came as aid from Europe to the colonies in the form of grants or loans on non-commercial terms.[9] According to Gifford and Louis, the determinant terminant of all aid before 1939 was the capacity of a colony to pay interest or of enterprise to pay dividends.[10] They noted that after 1945, while private investors retained the same commercial criteria, the bulk of public investment was related to planning for "growth" by the metropolitan and colonial governments rather than to colonial revenues.

In terms of aid and investments, the policies of Britain and France were for the most part similar. In both systems, economic development in the colonies was geared to the needs of the metropolitan powers.[11] Both powers expected their colonies to absorb manufactured goods and to produce raw materials. Both powers encouraged production of cash crops and paid little or no attention to the development of industries except for mining industries financed by metropolitan companies.[12] Both Britain and France possessed the power to determine the character of economic development in their respective colonies. In both systems, imperial objectives or interests were the main reasons for sponsoring economic programs aimed at achieving development. Finally, both imperial powers received a fair reward for their African investments. They managed to secure and dominate a remarkably large share of the African markets.[13]

Gifford and Louis pointed out that trade and currency restrictions after 1939 ensured that Africa's bullion and hard currency earnings were available to each metropolis to bolster the sterling and franc currency pools.[14] Thus, these benefits were quite substantial indeed.

The impact of European investments on African economic development after independence is a question subject to dispute. In other words, did economic development of the colonial period provide a satisfactory basis for growth after independence? Researchers have provided contradictory answers. While some writers claimed that both the colonizers and the colonized benefited from their association or relationship, outspoken critics of imperialism have suggested that investment and trade profited only European powers; that Britain and France reaped huge profits from their investments. These critics, such as E. A. Brett and Walter Rodney, to name but a few, insisted that Europeans removed wealth from Africa without contributing to the economic development of the colonies. Furthermore, they pointed out that agriculture was not developed in the sense that it simply perpetuated a situation which made Africans producers of raw materials. They characterized this situation simply as, "growth without development." It can be argued that, with the exception of mineral production, transportation, and communications, far too little capital was invested in the African colonies to promote rapid economic development. What was considered as economic development then simply meant or implied an overseas demand for African products at remunerative prices,[15] and thus, shifted the terms of trade in favor of European powers. This criticism is justified. Investments were indeed inadequate and thus tended to retard the economies of the African dependencies instead of stimulating their growth.

The principles which governed the investment policies of Britain and France were similar, though differences in terms of national style and emphasis existed in the application of investment programs. The amount of money invested in Africa was a small portion of British and French overseas investments as a whole. Black Africa was considered neither a major nor a necessary field for British or French investors, who preferred to invest elsewhere. For example, in 1928, French total investments abroad amounted to approximately £719 million, with just over £70 million of this amount placed in French tropical Africa.[16] Similarly, British total investments overseas stood at about £4.500 million in 1938, of which just under £373 million went to British Africa.[17] In both Anglophone and Francophone areas, investments were usually made in the building of infrastructure projects such as transportation and communications systems, agriculture, mining, and labor training.

Between the wars (1919-1939) there was a recognition on the part of the two imperial powers that most colonies could not afford to pay for their own development and, as such, that the metropole must be actively involved in the process of development. Despite the recognition of metropolitan aid in colonial development, the amount of aid coming from the metropole remained small.[18] Thus, David Fieldhouse claimed that before 1939, neither Britain nor France was prepared to make any substantial effort to accelerate development in Africa from metropolitan funds; the initiative and burden, he explained, were still left to colonial governments and private enterprise.[19]

The post-war period witnessed some major efforts made by Britain and France to improve upon their earlier performances as far as investments in the dependencies were concerned. Before 1945, it was generally believed that both imperial powers either lacked the resources or the commitment to embark on dramatic investment programs in the respective dependencies. Upon their recovery from that devastating war, Britain and France were determined to make improvements. Five- and ten-year plans were instituted to achieve economic growth in Africa.[20] Metropolitan "aid" on essentially non-commercial terms was provided as a substitute for pre-war colonial loans and to augment private investment.[21] Thus, in the post-war decades, the annual rate of investment increased to several times the pre-war rate, but private investment continued at less than half the total amount. Investments centered around educational and social services, which were expanded considerably. Thus, new airfields, ports, roads, railroads, and communications systems were constructed; the greater part of these investments came from public services. It is estimated, for example, that between 1946 and 1964 the French Government placed about $8,293 million in grants and aid in its Black African colonies.[22] Britain's grants and loans amounted to approximately $1,417 million for the same period.[23] As political independence approached, and on into the early 1960's, aid from the metropolitan countries in the form of grants and loans at low rates of interest became increasingly important.

Britain's Investment Experience

Britain's major goal, as far as the administration of colonies was concerned, was to make sure that colonial self-sufficiency and balanced budgets were attained. Thus, the first objective of any colonial administration was to pay for all its services out of recurrent revenue and to ensure that it maintained sufficient reserves. As Basil Davidson put it, these territories had to be administered, but not at the expense of the metropolitan taxpayer.[24] This situation meant, therefore, that the dependencies had to pay for their own administration and also, in large part, for their infrastructure.[25] To the British authorities, the ideal colony was not so much one that could provide raw materials as one that could be self-supporting financially.[26] This British policy frowned on or discouraged deficit financing, and the more affluent colonies were forced to accumulate reserves by underutilizing their resources. The need to build up large surplus balances was to remove, finally, the reliance on British aid. Thus, in colonial times, countries such as Ghana, Nigeria, and Uganda accumulated huge reserves in the British Treasury.

The British Colonial Development Act of 1929 was indeed an important landmark in Britain's efforts to develop its colonies. This Act set aside public funds for loans and grants to the poorer colonies and grants-in-aid were given occasionally.[27] For loans under the Colonial Development Act, the "borrower" government was required to accept full responsibility for servicing or repaying the loan after ten years. When grants were extended to a colony, its government was expected to bear a portion of the expenditure and to express its ability to make the annual charges resulting from the capital investment. The Colonial Development and Welfare funds, whether loans or grants, were administered very stringently by the British Treasury, and severe restrictions were imposed on the independence of the local administrations with regard to the management of the funds until they had balanced their budgets.[28] Through this Act the British Government made available free grants or loans of up to £1,000,000 per annum for all British dependencies, with relief on interest charges. Thus, in spite of the severe limitations imposed on the loans, the sum of £8,875,000 was committed in eleven years of its operation, of which £3,000,000 was in loans, the rest in outright grants.[29] From 1946 to 1955, total Colonial Development and Welfare grants amounted to £43 million. This showed a steady increase of funds committed to colonial projects.

The next important landmark in Britain's efforts to develop the colonies occurred in 1940 when the Colonial Development and Welfare Act was introduced. This Act made £5,500,000 available annually, of which £500,000 was set aside for research.[30] The Colonial governments were called upon to submit ten-year development plans. Furthermore, the Act of 1945 increased the sums for development and welfare to £120 million for the ten years 1946-1956; the funds allocated to research were increased to £1 million in any financial year. For purposes of efficient management, boards were established to determine priorities and to allocate resources. Unlike its predecessor, the new Act did not impose limits on expenditure on educational and social services.

In all, total expenditure contemplated in the original ten-year plan was £178 million, of which £56 million was to be provided by the Colonial Development and Welfare sources, £51 million from loans and £71 million from colonial revenues. As independence approached, the British Government increased the aid budget by the Acts of 1950 and 1955. For example, the projected expenditure for 1953 was £282 million.

A region where Colonial Development and Welfare operations were successful was East Africa, where the three dependencies – Kenya, Uganda, and the Trust Territory of Tanganyika, now Tanzania – experienced common services. The British Government, in cooperation with private enterprise, worked toward economic development in the area.

In response to the interests of the European settlers in Kenya Colony, the British Colonial administrators pushed for infrastructural development. The British Government provided funds through grants-in-aid which were designed to promote the establishment of infrastructure projects such as railroads, roads, and ports, which were considered necessary for the effective exploitation of the resources from the interior. As E. A. Brett explained, the British Government and private enterprise seemed to have a division of labor between them in terms of programs for developmental purposes in the area. For example, the government provided infrastructure services, agricultural extension, and research, as well as control over the legal framework of marketing and production, while private enterprise was given the right to develop production, processing, and marketing through either expatriate capital or African peasant production.[31] The British aid policy in Kenya particularly was tried in other regions with large concentrations of white settlers, such as Zambia and Zimbabwe. The interests of these white supremacist groups prevailed over those of the indigenous Africans.

In addition to the Colonial Development and Welfare Acts which provided direct aid in the form of grants and loans from Exchequer funds given to colonial territories, another form of assistance came through the Colonial Development Corporation. This was a public corporation set up in 1948 under the Overseas Resources Development Act whose purpose was to assist colonial territories in the development of their economies. This corporation did its work either on its own initiative or in association with private enterprise or even colonial governments. Its borrowing power was originally up to £100 million on a long-or medium-term basis and £10 million on a short-term basis. Later, its borrowing powers were raised to £150 million.

Most of CDC's loans are now made at interest rates of 3-10 percent, although it can lend at 5 to 6 percent for agricultural projects. The Corporation's investments in Kenya have been very substantial. For example, the value of its outstanding investment in Kenya in 1973 exceeded £30 million. Its funds are concentrated in projects such as agriculture, mining, housing, electricity, and water supply. Other large schemes included the Bura Bura housing estate in Nairobi, mortgage loans to buyers, and the Mumias sugar factory.

Britain reaped huge profits as a result of her African investments. For example, British merchants and investors were beneficiaries. They dominated the colonial market; their financial investments were safe and could not be nationalized. They controlled banking and instituted currency controls. They paid little or no taxes in the colonies and were not obligated to reinvest their profits there. Considering all these advantages, critics charged that metropolitan companies drained African resources while African countries obtained only minimal benefits from development.

Like the British, the French investments in France's African colonies were motivated by political and economic interests of the metropole. The main principles which governed the financial relations between France and her dependencies were laid down in the Finance Act of April 13, 1900. Article 33 of that Act provided that subsidies could be granted to the colonies out of the state budget.[32] Conscious of her special civilizing mission in Africa, France spent more money than her arch rival, Britain, in terms of investment capital for developmental purposes in the colonies. In the colonial period, French policy was the decisive factor in the determination of private and public investments placed in the colonies.[33] Thompson and Adloff outlined very precisely the features which characterized France's financial policy in Francophone Africa during the colonial era. These included: the exclusively French origin of all the colonial investments; the predominance of public over private capital, with the concentration of public funds in the colonial infrastructure, and of the private in commercial and related enterprises; colonial currencies tightly tied with the franc zone; and the sparsity of African revenues.[34]

French public investment was by far larger than private investment and was heavily concentrated in public works.[35] The public investments took the form of loans which were repayable with interest from colonial revenues. In terms of volume, French private investment in colonial Africa was quite considerably smaller and was placed in commercial enterprises whose monopolies the state enforced rigidly.[36] The 1930s witnessed a dramatic increase of French private capital invested in the African colonies. It is estimated that French private capital invested in tropical Africa within this period amounted to approximately 33 billion francs.[37] A breakdown of this total showed that about 30 percent was invested in trading firms; 9.5 percent in banking and real estate companies; industry, 17.1 percent; and transport, 3.6 percent. The analysts explained that the comparatively small allotment to industry and transport reflected the French investors' preference for investments that yielded quicker returns and which also involved minimal risks, as well as the limitations of the African markets.[38] Like their British counterparts in Anglophone Africa, French firms based in the Ivory Coast, Gabon, and Senegal benefited quite considerably because they usually preferred to repatriate their profits which were easily convertible inside the franc zone instead of reinvesting their profits locally.

The post-war period was characterized by a determined effort on the part of France to improve on her earlier records. This period witnessed a relatively heavy dose of public capital investment, the greater part of which came in the form of grants from France.[39] Thus, because of French investments, French colonies in Africa expanded their transportation, communications, education, and health programs in the post-war period. Between 1947 and 1956, for example, public capital investment in French West Africa alone totalled 170 billion cfa francs.[40] As Elliot Berg explained, about 106 billion francs, or over 70 percent of the total came from the French Treasury, most of it in the form of grants, and the rest in long-term, low– interest loans.[41] Compared with pre-war years, one will reach the conclusion that French efforts during the post-1945 period were very outstanding. It is estimated that between 1903 and 1946, only 46 billion cfa francs came from French sources to public authorities in West Africa alone.[42] All these came by way of loans, not grants. Thus, Elliot Berg concluded that in the ten post-war years more than twice as much public capital investment took place in French West Africa as had been made in the 43 previous years.[43] A major difference between the pre-war and the post-war efforts involved the fact that earlier public investments by France were repayable loans, while most of the most recent investments were outright grants.

The French contributions toward colonial development were indeed significant, though some critics point out that these were inadequate. The territories contributed between 30 to 35 percent of the total public investment from their own resources. France paid a substantial portion of their basic administrative expenditures. Thus, between 1950 and 1956, France paid over 37 percent of French West Africa's civil and military expenses. This included specific items of expenditure such as operating costs, pension payments, and the armed forces. In monetary terms, France paid 97 billion cfa francs out of a grand total of 260 billion.[44]

Thompson and Adloff claimed that a major cause of France's African colonies' inability to contribute more to their own economic development was the plan's failure to bring about an overall improvement in the living standards of farmers, herders, and fishermen.[45] In other words, there was change in the source of revenues. They pointed out that revenues continued to depend overwhelmingly on the fluctuating fortunes of foreign trade, while about half of all expenditures was accounted for by the salaries of a rapidly growing bureaucracy.[46]

During the post-1945 period, the French Government channeled its investments through the Investment Fund for Economic and Social Development (FIDES), which was established on April 12, 1946. This fund, financed from the metropolitan budget, was to make long-term loans for overseas development at a rate of one percent. FIDES funds were used in various projects ranging from communications infrastructures to education and public health. This fund made it possible to tackle the most difficult problems of the French-speaking African countries on a very large scale. The fund was supplemented by far smaller contributions from African territorial revenues.

The Investment Fund was managed by the Central Overseas Bank known by its initials in French as CCFDM. The CCFDM was a multi-functional body with such responsibilities as the issuing of currency in the Overseas Territories and the control of foreign exchange operations. Besides FIDES, it also had funds of its own available for low-cost loans to help finance overseas enterprises. The French Parliament appropriated the funds required by FIDES to carry out, year after year, the long-range plans which it had previously approved. The Executive Committee of FIDES usually distributed the funds according to the needs of each dependency on the basis of development projects presented by the individual territories after having been approved by the territorial assemblies. As the fund operated, it seemed as though the local people had an input in terms of planning at every stage, through their deputies and senators in parliament and, finally, through their members in the Executive Committee of FIDES, which represented Overseas Committees of Parliament. But it must be noted that France reserved the power to decide which projects had priority. This right, which was exercised by France, was vigorously criticized by various groups for many years. These critics pointed out that French and not colonial interests were predominant in determining which projects had priority.

The operations of FIDES fell into two main parts: (a) the general section, and (b) the overseas section. The former financed on a straight grant basis such undertakings which benefited all or more than one territory. This included such projects as scientific research, public development corporations, and major public works studies. The latter, financed through grants from FIDES, or loans (with interests from 1.5% - 2.5%, repayable in 25 years) from FIDES or the CCFDM, was used to secure for basic local equipment expenditures such as roads, railroads, airports, schools, hospitals, and housing.

For the period 1948-1958 (which the French have described as a decade of progress), FIDES, General Section, gave out grants approximating $305 million to French West Africa. This amounts to about 46% of the whole sum. FIDES, Overseas Section, 1948-1958, Public Investment, Country by Country was as follows:[47]

(a)	Mauritania	$ 15,100,000
(b)	Senegal	140,500,000
(c)	Guinea	78,700,000
(d)	Ivory Coast	109,000,000
(e)	French Soudan	79,400,000
(f)	Upper Volta	44,700,000
(g)	Dahomey (Benim)	49,900,000
(h)	Niger	25,200,000

FIDES made large contributions to the economic development of Francophone Africa by way of grants and low-interest loans. From its grants, new harbors were built in Conakry, Guinea, and Abidjan in the Ivory Coast. Since 1947, FIDES funds were used for the improvement of existing railroad systems by means of extending the lines to several parts of French Africa. Similarly, road-building projects were pursued with great vigor. Many international airports such as those at Abidjan, Bamako, Conakry, Dakar, and Niamey were built.

FIDES funds were also employed in the field of public health. This involved the establishment of institutes which specialized in medical research, such as the Leprosy Institute of Bamako, and the Trypanosome Institute of Bobo-Dioulasso. General hospitals were built in the major cities. Clinics, maternity homes, dispensaries, and mobile medical units were fully supported by FIDES funds.

Education and agriculture took the lion's share of FIDES funds. Marked improvements were registered in these two areas. For example, high schools, vocational schools, and teacher-training colleges were built as a result of FIDES participation in these developmental projects. Similarly, a large portion of French private investments were made in the field of agriculture. This was directly aimed at increasing production of cash crops such as palm produce, peanuts, bananas, cocoa, coffee, and wood; hence, critics asserted that, "all the aid went back to France."

FIDES' greatest success was in the fields of transport and urbanization. The main failure, its critics noted, was its inability to promote industrial and agricultural development, and eventually, productivity sufficient to keep pace with the growth in African population.[48]

By the late 1950s, much of French Africa was so linked with France by investments and trade benefits that independence brought little freedom to choose future economic policy.[49] Thus, in varying degrees, the new states which emerged in 1960 were still heavily dependent on French capital and skills. France continued to make its financial contributions to the new political entities. In spite of their membership in the EEC, French financial commitments to the former colonies have continued without any major cuts.

Foreign investments and aid have been very prominent in the post-colonial relationships between Britain and France on the one hand and the new African states on the other. Since 1960, when most of these ex-colonies emerged as sovereign states, investments and aid from Britain and France have continued to flow into Africa steadily. Since that time, the former imperial powers have felt that they could not be indifferent to their ex-empires. Thus, Britain and France have now changed quite drastically many of the old attitudes and actions involved in their national policies affecting the new African states. Both countries have increased their investment and aid programs in their former colonial territories without any major public debate.[50] These two European powers are now seeking new relationships with the developing African states. The old institutions have been modified to accommodate the new political situation. Having relinquished political control over the colonial peoples, they began to establish their influence by adopting specific programs designed to assist their former dependencies in their development projects. Thus, a large percentage of the investment capital needed for economic development is owned by British and French investors. In other words, foreign investment tends to control the most important sectors of production, namely, raw materials, export industries, and what observers have characterized as the dynamic sectors of the economy.

Although most African countries are rich in terms of natural and mineral resources, they are desperately short of the capital and technical know-how to exploit them. The direct effect of this weakness has simply meant dependence on the industrialized states for support. For purposes of securing the badly needed capital investment and aid, many of the African states have sought close ties with the former colonizers. The result of all this is that the nature of African states' economies has remained colonial, though one can assert that the more naked forms of colonial exploitation and capital transfer are ended. But more subtle methods of control have been instituted, such as, for example, the creation of huge multinational corporations, the system of patent rights, and technological know-how closely guarded by these foreign firms.[51] Since the foreigners control all the means of production, attempts at industrialization on the part of African states have not yet altered in any significant way the fundamentally complementary character of African economies and their dependence on the economies of former metropolitan powers. Thus, some critics have charged that the European ex-colonial powers have preferred not to disengage completely from their former dependencies and therefore have attempted to perpetuate their institutions and thereby protect their commercial and investment interests as long as possible.

In their attempts to achieve rapid economic development, both Anglophone and Francophone African states have been counting on the need for massive external assistance in finance, management, and in entrepreneurship, in project preparation, technology, and in skilled personnel.[52] They have to take into consideration the external assistance particularly from the former metropolitan countries when they draw up their national development plans. They realize that without external support, their development plans would not materialize.

British and French investors have been very selective in terms of countries where they place their capital investments. In other words, some countries are preferred over others for purposes of capital investments. Because of their favorable investment climate, Britain has invested heavily in Nigeria, Kenya, and Zambia. Similarly, France has placed its investments in such countries as Senegal, the Ivory Coast, and Gabon, and has refrained from investing heavily in areas like Mali and Guinea where the Governments in power have pursued active programs of nationalization of foreign investments in their land.

In order to attract foreign investment, African states which are striving for rapid industrialization, such as Kenya, Ghana, the Ivory Coast, Nigeria, Gabon, and Senegal, have taken steps to attract foreign investment. However, the potential investor usually takes into consideration risks involved in making an investment in a developing economy, emanating especially from political considerations such as instability of the political system, or economic factors, such as the instability of the exchange rates, both of which put a higher profit requirement upon the investment.[53] Thus, Richard Eglin points out that the potential investors will have to take into account the size of the host economy market relative to the technological threshhold of the industry in which they wish to operate.[54]

To a large extent, these risks are inevitable results of the turbulent currents of political, economic, and social change which are surging in these developing countries. Examples of these risks include: expropriation by the host government without adequate compensation; violation by the host government of a concession or other agreement; imposition of foreign exchange restrictions that prevent remittance of profits abroad; and import restrictions that prevent the importation of necessary equipment or raw materials.[55] Writers have used the term "creeping expropriation" to characterize the variety of more subtle measures which are employed by host governments to interfere with business operations and impair the rights of the foreign investor. These include the requirement of residence and labor permits for key personnel, and the unreasonable delay or refusal of import permits for essential materials and equipment. In addition to all this, taxes that discriminate, in substance if not in form, against foreign-owned business may be imposed. Profits may be restricted by governmental price controls or reduced as a result of governmentally-subsidized competition.[56] Finally, devaluation of the local currency may seriously diminish the real return on the investment.[57]

Recognizing that non-commercial risks pose an important obstacle to foreign investment, most of the developing African countries have taken measures to grant special assurances to foreign investors. Such assurances are usually negotiated either on an ad hoc basis and embodied in a concession agreement or a guarantee agreement.[58]

Occasionally, as Professor Friedmann pointed out, the capital importing countries might grant "investment encouragement programs," which include positive incentives such as tax reductions or holidays, assurances against tax increases, low interest loans supplied or guaranteed by the government, establishment of tariff barriers to protect the investment from foreign competition, and finally, a special guarantee against expropriation without compensation.[59] The need to acquire badly needed foreign investments has forced some capital-importing countries to accept, either in ad hoc concession or guarantee agreements or under investment incentive programs, arbitration of disputes with foreign investors.[60]

The desire to attract foreign investment has indeed become a preoccupation for many of the African states. They are now concerned with the idea of maintaining a good economic atmosphere conducive to private investment. Even now, African socialists have demonstrated pragmatism in the way they have been courting private investment. For example, Ghana, under the late President Kwame Nkrumah's leadership, and Tanzania, are two states which committed themselves to the ultimate achievement of a socialist society, yet both countries sought private investment. The goals of these governments, as stated in their Economic Development Plans as well as their official publications and pronouncements, are to create socialist states and also to attain a rapid rate of economic development. However, these two governments acknowledge that, during the transition to socialism, the economy of their countries will have to remain a mixed one in which the contribution of private enterprise will be essential to the attainment of substantial industrial growth. With this goal in mind, the government in

Tanzania secured the passage in 1963 of the Foreign Investment Protection Act which provided certain guarantees for approved foreign investments in the event of nationalization. But this Act has failed to inspire investor confidence of British nationals. It is true that international norms and agreements between investors and governments are legal bulwarks of foreign investment against injurious governmental intrusion, but some observers are skeptical about the efficacy of international norms and agreements as incentives to the flow of private capital to less developed countries.

Similarly, the development plans for Kenya and Uganda call for substantial investment of private foreign capital. Under Kenya's plan, government capital is to be concentrated primarily in social services, infrastructures, and security, leaving private capital – a significant proportion of which must come from abroad – to develop manufacturing, agriculture, tourism, fishing, and housing.

A warning note must be expressed. Attracting the foreign investors without considering the possible requirements of future policies could be extremely dangerous. Jonathan Mallamud warns that it must be borne in mind that the creation of a class of foreign investors with privileges and immunities considerably more extensive than those of the indigenous population can be counterproductive, since it will lead to an ultimate deterioration in the investment climate.[61]

Britain has remained a very reliable source of bilateral support to Commonwealth African countries. When African countries became independent sovereign states, the problem of financing economic development projects assumed new dimensions. Before independence, virtually the entire development budget or plan was supported by Britain. In other words, the proposed level of support from the United Kingdom was the principal determining factor in drawing up plans for development. At this time, the British Government exercised great flexibility in its provision of loans and grants to the dependencies. For example, capital funds from Britain were not always tied to British exports, and even when this policy was modified, the tie was never very comprehensive. Furthermore, Exchequer loans, for example, were not tied to projects at all and thus could be used as general support for the development budget.

Since independence, however, British capital investment has changed in two major patterns. The first one involves the simple fact that the independent countries have undertaken economic development plans on a more comprehensive basis, under which British support is no longer the only source, though, of course, it has remained an important one. The second change has involved the fact that new restrictions have been placed on the use of British funds, most notably that they be used more completely than in the past to finance imports from Britain and that they be used for projects more strictly defined than was the case in the past. As a consequence of the increasing rigidity of the link between British aid and export promotion, the new African states are forced to look for additional sources of overseas development finance. Thus, the International Bank for Reconstruction and Development and its affiliated banks, particularly the International Development Association, have served as sources of support. Similarly, the United States Agency for International Development and a variety of unsponsored programs, have served as sources of development finance for the new African states. The more radical states, such as Tanzania, Guinea, the Congo, and Mali, have not hesitated to seek aid from the Socialist states.

The post-colonial British investment in Africa has concentrated more on the primary producing industries such as rubber, tea, copper, uranium, palm produce, and petroleum. Private investment, which is the larger proportion of Britain's financial stake in overseas development, is of two types: namely, new money raised in the London market and direct investment; that is, investment financed from the existing resources of British firms or companies.

Although the bulk of Britain's overseas investment is carried out by private sources and is therefore not subject to government control or direction, the British Government is in a position to exert an encouraging influence on the nature of that investment by the attitude it adopts and by its regulations. For example, the Finance Act of 1957 afforded a substantial measure of tax relief to Overseas Trade Corporations which has enabled them to increase the amount available for reinvestment overseas and has encouraged them to expand further in those fields in which they have expertise. Similarly, all borrowings of more than £50,000 on the London market require treasury consent; since 1953, the conditions under which that consent is given have been eased.

Britain's support of investment programs in the new African states has been channeled through the Commonwealth Development Corporation. Through a Parliamentary Act of 1963, the Colonial Development Corporation was transformed into the Commonwealth Development Corporation. Its main objective is to cater to the economic needs, particularly investment needs, of the new members of the British Commonwealth. The change in terms of the title of the new institution was purely a technical one. It was simply a recognition on the part of Britain that all Commonwealth countries are theoretically equal and sovereign. Thus, the change was indeed a way of showing Britain's acceptance of their newly-acquired status as independent states.

Britain had earlier been criticized for excluding Ghana from benefits derived under the Colonial Development Corporation programs as soon as the latter achieved her independence in 1957. Taking into account this criticism, Britain realized that the new states had big problems confronting them and therefore took steps to create the Commonwealth Development Corporation in 1963. Under this Act, the CDC has been managing and advising on projects in independent Commonwealth countries. In partnership with private enterprise, it has undertaken a wide variety of projects such as agriculture, fisheries, water, gas, electricity, supplies, and marketing in Africa. The CDC has the authority to invest in Commonwealth countries directly. Its funds are used mainly to supplement development expenditures from local sources or from London market borrowings.

Commonwealth Assistance Loans have remained not only the most plentiful source of funds to African states, but also the most flexible. These funds must be used mainly to finance imports from Britain. However, under certain circumstances, they could also be applied against local costs, but never to finance imports from countries other than Britain. The interest rates generally range between 5 and 6 percent. The average life of the loan is over 25 years, including a five-year period of grace.

Another important source of support, particularly for projects involving large equipment, is the Export Credit Guarantee Department, which is authorized to guarantee loans for the purchase of British equipment. These loans may exceed ten years. Their rate of interest is between 5 and 6 percent.

A comparatively new channel for investing private capital in Commonwealth development programs is the Commonwealth Development Finance Corporation (CDFC). Its purpose is to invest in programs likely to benefit the sterling area's balance of payments, and in particular those for which adequate capital cannot be raised from ordinary sources.[62]

In addition to facilitating finance (capital) from private sources, the British Government is itself an active investor in overseas development. Finance is provided for beneficiaries in the form of grants and loans from Exchequer funds mainly for public development projects.[63]

Britain has invested more capital in some countries than in others. Nigeria, Kenya, Zambia, and Zimbabwe have attracted the largest portion of these investments. These countries are usually ones with natural resources, either minerals, petroleum, or cash crops, needed by British manufacterers. These states have generally allowed private capital to operate freely. They have offered inducements to industrial investors such as a greatly accelerated depreciation allowance, the "pioneer" certificate which grants relief from company tax for a certain period of years, tariff protection for the finished products, and the relief from duties on imports required as raw materials.

Since the late sixties and early seventies, African countries in general and Commonwealth countries in particular have joined other Third World countries in asserting full permanent sovereignty of every state over its natural resources and all economic activities. This assertion has resulted in tighter regulation of private capital flows as well as the unrestricted right to nationalize foreign-owned property and to pay compensation according to national laws. These states are taking concrete measures to decolonize their economies. They have expressed the view that foreign capital are investing only in export activities, in mines and plantations, and are deliberately neglecting manufacturing industries which, they claim, could help a great deal in the promotion of a diversified economy. In other words, they blamed foreign capital as being responsible for the lopsided structure of the economy where only the export market is efficiently developed.

In Nigeria, the Military Government led the way in the drive to achieve economic independence and thereby eliminate the exploitation of the country's national resources by foreign interests. The government believed that complete national control of the economy was indeed a necessary precondition for sustained economic growth which could only be achieved if the state had a firm grip on its economy. Thus, in Nigeria, the process of nationalization has been massive but selective. The Government has increased its shares in major industries. For example, in petroleum production (Shell-B.P., Phillips, Agip, Safrap, Mobil, Gulf), the government's share is 55 percent; in banking, 40 percent; in insurance, 49 percent; and petroleum (Shell), 60 percent. In Schedule I, the government listed 22 items or enterprises exclusively reserved for Nigerians.[64]

1. Advertising agencies and Public Relations business.
2. All aspects of pool betting business and lotteries.
3. Assembly of radios, radiograms, record changers, television sets, tape recorders, and other electric domestic appliances not combined with manufacture of components.
4. Blending and bottling of alcoholic drinks.
5. Blocks, bricks, and ordinary tiles manufactured for building and construction works.
6. Bread and cake-making.
7. Candle manufacture.
8. Casinos and gaming centres.
9. Cinemas and other places of entertainment.
10. Clearing and forwarding agencies.
11. Hairdressing.
12. Haulage of goods by road.
13. Laundry and dry cleaning.
14. Manufacture of jewelry and related articles.
15. Newspaper publishing and printing.
16. Ordinary garment manufacture not combined with production of textile materials.
17. Municipal bus services and taxis.
18. Radio and television broadcasting.

19. Retail trade (except by or within the department stores and supermarkets).
20. Rice milling.
21. Singlet manufacture.
22. Tire retreading.

In Schedule II, the government listed 33 Enterprises Barred to Aliens Under Certain Conditions.[65] The Government of Nigeria confiscated 120 foreign firms that defied Schedule I of the Nigerian Enterprise Promotion Decree and put Schedule II into operation. For example, during 1976, Amalgamated Tin Mines surrendered 40 percent of its shares to the Government. The critics have viewed Nigeria's Schedules I and II as indirect nationalization. Other Commonwealth countries such as Ghana, Tanzania, and Zambia have also established comprehensive nationalization programs of their own. Even Kenya, which has shown little interest in nationalizing foreign-owned property, has increased its shares in alien enterprises operating in the country. The Government now controls a 60 percent share in banking, 50 percent of petroleum refining, and 51 percent in electric power.

The leaders of these African States are convinced that foreign domination is particularly strong in the consumer and capital goods industries and are therefore committed to reduce or eliminate it. By acquiring greater control over the financial sector, the African states have demonstrated their commitment to adopt such measures which are designed to help their own indigenous entrepreneurs and companies that find it extremely difficult to raise capital from external sources. Thus, they encourage local banks to lend more to these individuals and companies.

French private and public investments, which were considerably heavy between 1946 and 1958, continued after decolonization. As a result, the African countries soon grew accustomed to these vast investments from France. The leaders of Francophone Africa have valued French support a great deal and have reached the conclusion that continued French support could only be assured if they remained very close to France. Like their British counterparts, French investors have been very selective in terms of countries where they invest their capital. Thus, French investments are concentrated in such countries as the Ivory Coast, Gabon, Niger, and Senegal, but very little in Guinea and Mali. Economic and political considerations explain this phenomenon. Senegal, for example, has always enjoyed a privileged position within French– speaking Africa chiefly for historical reasons. The Ivory Coast is the richest of Francophone African states and is considered the "darling of the French." Its major exports include cocoa, coffee, ivory, iron ore, bananas, and timber. Because of its relative affluence when compared with other Francophone African states in the region and the influence of its president, Dr. Felix Houphouet-Boigney, the French have been attracted to invest their capital. Similarly, Gabon's privileged position in French Equatorial Africa is the result of its natural resources. Its exports include plywood, timber, manganese, petroleum, and uranium. Gabon is now among the very few French-speaking African states with a favorable trade balance. These three states, which have attracted the largest amount of French capital investments, have offered considerable scope for private enterprise. Thus, French businessmen enjoy the favorable investment climate in these countries. For example, they do not encounter difficulties or restrictions in terms of capital transfers or the repatriation of profits to France. Frenchmen who live in these areas can easily send their earnings' profits to France or elsewhere without much difficulty, since there is no need for foreign exchange. This free-flow of capital permits capital repatriation to France.

By contrast, Guinea and Mali have attracted the least amount of French investments. Both countries have pursued active programs of nationalization of foreign-owned property. French businessmen in these two countries have the fear that these governments might impose new regulations of unfair taxes which should lower profits. They are also concerned about political instability in the areas where they invest their capital. Because of these considerations, French investors are leaving these countries which are rapidly nationalizing their economies. Guinea, after the break with France in 1959, has made new efforts to attract capital investment from other sources, particularly from the Soviet bloc countries. She designed a new investment code aimed at attracting foreign investors. This liberal code has not, however, been successful in drawing Frenchmen to invest in Guinea. French capitalists invest in areas where they feel secure that their investments would be adequately protected.

French investments are indeed very crucial to the post-independence development programs of Francophone African states. Just as the British Colonial Development Corporation was transformed to the Commonwealth Development Corporation, the Investment Fund for Economic and Social Development (FIDES) was replaced by the Fund for Aid and Cooperation (FAC). FAC has become an agent through which investment funds for French-speaking African countries are channeled. Like its predecessor, FAC's operations are divided into two main categories. The first category has involved operations carried out at the request of the African countries or by France itself, or even international bodies such as the United Nations and its various organs. The second category of operations involves those carried out by the states themselves under economic and social development programs formulated by them.

FAC's funds handle such projects as research, productivity, and technical training. The Central Fund for Economic Cooperation is in charge of the financing and administering of the Fund. It possesses its own funds which are used for long-range loans to African states.

In an attempt to stimulate the flow of capital investment in the former dependencies, the French government, in October 1970, established a plan to guarantee private French investments in the African and Malagasy states. This program ensures capital from 75 percent to 90 percent against several risks. This program is nevertheless limited to new investments with the exception of oil, agriculture, and buildling, which are not covered. It operates only for investments whose economic priority is officially recognized by the state concerned.[66]

French investors put their capital mainly in mining enterprises such as the iron ore and copper in Mauritania, the manganese, petroleum, and iron ore in Gabon, and the bauxite in Guinea. Thus, they emphasized extractive industries but cared very little for manufacturing, agricultural development, or even processing industries related to extractive activities. A major consequence of this situation is the fact that France controls the productive resources of Francophone Africa through her investments. French ownership and management of a large productive sector of these countries' economies give French investors power to participate, in a dominant fashion, in the decision-making process affecting these new states. For example, Frenchmen make decisions regarding the use of profits earned from the extraction of resources. Low taxes, free repatriation of capital, and free transfers under the franc zone system simply mean that investors can very easily return earnings to France.

The French have enjoyed many important contractual rights in Francophone Africa. These special contractual arrangements provide France with several benefits. They were part of the cooperation agreements which accompanied the granting of independence to the new states. For instance, there are provisions which give French investors equal rights of establishment with the nationals of these African states. Upon becoming associate members of the EEC, the African states extended to France's Common Market partners the same privileges which France had earlier enjoyed all alone.

France's national interests are among the main determining factors that have influenced its investment policies in Africa. Under special agreements, the uranium deposits in Gabon, the Central African Republic, and Niger are preserved for the French nuclear program. France is assured priority of the sale of certain strategic raw materials, including uranium.[67] Other strategic raw materials include liquid or gaseous hydrocarbons, thorium, lithium, beryllium, helium, and their minerals and compounds. Through these accords, France secures the right for information regarding research, exploitation, and foreign trade of these strategic raw materials. Thus, the arrangements assure France the priority of sale of these raw materials, facilities stockpiling of these materials for the benefit of the French armed forces, and provides the limitation or prohibition of export of these materials to other countries when French defense interests require.[68]

The participation of the French Atomic Energy Commission in exploiting companies further assures French control of uranium in Gabon, Niger, and the Central African Republic. The BRCM and the Commissariat

Française à l'Energie Atomique are involved in investment projects in French Africa.

In spite of the fact that the French have made sizable investments in French Africa, there are significant limits to investment opportunities for France in Africa. In the period 1963-1966, there was steep decline in private capital flows to the area. Since the mid-1960s, French investors have been turning to other industrial developed countries for purposes of investments.[69] In contrast, investment in industry in the African states has not proven to be attractive to French investors. This is explained in terms of relatively low investment returns which result from the constraints of narrow markets that limit economies of scale.[70]

The desire to reduce their dependence on France has led to the formation of regional unions in French Africa. The most important are the Union Douanière des États d'Afrique Occidentale (UDEAO) composed of all the former French West African dependencies with the exception of Guinea.

In 1965, the Organization of Senegal River States, made up of Guinea, Mali, Mauritania, and Senegal, was established for the joint development of the Senegal River basin. Upon Guinea's withdrawal following disagreements with Senegal, the other three members created the Organisation pour la Mise en Valeur du Fleuve Senegal (OMVS) in November, 1971.[71] The reason for the creation of these unions is the determination of these new states to preserve their identities as well as to further economic cooperation among them.

The European Economic Community is another major source of investment funds for the associated African members. Apart from guaranteed preferential access to the markets of the EEC for their products, the associated African states benefit under the aid provided through the EEC Development Fund. Article 132 of the Treaty of Rome provided that member states should contribute to the investments required for the progressive development of these "associate" countries and "territories." A total of $581,250,000 was to be contributed over a five-year period: $200 million each from France and the Federal Republic of Germany; $70 million each from Belgium and the Netherlands; $40 million from Italy; and $1.25

million from Luxemburg.[72] The distribution of the funds during the first five years favored Francophone African countries. For example, out of the grand total of \$581,250,000, they received the lion's share, \$511,250,000; Netherlands territories received \$35,000,000; Belgian territories, \$30,000,000; and Italian Somaliland received \$5,000,000.[73] From these figures, one can suggest that French territories were in effect being subsidized by the other five members' states. All assistance from the Development Fund is in the form of non-repayable grants. The EEC's Council of Ministers, on June 21, 1962, made further commitments to the associated Francophone African countries for the sum of \$780 million in aid for investment purposes.

Under the first Yaoundé Convention of 1969,[74] of the total \$1 billion committed, \$900 million was provided through the European Investment Fund, while \$100 million was provided through the European Investment Bank. Of the total sum made available by the European Investment Fund, \$748 million went in the form of grants to the eighteen associated African countries while another \$80 million was provided as loans on especially favorable terms for these states. These special loans are usually made to price-stabilization funds for commodities. A provision was made to accommodate difficult times such as economic crises or natural disasters. The "Disaster Fund," as it is generally called, was established to make grants available to the associated countries in the event of (a) exceptionally severe drops in world prices for their exports; or (b) natural calamities such as famine, drought, or floods. Thus, in time of trouble, the EEC could rescue the distressed associates as it did early in 1971, when it provided an emergency grant of \$7.2 million to Senegal to cope with the effect of drought and low world prices of peanuts.[75]

In addition, the European Investment Bank was authorized to make loans totalling \$90 million to the associated states out of funds obtained from bond issues on the international capital markets. From all these figures, one can safely assert that the support funds from the EEC donor states increased steadily. The overall aid total of the second Yaoundé Convention was \$1 billion, compared with \$800 million under the first Yaoundé Convention and \$581 million under the Treaty of Rome.[76]

The two Lomé Conventions provided the most ambitious and comprehensive capital investment schemes for the associated African states. A major innovation of the Lomé II Convention is a scheme to safeguard and develop mineral production. This new program attempts to bring to minerals the benefits that the STABEX scheme has brought to agricultural raw materials.[77] As explained earlier, STABEX was created to stabilize the export earnings of associated member states. The intent of the organizers of the new scheme was to increase the security of countries whose economies were at the mercy of sudden drops in prices or production.[78] The scheme covers copper, cobalt, phosphates, manganese, bauxite, aluminum, tin, and iron ore. Analysts describe the new scheme as an accident insurance scheme backed by finances amounting to $372 million. The scheme is set into operation if an "accident" causes a significant drop in a country's production, export capacity, or export earnings. The "accident" may be caused by local circumstances such as natural disasters or grave political events, or economic factors such as price collapses.[79] The assistance to a victim takes the form of special loans to finance projects or programs proposed by the recipient ACP country to restore its production and export.[80]

STABEX, which operated under Lomé I, has been expanded under Lomé II. Originally, it covered twenty-six products. The list grew to thirty-four items during the life of Lomé I, and now the other items have been added. They include cashew nuts, pepper, shrimp and prawns, squid, cotton cakes, oil cake, rubber, peas, beans, and lentils. STABEX transfers are made in the form of grants or interest-free loans whose terms are made even more flexible under Lomé II.

An issue which was seriously debated during the negotiations was over the total funds available. Under Lomé I, this was $3.466 billion units of account. At the time of negotiations for Lomé II, the EEC donor states pledged $5.1 billion, while the ACP countries were demanding $10 billion. A bone of contention involved the demand of the donors that new rules be laid down about investment protection which should make private capital more available, including an understanding to give the same treatment to investors from all members states of the EEC. They wanted investment guarantees to be retroactive and cover all investments; the ACP countries wanted the new rules to cover only the new investments.

The character, direction and flow of capital investment in both Anglophone and Francophone Africa in the post-colonial times have been remarkably similar. In the two areas investments have been very modest. On the basis of investments which the two metropolitan powers made in other parts of the world, the African investments were indeed on a very modest scale. In the early stages of the colonial enterprise, capital was necessary for the development of trade and for establishing infrastructure projects such as roads, railroads, communication systems and public works. However, as the concession firms gained great financial power, investments were for the purpose of exploiting readily accessible resources such as minerals. Thus, the main investments were made in those countries with extensive mineral wealth where the industries utilized large masses of unskilled labor. In dependencies where these resources were absent, development depended on the introduction of new cash crops such as cocoa, palm produce, groundnuts and coffee, either through the establishment of European plantations or by the adoption of systems of peasant production.

Since the time of political independence, the African states have continued to rely heavily on European industrial powers for investment capital. Researchers and analysts who support foreign investment for the new states point out that by transferring capital and technology, by bringing organizational and managerial skills and by opening up new export markets for African products, the European powers help to draw the African countries into the world economy and thus contribute to their economic growth and development. However, critics point out that too much reliance on foreign investment capital may prove to be counterproductive and warn that benefits and costs must be carefully weighed. They note that the developed industrial powers of Europe indeed have a considerably greater leverage over political life in the developing countries. For example, their economic power, their fiscal capacity and access to skills and information give them unusual advantages in their dealings with weak and fragile African governments. The end result will be a loss of responsible political control and self-determination on the part of African states.

Both Anglophone and Francophone African states have tried to diversify their contacts for capital investment. The radical states which adhere to a policy of positive neutrality are opening up new links with the Communist world. For example, in September 1960, hard-pressed Guinea secured a loan of some £9 million from the People's Republic of China. Similarly, Mali signed an agreement in March 1961 with the Soviet Government which provided 40 million rubles worth of credits and support for various industrial projects in Mali. Ghana signed a similar agreement in September 1961 with the USSR in which the Soviet Government pledged to assist in setting up state farms, increasing rice, maize and cotton production and building a tractor and ferro-manganese works.

This author strongly believes that the alleged economic benefits of European investments and marketing must be thoroughly weighed against the political and cultural consequences resulting from foreign corporate activities. In order to supervise effectively foreign investments in Africa the following policies must be adhered to. First, there should be improved national regulations on (a) capital and technology transfers, (b) recruitment and training of local personnel, (c) export restrictions, (d) taxation policies, and (e) the reinvestment of profits and the use of local shareholding.

These recommendations can make foreign investments more responsible to the special developmental needs of the developing African countries.

Endnotes Chapter 3

1   E. A. Brett, *Underdevelopment in East Africa: The Politics of Economic Change 1919-1939* (New York: NOK Publishers Ltd., 1973), p. 71.

2   *Ibid.*

3   *Ibid.*, p. 75.

4   *Ibid.*, p. 76.

5   *Ibid.*, pp. 72-73.

6   *Ibid.*, p. 73.

7   See Herbert Frankel, *Capital Investment in Africa* (London: Oxford University Press, 1938), pp. 158-159.

8   Prosser Gifford and William Roger Louis, eds., *France and Britain in Africa: Imperial Rivalry and Colonial Rule* (New Haven: Yale University Press, 1971), p. 627.

9   *Ibid.*

10   *Ibid.*

11   Joseph C. Anene and Geofrey N. Brown, eds., *Africa in the Nineteenth and Twentieth-Centuries* (London: Ibadan University Press, 1968), pp. 309-310.

12   *Ibid.*

13   Gifford and Louis, *France and Britain in Africa*, p. 637.

14   *Ibid.*

15   *Ibid.*, p. 636.

16   See Peter Duignan and L. H. Gann, "Economic Achievements of the Colonizers: An Assessment," in *Colonialism in Africa, 1870-1960, Vol. 4, The Economics of Colonialism*, eds. Peter Duignan and L. H. Gann (London: Cambridge University Press, 1975), p. 675.

17   *Ibid.*

18   *Ibid*

19   See David K. Fieldhouse, "The Economic Exploitation of Africa: Some British and French Comparisons," in *France and Britain in Africa: Imperial Rivalry and Colonial Rule*, eds. Prosser Gifford and William Roger Louis (New Haven: Yale University Press, 1971), p. 624.

104

20   Gifford and Louis, *France and Britain in Africa*, p. 624.

21   *Ibid.*, p. 600.

22   Duignan and Gann, *Colonialism in Africa*, p. 677.

23   *Ibid.*

24   Basil Davidson, *Let Freedom Come: Africa in Modern History* (Boston: Little, Brown and Company, 1978), p. 82.

25   *Ibid.*

26   B. W. Hodder, *Africa Today: A Short Introduction to African Affairs* (New York: Africana Publishing Company, Inc., 1978), p. 19.

27   Fieldhouse, "The Economic Exploitation of Africa," p. 624.

28   Cf. R. Oliver and J. D. Fage, *A Short History of Africa* (Harmondsworth: Penguin Books, 1962), pp. 196-205; taken from E. A. Brett, *Colonialism and Underdevelopment in East Africa*, pp. 28-30.

29   Overseas Development Institute, *British Aid*, vol. 5, *Colonial Development* (London, 1964), pp. 28-30.

30   Overseas Development Institute, *British Aid*, vol. 2, *Government Finance* (London, 1964), p. 96.

31   Brett, *Colonialism and Underdevelopment in East Africa*, p. 80.

32   See Jean Suret-Canale, *French Colonialism in Tropical Africa 1900-1945*, trans. Till Gottheiner (New York: Pica Press, 1971), p. 342.

33   See Virginia Thompson and Richard Adloff, "French Economic Policy in Tropical Africa," in *Colonialism in Africa 1870-1960, Vol. 4, The Economics of Colonialism*, eds. Peter Duignan and L. H. Gann (London: Cambridge University Press, 1975), p. 133.

34   *Ibid.*

35   *Ibid.*

36   *Ibid.*, p. 129.

37   *Ibid.*, p. 136.

38   *Ibid.*

39   See Elliot J. Berg, "The Economic Basis of Political Choice in French West Africa," in *Independent Black Africa: The Politics of Freedom*,

ed. William John Hanna (Chicago: Rand McNally & Company, 1964), p. 613.

40   *Ibid.*

41   *Ibid.*, pp. 613-614.

42   AOF, 1956, p. 340, taken from Berg, "The Economic Basis of Political Choice in French West Africa," p. 614.

43   Berg, "The Economic Basis of Political Choice in French West Africa," p. 614.

44   AOF, 1957, p. 376.

45   Thompson and Adloff, "French Economic Policy in Tropical Africa," p. 137.

46   *Ibid.*

47   See *French Economic Assistance in West and Equatorial Africa, "A Decade of Progress, 1948-1958,"* pp. 16-27.

48   Thompson and Adloff, "French Economic Policy in Tropical Africa," p. 133.

49   Gifford and Louis, *France and Britain in Africa*, p 641.

50   William Clark, "New Europe and the New Nations," *Daedalus: Journal of American Academy of Arts and Sciences* 93, no. 1 (Winter 1964): 151.

51   See Amiya Kumar Bagchi, *The Political Economy of Underdevelopment* (New York: Cambridge University Press, 1982), p. 39.

52   See Arthur F. Ewing, "Industrial Development in Africa: The Respective Roles of African Countries and External Assistance," in *Africa and the World*, eds. Robert K. A. Gardiner, M. J. Anstee, and C. L. Patterson (Addis Ababa: Oxford University Press, 1970), p. 110.

53   Raphael Kaplinsky, ed., *Readings of the Multinational Corporation in Kenya* (New York: Oxford University Press, 1978), p. 102.

54   *Ibid.*, p. 103.

55   See Wolfgang G. Friedmann, Oliver J. Lissitzyn, and Richard Crawford Pugh, *Cases and Materials on International Law* (St. Paul, MN: West Publishing Co., 1969), p. 797.

56   *Ibid.*, pp. 797-798.

57   *Ibid.*, p. 798.

58   *Ibid.*, p. 800.

59   *Ibid.*

60   *Ibid.*, p. 801.

61   See Jonathan Mallamud, "Legal Safeguards for Foreign Investment," in *Financing African Development*, ed. Tom J. Farer (Cambridge, MA: M.I.T. Press, 1965), p. 190.

62   Duncan Crow, *Investment in Progress: British Contribution to Overseas Development* (London: Fosh and Cross, Ltd., 1958), p. 10.

63   *Ibid.*, p. 13.

64   See P. Collins, *The African Review 4, no. H, A Journal of African Politics, Development and International Affairs* (Department of Political Science, University of Dar-es-Salaam, 1974).

65   *Ibid.* These enterprises are as follows: 1. Beer brewing, 2. Boat building, 3. Bicycle and motorcycle tire manufacture, 4. Bottling soft drinks, 5. Coastal and inland waterways shipping, 6. Construction industries, 7. Cosmetics and perfumery manufacture, 8. Departmental stores and supermarkets, 9. Distribution agencies for machines and technical equipment, 10. Distribution and servicing of motor vehicles, tractors, and spare parts thereof or other similar objects, 11. Estate agency, 12. Furniture making, 13. Insecticides, pesticides and fungicides, 14. Internal Air Transport (schedule and charter services), 15. Manufacture of bicycles, 16. Manufacture of matches, 17. Manufacture of cement, 18. Manufacture of metal containers, 19. Manufacture of paints, varnishes, and other similar articles, 20. Manufacture of soaps and detergents, 21. Manufacture of suitcases, briefcases, handbags, purses, wallets, portfolios, and shopping bags, 22. Manufacture of wire, nails, washers, bolts, nuts, rivets, and other similar articles, 23. Paper conversion industries, 24. Passenger bus services (interstate), 25. Poultry farming, 26. Printing of books, 27. Production of sawn timber, plywood, veneers, and other wood conversion industries, 28. Screen printing on cloth, dyeing, 29. Slaughtering, storage, distribution, and processing of meat, 30. Shipping, 31. Travel agencies, 32. Wholesale distribution.

66   See N. Ngoue-Ngabissie, "Finances zone franc: les africains sont satisfaits," *Jeune Afrique* 509 (October 7, 1970): 40; *Le Monde* (16 December 1970).

67   See Maurice Ligot, *Les Accords de coopération entre la France et les états africains et malgache d'expression française* (Paris: La Documentation française, 1964), p. 91.

68   "Journal officiel de la République Française Textes d'Interét Général Communanté Accords Franco-Gabonais" (November 1960) no. 60, 278S, pp. 16-17.

69   Pierre Jalée, *Le Pillage du tiers monde* (Paris: Maspero, 1970), p. 110.

70   *Ibid.*

71   *West Africa*, 21 April 1972.

72   Vernon McKay, *Africa in World Politics* (New York: Harper and Row, 1963), p. 147.

73   *Ibid.*

74   *West Africa*, 2-8 January 1971.

75   *West Africa*, 16 April 1971.

76   For a detailed discussion, see Keesing's Research Report, *Africa Independent* (New York: Charles Scribner's Sons, 1972).

77   *West Africa*, November 1979, p. 2021.

78   *Ibid.*

79   *Ibid.*

80   The term ACP refers to the 58 African, Caribbean, and Pacific states which are signatories to the second Lomé Convention. These are the ACP signatories to the Lomé Convention: Bahamas, Barbados, Benin, Botswana, Burundi, Cameroun, Cape Verde, Central African Republic, Chad, Comoro Islands, Congo, Djibouti, Dominica, Equatorial Guinea, Ethiopia, Fiji, Gabon, The Gambia, Ghana, Grenada, Guinea, Guinea-Bissau, Guyana, Ivory Coast, Jamaica, Kenya, Kiribati, Lesotho, Liberia, Madagascar, Malawi, Mali, Mauritania, Mauritius, Niger, Nigeria, Papua New Guinea, Rwanda, St. Lucia, Sao Tomé and Principe, Senegal, Seychelles, Sierra Leone, Solomon Islands, Somalia, Sudan, Surinam, Swaziland, Tanzania, Togo, Tonga, Trinidad and Tobago, Turalu, Uganda, Upper Volta, Western Samoa, Zaire, and Zambia. *West Africa*, November 1979, p. 2021.

CHAPTER 4

ECONOMIC AND TECHNICAL ASSISTANCE

In addition to public and private capital investments placed in African states, Britain and France have also provided other forms of direct economic aid and technical assistance to enhance the cause of post-independence development in these countries. Financial and technical assistance provided by Britain and France to the new African states have played a key role in governmental operations, the functioning of the economy, and economic development in recipient countries. However, it is generally believed that aid creates dependence. Foreign economic assistance to African states is often concentrated on one European source and thus allows manipulation, management, and decision-making from the outside. As Professor Spero put it, aid may also reinforce European trade and investment dominance.[1]

The aid policies of Britain and France grew out of the history of colonialism.[2] During the colonial period, close economic and political links were established between the metropolitan powers and their African dependencies. These ties were not necessarily severed at the time of political independence; instead, in most instances, these links were reinforced after the colonial subjects had become sovereign states. Thus, the combination of historical connections, the desire to maintain spheres of influence, and economic self-interest led to the development of policies of foreign aid by these two former imperial powers.[3] Professor Cowan, in an unpublished article, "Imperialism, Colonialism and After," pointed out that of all the sources of charges of neo-colonialism, the greatest is often seen as the continued domination of the former colonies by the subtle exercise of economic control through aid, investments, and loans by business interests of the colonial power.

Two outspoken African statesmen expressed their opposite views about aid. The late President Kwame Nkrumah of Ghana once observed that aid was one of the commonest channels through which the former imperial powers exercised control of the new African states. Dr. Nkrumah described aid as an instrument of neo-colonialism, sinister in its subtle and insinuating implications and imposing a client status on supposedly free states. He argued quite persuasively that the acceptance of aid usually led to intervention in the domestic affairs of the receiving states by the donor states.

By contrast, President Felix Houphouet-Boigny of the Ivory Coast dismissed Dr. Nkrumah's interpretation of aid and claimed instead that the new African states must get aid from abroad and, preferably, from the former metropolitan powers. Although the attitudes of the two men toward aid contradicted each other, experience has demonstrated that aid is indeed essential to these countries' development and has therefore been sought and accepted as such by all, including even the bitterest attackers of aid donors.

Aid-giving is indeed a very complex activity and it seems plausible that donors are trying to do many different things in different places.[4] The critics of aid have pointed out the fact that it has not always been entirely clear what the donors are trying to achieve. In other words, the motives which have prompted donors to provide aid to the poor countries are subjects which have generated a lot of debate. The simple view of donors as villains engaged in an organized conspiracy, pursuing their self-interest and dominance over the poor countries, and keeping them in a condition of dependence has gained support in many circles. The equally simple view of donors as mere disinterested distributors of charity is also controversial. According to John White, the question of what donors do is often discussed in terms of their motives – commercial self-interest, the desire for power, prestige and influence, a belief in global interdependence, concern for poverty, and so on.[5] He noted that most, if not all, of the commonly mentioned motives are present in varying degrees in most, if not all, donor countries.[6] Hazelwood and Holtham explained the shortcomings of these two positions. For example, they pointed out that the naive altruistic view of aid is inadequate because it ignores the mixture of motives in the donor country, assuming a single-minded benevolence, and ignores the possibility that aid can have detrimental effects on the recipient. Similarly, they rejected the Machiavellian view of aid based purely on a single-minded and narrow self-interest, and thus ignoring the beneficial effects of aid.[7] In conclusion, they noted that, in reality, donor policies reflect a balance of diverse views and interests.[8]

Foreign aid has been used by Britain and France to retain political influence and win friends in the newly independent states. When the two European powers relinquished imperial control by granting independence to their African dependencies in the late fifties and early sixties, they traded positions of political control for positions of influence. A proposition about the distribution of aid which this author is willing to support is that aid is given to compliant governments; that is, those that follow the dictates and support the policies of the donor state. As Hazelwood and Holtham put it, such a government receives aid because it is compliant, and is compliant because it receives aid.[9] Thus, British and French aid to Kenya and the Ivory Coast, respectively, are by far greater than the aid which both countries provide for Tanzania and Guinea, for that matter. The countries which receive the most aid are usually those which have established in the past, and perhaps still have, a special relationship with some particular rich donor state either as a dependency or as a traditional area of trade or investment.[10]

A major difficulty which confronts aid recipients involved the fact that their acceptance of economic aid may imply at least tacit approval on their part of the general policies of the donor state and, as a result, jeopardize their own choice of policies.[11] However, the proliferation of sources of foreign aid these days has led several developing African states to play one donor against the other in order to obtain aid on the most favorable conditions. By doing this, they have managed to preserve their independence and their so-called nonaligned posture.

The critics of British and French aid to African states have attacked it on several grounds. John White mentions such donor practices as procurement-tying and their demand that recipients specify the uses to which their resources are to be put as good examples of this criticism. He cites instances where British loans to Kenya, Ghana, and Nigeria have been made available for capital and semi-capital goods only. He also cites other situations where a donor has provided a loan to finance a specified single project and, in addition, specified where the investment was to be located, what kind of equipment was to be installed, and how the undertaking was to be managed.[12] Thus, the donors are accused of having the power to preempt domestic resources and thereby alter the entire development program, eventually substituting their preferences for those of the recipient governments.[13] Thus, aid may have retarded development by simply distorting the composition of investment[14] and frustrating the emergence of an indigenous entrepreneurial class.[15]

Finally, the opponents of aid have accused it of fostering corruption. They claim that the availability of aid funds makes their misappropriation possible.[16] Aid, they claim, corrupts morally; it establishes dependency, destroys self-reliance and enervates government and society.[17] They argue that part of the explanation of why foreign aid has not resulted in faster development is simply that it is not designed for the best interests of the recipients, but rather to further the selfish interests of the donors.[18] From these observations, one can conclude that aid from the former metropole to its dependency or satellite is meant to safeguard relationships with client states.[19]

Britain and France have not been indifferent to the development needs of their former dependencies. Both states have made concerted efforts to bring about economic development in their zones of influence. But the French have followed a more liberal tradition. They have a more enviable record than their British counterparts. In 1955, for example, France's national income was $40 billion and her annual investment (public and private) amounted to $600 million, i.e., 1.5 percent. The United Kingdom's national income in 1956 was $47 billion. Her annual investment (public and private) was $300 million, i.e., 0.6 percent. Thus, France has continued to be in the front ranks of industrialized countries that are making a national effort to assist developing regions of the world and especially former French dependencies. According to the statistics published by the Development

Action Group (DAG) of the Organization for Economic Cooperation and Development, funds allotted by France to the developing countries and multilateral bodies in 1961 represented 2.41 percent of its gross national product. This is to be compared with 1.3% for the United Kingdom, 1.17% for the Federal Republic of Germany, 0.97% for the United States, and with an average of 1.1% for the OECD member countries.[20]

In order to achieve and sustain economic development and thereby raise the standards of living of their people, Anglophone and Francophone African states have relied quite heavily on aid coming from Britain and France. As a general rule, these new states are suspicious of foreign aid lest political strings be attached to it. All of them have professed to favor a policy of nonalignment in their dealings with the two hostile ideological blocs to avoid jeopardizing their countries' newly won independence by way of committing themselves deeply to one or the other bloc. But, in practice, these African states have always made first approaches to their former mother-countries before turning to other states for aid. The assumption is that aid from this source has not many political strings attached to it. Britain and France have reacted favorably to the new states' financial and technical needs. The political motives of both countries are quite simple. – they would like to maintain and consolidate their economic, cultural, and political spheres of influence.[21] Thus, the foreign aid policies of these two former imperial powers were essentially an extension of the assistance which they had previously granted to their former colonies. When these countries achieved their independence, this aid was continued to some extent and grew in scope to also include other developing countries.[22]

French Aid

After the former colonies had achieved the status of independent states, French aid continued to flow into the area. Thus, after relinquishing political control over her colonial African territories, France still recognized the fact that the new states needed continued French assistance. The Francophone states entered into agreements for cooperation with France under which her assistance in loans for development, grants for the expansion of services, and the supply of administrative and technical personnel would continue.[23]   Other agreements covered reciprocal preferential trade relationships, the stabilization of prices for primary agricultural commodities, provisions for balancing domestic budgets, and the use of the French monetary zone to facilitate commercial dealings.[24] Analysts have pointed out that although France gained certain commercial benefits from these arrangements, on balance they were a burden rather than an asset.[25] This burden was offset considerably as a result of arrangements with the European Common Market obliging the other EEC members to share the cost of giving former French dependencies aid.[26]

These cooperation agreements were two-sided.   First, France conceded its political and administrative privileges in favor of the new African states and committed itself to continuing economic, financial, and technical assistance. African governments, for their part, acknowledged that they were administratively and economically weak and thus required aid. In other words, political independence did not mean economic independence. They pledged themselves to protect French interests in Africa as a sort of *quid pro quo* for the aid they received from France.[27]

Since 1960 when these states emerged as independent sovereign states, France has remained the main source of foreign aid to them. This aid has been most extensive in the Ivory Coast, Senegal, Gabon, and Cameroon, and least in Guinea and Mali. For all these Francophone states, with the exception of Guinea and Mali, French aid has been very essential if not crucial for their post-independence development. French aid to French Africa is by far greater than all other aid coming from other countries combined. To the leaders of these states, French aid seemed to be less risky than aid from other sources. This aid has been described as "clean" aid, one that has no political strings attached to it. French aid plays a crucial part in the economies of Francophone African states as they are confronted with economic development problems. Thus, foreign public aid from France comprised a sizeable part of receipts for development plans. It provides a large part of all infrastructure projects.

In tune with its policy of paternalism, France has continued to assist in balancing the budgets of these new African countries. Without this assistance, the governments could not perform the general basic services which are essential for the national economy; that is, the operation of existing infrastructures such as airports, electrical plants, water works, health, and education. African states have received direct budgetary assistance to pay directly large numbers of personnel who serve in regular administrative posts in these countries. In recent years, however, some proud leaders in Francophone Africa are beginning to realize that it is indeed an unhealthy situation for one sovereign state to pay for the cost of administration for another. The result is that many of them have pledged themselves to balance their own national budgets from local resources and thus use French aid solely for national development projects.[28]

Because of this strong financial backing from France, the former French colonies, with a few exceptions, have not moved as far from France as the former British dependencies have moved from Great Britain.[29] The French-speaking states have maintained important economic and financial ties which had their origin in colonial days.

Technical Assistance

The French aid program for Francophone African states is more impressive than the British aid program for Anglophone Africa. French aid has indeed promoted a lasting two-way cultural relationship between France and the new states. Thus, French-speaking African countries have appreciated French efforts on their behalf in the fields of education and technical assistance which they have generally characterized as purely philanthropic. By contrast, relations between the Anglophone African states and Britain, though not uncordial, fell far short of the intimacy that characterized the relationship of France with most of the ex-French colonies. However, all the former British dependencies chose to continue association in the British Commonwealth immediately after independence and continued to receive fluctuating amounts of financial aid and technical assistance from Britain.

The essential link between France and its former colonies is in the aid it has provided to them. France ranks very high among donor states which provide aid to poor underdeveloped countries. The United Kingdom, the other major ex-imperial power, has averaged less than half of the French contribution. Within the period 1962 to 1968, African states received an average of 32 percent of all French aid, the highest percentage of any recipient group.[30] DeLattre points out that the figures would still be higher if figures for multilateral aid were included, for most of French multilateral aid is made up of European Development Funds which go primarily to Francophone African states.[31] Since the sixties, aid to these states has remained relatively constant, while aid to other former colonies under different colonizers declined considerably. For example, Senegal, an ex-French colony, received in aid both bilateral and multilateral, in the years 1964-1967, an annual average of $13.90 per capita of population; comparable figures for two ex-British dependencies, namely, Ghana and Nigeria in the same period, were $7.70 and $2.10 respectively.[32] According to Robin Halbett, the price to be paid for this assistance was the continuation of a massively visible French presence and influence – French banks, French businesses, French civil servants, French teachers – which seemed by its very nature to deny the reality of independence.[33]

The main channel through which French aid to French Africa is made is the Fund for Aid and Cooperation (FAC). The Fonds d'Aide et de Cooperation and its paying agent, the Caisse Central de Cooperation Economique, were created to cater to the economic needs of the new states. FAC operations totalled some $270.7 million between 1959 and 1961; $92.8 million of this amount being granted in 1961 alone.[34] French aid dispensed through FAC is mainly in the form of grants. Since 1962, it has also been disbursing long-term loans, with a very low rate of interest. Such loans represent approximately 6-8 percent of all funds provided since 1962. Between 1962 and 1968, an average of 94 percent of French aid to Francophone African countries was in the form of grants and only 6 percent in the form of loans.[35] FAC's operations handle such projects as general technical surveys and studies, research into agriculture and mining, cultural and social activities, and school buildings.

A major problem which confronted the Francophone African countries after independence involved the lack of trained technical and administrative personnel to man important positions in government and business. During the colonial period, relatively heavy use of French personnel was made. Frenchmen were used in large numbers for manning the various branches of the administrative and business bureaucracy. Skilled and lower level supervisory positions were similarly dominated by French nationals. Africans held a relatively small proportion of managerial posts in their various countries. Even the ranks of sales clerks and office secretaries were filled up by the wives of French servicemen. This situation led to a retardation in the development of skills and the gaining of experience in governmental duties on the part of the indigenous Africans. Thus, unlike Anglophone African states, the process of Africanization of the civil service in Francophone Africa was very slow.

Having depended on France so heavily as a source of governmental as well as business personnel, the new states realized that chaos would be the result if Frenchmen and women were all withdrawn immediately once independence was achieved. France realized this situation and took concrete measures to cope with this problem. Thus, France demonstrated once again her principle of carrying out a civilizing mission. For example, the Frenchmen who had been civil servants administering and developing French Africa remained on the French payroll as before, but automatically became advisors to the new indigenous civil servants until such a time when these states would be able to produce their own technical as well as administrative experts. As a consequence, many French nationals remained in the new countries serving in various capacities such as teachers, administrators, and business executives. Table 13 shows that there was a slight reduction in the number of French civil servants in French-speaking Africa. French technical assistance after independence continued to supply many of the specialists needed to meet the requirements of the ambitious development plans initiated by the new states. Thus, after independence was attained, the administrative and economic structures of these African states was still in the hands of the French cooperation officers. With the exception of Guinea and Mali, it was the Frenchmen who dealt with important administrative or technical problems. Through bilateral arrangements, the Minister for Cooperation sent out French personnel on Technical Assistance Missions in 1961 to fourteen French-speaking African and Malagasy states. The personnel in question were distributed in many ministries which included

Justice, Administration, Health, and Technical Services.[36] France placed trainees from these new states in French research centers, Institutes of Technology, and industrial plants. In 1967 for example, the cooperation officers numbered 13,386 as compared with 9,324 Britons in Anglophone Africa.[37] Furthermore, every level of African education–primary, secondary, and university–was greatly dependent on French teachers whose military service took the form of teaching in overseas countries.[38] By 1982, the French Ministere de la Cooperation et du Developement reported sending some 10,000 French cooperants to Africa, 80 percent of whom were schoolteachers.[39]

As indigenous personnel developed, there was a slight decline of French personnel in the field of administration. These new African elite groups had either been trained overseas or trained on the spot by French advisors who had been induced to stay in the indigenous civil service. Despite the decline of French personnel in the field of administration, there was a remarkable increase in the field of education. The reason for this phenomenon is perhaps simply the importance France has placed on cultural relationships between herself and Francophone Africa.

In the late 1960s and early 1970s, the French authorities resumed an aggressive training program for the new states. It is estimated that France had about 20,000 French Government paid technicians assisting Francophone African states on a "permanent" basis and thousands more on short-term contracts.[40] In Gabon alone, in 1968, there were 645 French personnel paid by FAC serving in the Gabonese Government; in 1969, 661; and in 1970, 620.[41] These so-called French advisors occupied the key positions in the decision-making process.

Government and private enterprise worked hand-in-hand in providing technical aid to African states. For example, French private industries such as the Mechanical Industries Federation and the Electricité de France organized technical training centers in many African countries for which the French Government provided and paid university professors who directed the programs. Other trainees were also sent to state establishments such as the Institute of Technology, Government Services, and National Enterprises.

Franco-Ivorian special relationships do illustrate France's deep involvement in Francophone Africa. In 1960, the two countries signed cooperation agreements establishing a special relationship. It is estimated that French public bilateral aid to the Ivory Coast, both in financial and technical assistance, subsidies, and loans, reached approximately 89.2 billion CFA francs between 1960 and 1970. The Ivory Coast has attracted substantial French private investment. Through its membership in the European Common Market, the Ivorian Government has tried to diversify its sources of aid. Under the Yaoundé and Lomé Conventions, it has drawn considerable benefits from aid disbursed by the European Development Fund of the EEC. Thus, between 1964 and 1970, for example, the share of the Ivory Coast in financial operations of the EDF in Francophone Africa amounted to 9.274 million CFA francs.[42]

French presence in the Ivory Coast has remained quite significant indeed. French nationals are still being trusted to handle or man the top administrative posts in their official capacity as advisors. They control the banks and private enterprises. Their experts formulate and implement the economic development plans for the Ivory Coast. A major consequence of this situation is the simple fact that it was decided that not until the early 1970s could all the "key posts" of the administration be taken over by Ivorians. Even by the late 1970s, the process of Africanization of the civil administration had not been completed.

What the Ivory Coast is to France, Kenya is to Britain. Kenya has continued to cultivate Britain as its major source of economic and technical assistance. Thus, between 1963 and 1972, Britain provided to Kenya aid amounting to £250 million.[43] It is estimated that Britain provided approximately 59 percent of technical assistance personnel to Kenya.

Francophone African states, with the exception of Guinea and Mali, decided to remain members of the franc zone in view of the economic benefits involved. The franc zone was created in 1939 and was meant to impose exchange control on the French franc for any resident of France or of the French Empire.[44] As Lusignan explained, by analogy with the franc area, a parallel currency known as the CFA (Colonies Françaises d'Africque) franc was established.[45] In recent years, this franc area within French-speaking

Africa became known as the Communauté Financiére Africane. The result has been that the fiscal affairs of these states has come ultimately under French control. France has claimed that her motives have been to ensure monetary stability in the area and thus has shouldered the responsibility for monetary decisions affecting the area. She has supported the African monetary systems in order to prevent inflation and imbalance in external finances.[46]

The French Treasury has opened an operational account for each central bank into which each bank transfers its entire holdings of CFA francs which are automatically converted into French francs.[47] The Bank of France usually guarantees that the currencies of the African states will be easily converted into French francs at a fixed exchange rate, and that they will extend to them unlimited credit, even if their operational accounts show a deficit.[48] In return for these guarantees, the African central banks must deposit all their foreign currency reserves at the Bank of France in the form of French francs. Thus, according to Lusignan, it is to the advantage of the African states to depend on the French Treasury. They can ignore any difficulties resulting from their balance of payments, and can remain totally unconcerned at any deficit in their trade balance. They remain secure with the understanding that any deficit they incur will eventually be met.[49] As Lusignan sees it,

> the franc zone indeed means much more than mere monetary cooperation; it is an entire system of economic and financial assistance. It makes provision for the entirely free transfer of capital which is a great asset for French private interests as incomes can be transferred and capital removed when deemed necessary.[50]

He therefore argued that such total freedom provides the incentive for private capital to take risks in investment in the economy of the African countries.[51]

Through the control of foreign aid, France is able to determine important decision outcomes in Francophone African countries. Her financial aid programs make it possible for her to determine to a large extent the general structure of development and investment in these new African states.

France draws other benefits resulting from the monetary system which she controls. For example, the franc zone system facilitates the return flow of francs to France, thus lessening the aid burden. French aid, like that of Britain, is tied so that expenditures for equipment, construction contracts, as well as research contracts are given to French interests. Finally, it must be noted that a large percentage of French aid is spent for the salaries of French technical experts who prefer to spend their money in metropolitan France itself.

France has exercised tremendous influence in Francophone Africa through the use of threats of either reducing or withdrawing aid to them. The French aid budget for the African states is usually voted upon by the French Parliament and this gives the Government the free hand to manipulate aid to each country to suit its purposes. Experience has shown that the distribution of this aid has depended more on political than economic considerations. The drastic French punitive measures imposed against Guinea when she voted to break away from the French Community in 1958 is still fresh in the minds of many leaders of French-speaking African states. Following Sékou Touré's decision to take Guinea out of the French orbit, Charles de Gaulle, the president of France at the time, reacted very swiftly by withdrawing all financial assistance and trade support, blocked the Guinea account in the French Treasury, and immediately terminated payment of pensions to Guinean war veterans.[52] However, after the Guinean experience, France has not utilized complete withdrawal of aid to punish any other state. For example, aid has continued to Mali and the Congo-Brazzaville, in spite of political deviations by these two states.

There are two other instances where France used the threat of cutting off aid to achieve desired French objectives. The first involved the Maghrib nations – Algeria, Morocco, and Tunisia. France has been very generous with both economic and cultural aid despite rifts witih President Bourguiba of Tunisia over such issues as the French naval base at Bizerte and the expropriation of French-owned investments in Tunisia. Morocco and Tunisia were also very critical of French policies during the Algerian war of independence which strained their relations with France. When the Algerian fiasco ended, the former friendly relationships were revived,[53] and President

Charles de Gaulle was bent on cultivating Ben Bella's Algeria. A significant portion of the cost of compensating displaced *colons* was subsidized by French economic aid and, despite continued confiscation of French assets, the French exercised patience. At the conclusion of the revolutionary war, there were over twelve thousand French teachers in Algeria under the sponsorship of France. Following the Evian Settlements the Algerians and the French shared the profits of a rapidly expanding oil industry in the Sahara. Thus, Algeria's return to the franc zone turned out to be a major economic asset to France's balance of payments position. Under President Boumedienne, the Franco-Algerian partnership became more secure.

The other known instance in which the direct public threat of aid withdrawal was made by France came in 1966 after a series of military coups hit Francophone African states. As a direct response to these military disturbances, the Minister of Information, Alain Peyrefitte, warned at that time that governmental changes such as had occurred in Benin, Upper Volta, and the Central African Republic could influence the French policy of aid and cooperation.[54]

In recent times, France has used more subtle aid pressures to demonstrate her displeasure and thus encourage political cooperation. One good example has involved the rejection of aid projects[55] or deliberate bureaucratic delays involving the loss of dossiers or program delays for countries not taking French interests at heart.

The intimate relationship between France and French-speaking African states has sharply been criticized not only by those Africans who look at it simply as a clear form of neo-colonialism, but also dissident elements within these countries who are seeking rapid personal advancement and thus regard the presence of French nationals in key posts of their administrative and business bureaucracy with indignation. African nationalists, including youth groups, consider French influence as the main cause of why these new states, with the exception of Guinea, Congo (Brazzaville) and Mali whose political relations with France are less close, are not in the forefront of radical African nationalism.[56] Leaders such as Léopold Senghor of Senegal and Felix Houphouet-Boigny of the Ivory Coast have been successful in silencing their critics by the use of raw force or by making them part of their administration.

Similarly, in France itself, the close ties with Francophone African states as well as the financial and technical assistance involved, has been criticized. The critics of aid to these African countries argue that money which could be better utilized in improving conditions in France itself has been wasted, and thus that aid should be drastically curtailed. Since the end of the Gaullist era, aid given to these African states has been diminishing, although the immediate successors of President Charles de Gaulle have pledged continued French support for the African countries.

British aid policy was influenced by three important factors; namely, the desire to maintain friendly relations with the new states, economic and political considerations. These factors determined some of the general features of aid a Commonwealth country received or to what extent aid was tied to specific projects and how far it was tied to the purchase of British goods. Nevertheless, it must be pointed out that Britain's aid to Anglophone African states was rather slow in developing. Following Britain's traditional doctrine of colonial responsibility, British policymakers in the late fifties generally believed that there was a cutoff point in political independence when help became mere interference. William Clark asserted that this policy was based on the analogy of the old Dominions which achieved full independence long after they had become self-supporting. He argued that, in the new African states where political independence was given as a gesture early in the process of becoming self-supporting, the doctrine had little relevance.[57] He cited the case of Ghana as a good example of this experience. Shortly after Ghana achieved its political independence in 1957, all aid provided by the CDC and other British agencies was stopped. Britain was criticized for excluding Ghana from benefits derived under the CDC programs. She learned her lesson well and eventually accepted the fact that independent Commonwealth countries were still economically dependent and, as such, needed assistance. Thus, when a host of British dependencies became independent in the sixties, plans were initiated to cope with the problems.

Britain's aid to Anglophone African states was considerably smaller than what France provided to Francophone African states. Britain's post-war economic difficulties accounted for the fluctuation of aid she provided to African Commonwealth countries. Analysts have noted that, until recently, British aid to Commonwealth Africa was less than a quarter of French aid to French-speaking Africa. Similarly, Britain's investment contribution in Africa was also comparably less.[58] Britain's economic problems meant that aid to the new states was drastically reduced, and the British Treasury began to insist that beneficiaries or recipients of British aid should spend large proportions of aid from Britain on British exports. For the new states, procurement-tying became an established practice. Britain justified its position by pointing out its balance of payments difficulties and also the fact that British aid to other countries was usually tied two-thirds to British goods.

It was at the Commonwealth Finance Minister's Conference held in Montreal, Canada in 1958, that an official policy statement was expressed in which the British Government made a commitment to continue financial and technical aid to the new, poor independent Commonwealth countries. By 1963, programs which provided assistance to the new states had been established. Elaborate plans were made to organize Britain's aid programs. For example, in 1963, British aid was placed under the control of the Foreign Office and the Commonwealth Office. A Department of Technical Cooperation in charge of technical assistance and jointly responsible to these two ministries was established. Similarly, in 1964, the Overseas Development Ministry, headed by a Cabinet Minister, was set up. This Ministry eventually took over the full responsibility for aid.

The planning and administration of British aid to Commonwealth countries became more systematic after 1969 with the introduction of the Country Policy Paper, CPP.[59] This Policy Paper was the product of economists attached to the relevant geographical department of Overseas Development Ministry. It is an internal working document which describes the economy and policies of the recipient country involved and usually examines the main constraints on development and other relevant factors in its relations with Britain.

The CPP usually sets out the proposed amounts and forms of British aid for the next five years indicating how this fits in with the recipient country's development priorities and the likely further aid programs of other donors.[60] The CPP also indicates the main sectors of the economy towards which the aid allotted should be directed and stipulates relative priorities. The British Mission in the recipient state has some responsibility for administering the aid program.

Commonwealth Assistance Loans are available to the new states. Thus, assistance is provided in the fields of research, education, and planning. Scholarships are provided in Britain for the training of teachers. Also, teachers are made available from the United Kingdom to African states which need them.[61] Countries such as Kenya and Tanzania have received substantial assistance both in finance and the supply of teachers and other technical personnel. Other projects which were handled by the Commonwealth Assistance Loans included agriculture, fisheries, hydroelectric schemes, and communications systems.

Furthermore, Britain expanded her aid program in Africa by the creation of a Special Commonwealth African Assistance Plan (SCAAP). All financial and technical assistance to Commonwealth states in Africa passed through this channel. The purpose of the new plan was to give particular attention to the needs of these new states and thereby provide aid bilaterally and through existing international monetary institutions such as the International Bank for Reconstruction and Development (IBRD), the International Development Association (IDA), and the International Monetary Fund (IMF). Capital assistance provided by Britain to African "independent" members of the Commonwealth under the new plan included a tied-loan of £5 million to Ghana towards the cost of the Volta hydroelectric project, and the Commonwealth assistance loans of £12 million and £10 million, respectively, to Nigeria.

The character of British financial aid to African states has been changing quite considerably since the mid-1960s. From that time on, approximately half of Britain's aid has been in the form of outright gifts and the rest in loans. About four-fifths of these loans are made available for twenty-year periods or more. The rate of interest on these loans has been the rate at which the Government can borrow from the capital market plus a small management charge to cover the expense involved.

Like France, Britain has supplied the trained personnel needed to man the higher levels of the administrative and technical services of her former dependencies during the period of transition until such a time as indigenous Africans themselves would take over full control. The status of the colonial administrators and technicians usually formed part of the devolution agreements reached between Britain and her former dependencies before independence was granted. Unlike France, which retained the colonial administrators on the French payroll and made them automatically advisors to the indigenous civil servants, Britain pursued a different policy. The new states retained the services of experienced expatriate administrators whose services they needed very badly by signing new contracts with them. By way of enticement, the salaries of these top administrators were increased and charged to the new states' governments. This served as a generous compensation for their loss of career in the colonial administration.

The Department of Technical Cooperation (DTC) was established primarily to coordinate, promote, and carry out arrangements for supplying other countries outside Britain with technical assistance, particularly in the fields of economic development, administration, and social services. The DTC became the single main channel through which all overseas countries, whether dependent or independent, could ask for assistance from Britain. Nevertheless, technical assistance from Britain to Ghana, Nigeria, Gambia, Sierra Leone, and the East African states, was given within the framework of the Special Commonwealth African Assistance Plan (SCAAP).

The Overseas Service Act Scheme (OSAS) was devised to enable all territories which achieved independence after September, 1960, to recruit and retain the services of experienced expatriate administrators and specialists before and after independence. Under this scheme, while the indigenous government was responsible for local rates of salary, Britain paid the cost of inducement and educational allowances for overseas officials and contributed toward passage costs plus half of any compensation for loss of career. Through this medium, Britain recruited highly qualified personnel for administrative, agricultural, engineering, medical, and educational appointments in the new states.

Britain assisted these new states in a number of other ways. One of these was the training of scientists from African Commonwealth countries and by making the results of scientific research available to them. The Department of Technical Cooperation has financed research bearing on the economic and social problems of these developing countries. Britain has remained the largest source of recruitment of university and secondary school teachers in Commonwealth Africa. The Commonwealth Scholarship and Fellowship Plan made it possible for Nigerians, Ghanaians, Gambians, Kenyans, Tanzanians, and Zambians to undertake postgraduate and research programs in universities in Britain as well as in other advanced countries of the British Commonwealth such as Canada, Australia, and New Zealand, which are assisting Britain with the burden of aiding the new members of the Commonwealth.

In terms of the financial and technical assistance which Britain has provided to Commonwealth Africa, Kenya has enjoyed the lion's share. It is estimated that Britain extends to Kenya slightly more aid per head than its average for Commonwealth Africa and three times the average for all Commonwealth countries.[62] Hazelwood and Holtham indicated that, in 1964, a year after Kenyan political independence, well over 80 percent of all its official aid receipts came from Britain. Although Britain's relative importance as a donor has declined since the early seventies, she has remained Kenya's principal source of economic and technical assistance. Between 63 and 1972 Britain provided £250 million to Kenya by way of aid.[63] In September of 1971, there were approximately 3,609 technical assistance personnel in Kenya from abroad, of which 2,130, or roughly 59 percent, were supplied by Britain.[64] These figures demonstrate that Britain has maintained a special relationship with Kenya since she became independent in 1963.

Hazelwood and Holtham have explained this special relationship in terms of political considerations. The two analysts have argued that any reductions in aid, not agreed upon with the recipient, could be damaging to political relations and thus, British policymakers have been cautious to see the volume of aid to Kenya maintained, at least in nominal terms. They pointed out that British authorities are fully aware of the problem of Kenyan Asians who are also British citizens. The expulsion of these Asians definitely would leave Britain with difficulties of immense proportions in absorbing the refugees. The two writers see this situation as a tacit bargaining counter for Kenya in relations between the two governments and provides the United Kingdom with an incentive to maintain friendly relations.[65] A second explanation is that foreign penetration and competition in a country and in markets that had previously been a British preserve, provided a reason for stepping up aid on commercial and political grounds.[66]

Right from 1963 when Kenya emerged as an independent state, Britain's aid policy towards it has been very generous indeed. For example, the "independence settlement" between Britain and Kenya included a commitment of £34.2 million in aid.[67] Between 1961 and 1965 British aid made it possible for the government of Kenya to purchase some 1,094 European settler farms containing 1,421,257 acres at a cost of £12,600,000.[68] These farms were distributed among indigenous Kenya farmers who were, in colonial times, excluded from the use of their land by white supremacists in their midst.

The United Kingdom has also aided Kenya by providing loans and grants to cope with the mounting debt incurred from long-term development loans received from the British Government which usually bear interest rates of between 5½ to 7% annually. Aid from Britain has assisted in handling the servicing charges of these loans. The servicing charge on Kenya's outstanding foreign debt was estimated to be about £5 million in 1966. Between 1967 and 1971 it rose to £7 million, or approximately 9% of total estimated exports for 1966.

British aid was also very crucial in financing the Kenyan Government's development budget in the early years of independence. For example, in 1963/1964, gross financial aid accounted for 87% of development revenue and 77% of that revenue was from Britain.[69] Also, Britain has contributed to Kenya's recurrent budget expenditure with technical assistance grants.

Technical assistance is indeed an important part of aid to the new African states and the East African state of Kenya is no exception. Technical assistance features very prominently during the early stages of independence. For example, it is estimated that about this time there were approximately 1,716 publicly financed British civil servants and specialists in Kenya; 1,674 were from the Overseas Service Act Scheme (OSAS), of whom nearly fifty percent were schoolteachers. Thus, technical aid accounted for approximately forty percent of gross British aid.[70]

In Kenya, there are two main categories of British technical assistance personnel, namely, (a) partly-funded and, (b) fully-funded personnel. The partly-funded personnel included British nationals who occupy established posts in the Kenyan administration. They are paid "local" salary while the British Government provides the inducement allowance to bring their salaries to the levels paid out in Britain. The terms and conditions of service for these personnel are generally covered by the Overseas Service Aid Scheme and the British Expatriates Supplementation Scheme. At the time of political independence, the OSAS program induced experienced British civil servants to remain at their posts while recruiting additional needed personnel. This scheme made it possible for Britain to support the Kenyan Government at the top levels of administration at a time when there were not many indigenous administrators and executives to man these positions.

The British Expatriates Supplementation Scheme (BESS) generally supported Britons who were employed outside the Kenyan central government, such as in local governments, state corporations, and universities. Due to the fact that Kenyans have begun to take some of these top administrative posts, British nationals in the administrative services in Kenya are now declining. Nevertheless, teachers, as a group, have continued to be in great demand because of the fact that Kenya is rapidly expanding its educational program. Thus, by 1973, Britain still supplied over half of expatriate personnel in the country.

The other group is the so-called fully-funded personnel. These British nationals serve in the capacity of advisors to the Government of Kenya. Their salaries are paid by Britain. Usually, they work for a contract period and, as such, do not occupy any established posts in the administration. They are mainly specialists with particular technical know-how rather than managers or administrators. The terms and conditions which govern their services are covered by the Special Commonwealth African Assistance Plan (SCAAP).

The presence of British expatriate technical assistance personnel in Kenya is indeed very impressive. This could be likened to French presence in the Ivory Coast. It is quite obvious that their numbers are relatively small when compared with the indigenous civil servants; however, they are concentrated in key ministries. For example, in 1972, their numbers in key ministries were as follows: Foreign Affairs, Cooperatives and Defense, zero; Agriculture, 31.76%; Finance and Planning, 30.43%; Works, 29.62%; and Education, 20.56%.[71] Thus, the Ministries of Finance and Planning as well as Education contain the largest numbers of British expatriates employed in Kenya in the period between 1969 and 1972. As Kenyanization of the civil services progresses, the number of British expatriates will also decline steadily.

British aid to Kenya is usually tied to the purchasing of British exports or goods produced in Kenya.[72] Thus, if the Government of Kenya wished to use British aid directly on goods from elsewhere, it must secure the approval of the Ministry of Overseas Development, which, in turn, requires clearance from the Department of Trade. These two ministries must be satisfied that no equivalent British good was available before any special dispensation was authorized. Such requests and dispensations, according to Hazelwood and Holtham were, however, rare.[73]

Critics of British aid to Kenya are fully aware of the fact that the practice of procurement-tying has been detrimental to the recipient state. In the case of Kenya, all technical assistance was tied to the acquisition of personnel in Britain. The practice of procurement-tying has involved costs for the recipient country which critics insist should be deducted from the nominal value of aid.[74] These critics note that the most obvious cost is the prevention of competitive international tendering for contracts. Thus, the price the recipient has to pay British suppliers for goods may definitely be well above the world market price. It is estimated that the recipient may pay up to 20% higher than the regular world prices in instances where procurement-tying is the case.[75] Nevertheless, procurement-tying seems to create no major problems for Kenya and other African states which generally take a high proportion of their imports from the United Kingdom.

The economic and technical assistance needs of African states since independence have remained great and urgent. In most cases, aid has been necessary to stimulate development; in some other instances, it has been quite indispensable to the preservation of orderly government.[76] Since the post-independence period, economic development or growth has quite often been achieved by the increased use of imported capital equipment and supplies without a corresponding expansion of export earnings, and this situation has quite often resulted in rising foreign debts.[77] The efforts of African countries to achieve economic development have been focused mainly on industrialization and the concerted efforts of these governments have been to attain economic growth and a more diversified economic structure through planning.

In recent years, some African states have expressed deep concern about the fact that they have continued to depend very heavily on the former colonizers for financial and technical assistance and have decided to find ways and means to reduce that dependence. These states have now realized that foreign aid is a familiar economic tool used by the "donor" states to achieve both diplomatic and strategic goals.[78] They understand also that foreign aid has been used by former colonial powers to retain political influence in the newly independent states.[79] The granting of aid and the conditions which are placed on that aid provided important avenues for influencing the internal as well as the external policies of recipient states. The simple fact that financial and technical aid to the new African states are often drawn from one major source, the donors are able to manage and manipulate the decision-making processes in the new African states. Thus, the providers of aid have used it to support preferred internal as well as external policies of recipient governments. Similarly, they have used the withdrawal, or even the threatened withdrawal, of aid to express disapproval or opposition to internal and external policies of recipient states.

The opponents of foreign aid have expressed reservations about its effectiveness in helping the recipients stand on their own feet. They have argued that, although it is generally considered as a necessary path to development for the new states, experience seems to demonstrate the fact that aid has not solved the economic problems confronting these African states. These critics point out that financial and technical assistance have provided neither a change in the management of resources nor a meaningful redistribution of economic benefits.[80]

Two major strategies have been adopted by both Anglophone and Francophone African states to reduce their dependence on the former metropolitan powers. These strategies are: (a) cooperative ventures, and (b) multilateral aid. The first strategy has involved the cooperative efforts of African states who believe that much by way of development can be attained if the states pull their resources together. Thus, the Francophone states under the leadership of President Felix Houphouet-Boigney of the Ivory Coast and French encouragement, established in 1965 the association called Organisation Commune Africaine et Malgache (OCAM). The goal of this organization was to achieve economic independence and solidarity amongst its members. Since its establishment, it has enabled its members to present a common united front in negotiations with France and other EEC members over financial and technical questions. Furthermore, it has encouraged the creation of a number of subsidiary agencies concerned with cooperation in specific fields such as management of ports and railways, research, and telecommunications.

Another joint cooperative venture has involved the establishment of the Niger River Basin Commission made up of both Anglophone and Francophone states. The declared goal of the participating members is to develop the Niger River Basin and thereby enhance the economic independence of the riparian states.

The second strategy involved more reliance on multilateral rather than bilateral aid. Radical groups among the new African states have expressed their suspicions of too much dependence on bilateral aid, attributing neo-colonial motives or economic imperialism to former colonizers.[81]

The Lomé Convention signed in February 1975 by the EEC and the associated African states introduced an innovation in terms of a new international economic order. The Convention increased aid to associated members and gave them a greater voice in aid management. The donor states of the EEC created a compensatory finance scheme to subsidize the export earnings of the associated countries.[82] Under this scheme, when the market price for certain marked commodities falls below a certain level, the associated states are paid compensations from the established fund. For the wealthier associated states, compensation usually takes the form of an interest-free loan, whereas, for the poorest states, compensation takes the form of a grant.[83] The Lomé Convention also provided for preferential access for the products of associated African states to EEC markets without requiring or demanding reciprocal advantages for EEC products.

The United Nations and its organs are other sources of bilateral aid for the new states. Since the early sixties, the UN has played a very significant part in the economic and technical development of the African states. Thus, it must be noted that the international organization has been called upon to carry a greater burden of responsibility in aiding the new African states during this period of transition from colonialism. This idea of multilateral aid for the new nations has been praised by those groups who see it as the best way to reduce complete dependence on the part of these new states on the former European imperial powers.

At the UN, African states joined other members of the so-called "Group of 77" which in 1974 and 1976 called for the development of and a coordinated program for a "New International Economic Order" (NIEO). They joined other Third World countries in demanding the restructuring of the International Economic Order in their own favor. Their proposed programs to achieve the New International Economic Order included many fields of international economic interactions. For example, in the field of aid, they called upon the developed industrial powers' commitment to the transfer of 0.7% of their GNP as stipulated by the United Nations Development Decade;[84] a greater flow of emergency funds designed to deal with the problems of food, energy and recession-inflation crises; a renegotiation of less developed countries' debts; and the implementation of the link in monetary reform.[85] They also demanded commodity agreements and the stabilization of their export earnings. However, their demands fell on deaf ears as the developed industrial powers refused to be pressured into making commitments they believed would hurt them in the long-run.

The two ex-imperial powers, Britain and France, have utilized the instrument of aid to establish friendships and maintain influence in the new states. In this regard France was the more successful of the two. She managed to involve her EEC partners in the provision of aid to her dependencies by making their participation in this predominantly European economic club a condition for her membership in the common market. Upon France's insistence, the French dependencies were granted associate status in the EEC in 1957. Thus, France transformed bilateral aid arrangements to a multilateral system of aid. Today, these new Francophone states continue to enjoy a generous program of aid to which France's EEC partners make contributions.

Compared with Britain, France has a more enviable foreign aid program for its former dependencies. It is indeed the only country among the industrial powers whose overseas aid program in the sixties and seventies consistently represented more than 1% of national income. Government grants and loans to African countries have amounted to approximately $300,000,000 annually. This aid is channelled through the Fonds d'Aide et de Co-operation. The poorer Francophone states such as Chad, Upper Volta and Benin still depend on French grants to balance their annual budgets as well as to pay for the costs of infrastructure projects such as airports, roads, railways, hospitals and schools. A large number of French personnel still man the various departments of the Civil Service in French-speaking African countries.

Like France, Britain did not leave the new Commonwealth members in the cold as soon as they attained the status of independent sovereign states. She realized that they faced rough times ahead and intensified her aid program as best as her shaky post-war economy could permit. British aid was mainly to supplement development expenditures from local sources or from market borrowing.

British aid to the English-speaking African countries was channelled either through the Commonwealth Development Corporation or the Special Commonwealth African Assistance Plan. Half of Britain's aid was in the form of outright grants and the rest in long-term loans. The rate of interest on these loans was the rate at which the government could borrow from the capital market plus a management charge to cover expenses.

Soviet economic aid began around 1949. Guinea'a decision to break away from the French Community following the de Gaulle Referendum of 1958 gave the Soviet Union and its East European allies an opportunity to establish contacts in Africa. The countries which signed Friendship Agreements with the USSR are usually the ones that receive Soviet aid. Thus, the geographical distribution of Soviet aid is very similar to that of trade. The countries which receive Soviet aid include Guinea, Ghana, Angola, Ethiopia, Mali and Nigeria.

China has maintained a low profile in terms of economic aid to African countries since the sixties. She selected a few states where her aid money was concentrated. The most outstanding economic contacts China has made included those with Guinea in 1959; Ghana and Mali in 1961; and Tanzania in 1961-1962. China's most ambitious project was the financing of the Tanzam Railway owned jointly by Tanzania and Zambia. The project was calculated to provide Zambia an outlet through Tanzania and thus reduce her dependence on transportation systems controlled by the South African government.

Endnotes Chapter 4

1   Joan Edelman Spero, *The Politics of International Economic Relations* (New York: St. Martin's Press, 1977), p. 15.

2   *Ibid.*, p. 139.

3   See Teresa Hayter, *French Aid* (London: Overseas Development Institute, 1966).

4   See John White, *The Politics of Foreign Aid* (New York: St. Martin's Press, 1974), p. 34.

5   *Ibid.*

6   *Ibid.*

7   Arthur Hazelwood and Gerald Holtham, *Aid and Equality in Kenya: British Development Assistance to Kenya* (London: Croom Helm in association with the Overseas Development Institute, 1976), p. 245.

8   *Ibid.*

9   *Ibid.*, p. 246.

10   White, *Politics of Foreign Aid*, pp. 37-38.

11   See Paul Alpert, *Partnership or Confrontation: Poor Lands and Rich States* (New York: The Free Press, 1973), p. 72.

12   White, *Politics of Foreign Aid*, p. 166.

13   K. B. Griffin, "Foreign Capital, Domestic Savings and Economic Development," *Bulletin* 32, no. 2 (May 1970): 160.

14   *Ibid.*, p. 326.

15   *Ibid.*

16   Hazelwood and Holtham, *Aid and Inequality in Kenya*, p. 254.

17   See T. Mende, *From Aid to Re-Colonization: Lessons of a Failure* (New York: Pantheon Books, 1973), p. 158.

18   K. B. Griffin, "Foreign Capital, Domestic Savings and Economic Development: A Reply," *Bulletin* 33, no. 2 (May 1971): 157.

19   K. B. Griffin and J. L. Enos, "Foreign Assistance: Objectives and Consequences," *Economic Development and Cultural Change*, 18, no. 3 (March 1970): 315-316.

20   DAG Statistics published in 1961.

21   See Alpert, *Partnership or Confrontation*, p. 73.

22   *Ibid.*, p. 71.

23   See Colin Legum, ed., *Africa: A Handbook to the Continent* (New York: Praeger Inc., 1962), p. 497.

24   Wolfram F. Hanrieder and Graeme P. Auton, *The Foreign Policies of West Germany, France and Britain* (Englewood Cliffs, NJ: Prentice Hall, Inc., 1980), p. 148.

25   *Ibid.*

26   *Ibid.*

27   Guy de Lusignan, *French Speaking Africa Since Independence* (New York: Frederick A. Praeger, Publishers, 1969), pp. 327-328.

28   Richard Adloff, *West Africa: The French Speaking Nations* (New York: Holt, Rinehart & Winston, Inc., 1964), p. 311.

29   Victor C. Ferkiss, *Africa's Search for Identity* (New York: George Braziller, 1966), p. 242.

30   De Lattre, [full citation], pp. 158-164.

31   *Ibid.*

32   Robin Halfet, *Africa Since 1875: A Modern History* (Ann Arbor: The University of Michigan Press, 1974), p. 406.

33   *Ibid.*

34   *France, Aid and Cooperation*, December 1962, p. 35.

35   *De Lattre*, [short title], p. 31.

36   *France, Aid and Cooperation*, December 1962, p. 47.

37   *Le Monde*, January 19, 1967.

38   *Ibid.*

39   *West Africa*, No. 3382, 1 May 1982, p. 1437.

40   R. W. Howe, *The African Revolution* (New York: Barnes and Nobles, Inc., 1969), p. 251.

41   French Governmental Statistics.

138

42   Nicole Delorme, *The Association of African and Malagasy States and the European Economic Community* (General Library of Law and Jurisprudence, 1972).

43 *Washington Post*, 7 January 1973, p. 20.

44   Lusignan, *French Speaking Africa Since Independence*, p. 329.

45   *Ibid.*

46   *Ibid.*, p. 330.

47   *Ibid.*

48   *Ibid.*

49   *Ibid.*, p. 331.

50   *Ibid.*

51   *Ibid.*

52   See Waldemar Nielsen, *The Great Powers and Africa* (New York: Praeger Publishers, 1969), p. 88.

53   Ferkiss, *Africa's Search for Identity*, p. 244.

54   *Washington Post*, 6 January 1966.

55   See Hayter, *French Aid*, p. 178.

56   Ferkiss, *Africa's Search for Identity*, p. 246.

57   William Clark, "New Europe and the New Nations," *Daedalus: Journal of the American Academy of Arts and Sciences* 93, no. 1 (Winter 1964): p. 149.

58   See Russell Warren Howe, *The African Revolution* (New York: Barnes and Noble, Inc., 1969).

59   See R. B. M. King. "The Planning of the British Aid Programme," *Journal of Administration Overseas*, January 1972.

60   *Ibid.*

61   Legum, *Africa: A Handbook to the Continent*, p. 497.

62   Hazelwood and Holtham, *Aid and Inequality in Kenya*, p. 84.

63   *Washington Post*, 7 January 1973, p. 20.

64   John Okumu, "Kenya's Foreign Policy," in *The Foreign Policies of African States*, ed. Olajide Aluko (London: Hodder & Stoughton, 1977), p. 157.

65   Hazelwood and Holtham, *Aid and Inequality in Kenya*, p. 84.

66   *Ibid.*

67   *Ibid.*, p. 76.

68   Okumu, *Kenya's Foreign Policy*, p. 152.

69   See *Economy Survey*, 1966; see also Table 8.

70   Hazelwood and Holtham, *Aid and Inequality in Kenya*, p. 76.

71   *Ibid.*, p. 49.

72   *Ibid.*, p. 55.

73   *Ibid.*, p. 57.

74   See Proceedings of UNCTAD, Feb.-March 1968, Second Session, vol. 4, *Problems and Policies of Financing*.

75   Bhagwati, UNCTAD, "The Tying of Aid," p. 46.

76   Legum, *Africa: A Handbook to the Continent*, p. 498.

77   See Sava S. Berry, "Economic Change in Contemporary Africa," in *Africa*, eds. Phyllis M. Martin and Patrick O'Meara (Bloomington: Indiana University Press, 1977), p. 261.

78   Spero, *The Politics of International Economic Relations*, p. 9.

79   *Ibid.*

80   *Ibid.*, p. 131.

81   Legum, *Africa: A Handbook to the Continent*, p. 497.

82   See Lomé Dossier, Reprinted from the Courier 31 Issue, March, 1975 (Brussels: Commission of the European Communities, 1975). See also Isebill V. Gruhn, "The Lomé Convention: Inching Toward Interdependence," *International Organization*, 30 (Spring, 1976): 240-262.

83   Harry G. Johnson, *Economic Policies Toward Less Developed Countries* (Washington: Brookings Institution, 1967), pp. 149-152; Marion Bywater, *The Lomé Convention* (European Community, March 1975), pp. 5-7.

140

84   The so-called UN Development Decade was 1961-1971. The
UN General Assembly passed a resolution calling for concerted efforts to
improve living conditions of poor states as well as bringing about economic
development in these areas.

85   "Declaration and Action Programme on the Establishment of a
New International Economic Order," in Guy F. Erb and Valeriana Kallab,
Beyond Dependency: The Developing World Speaks Out (Washington, D.C.:
Overseas Development Council, 1975), pp. 165-236.

CHAPTER 5
CULTURAL, DIPLOMATIC, AND POLITICAL RELATIONSHIPS

Cultural, diplomatic, and political ties have figured very prominently in the post-independence relationships between these two ex-imperial European powers and their former African dependencies. In spite of the fact that the African countries have attained the status of independent states, still they have continued to maintain cultural, diplomatic, and political ties with the former metropolitan countries. The most important of these ties are common languages, common administrative, educational, and legal systems, as well as informal personal relationships between politicians, clergymen, businessmen, and other professional groups of the newly independent states and their counterparts from Britain and France. These links have generally been formalized in institutions such as the British Commonwealth of Nations or the French Community. Thus, all kinds of direct and indirect cultural, diplomatic, and political relationships between former colonies and former colonizers have been reinforced since the dependencies achieved their "flag" independence. Commenting on this very question, George W. Shepherd, Jr., observed that the former metropolitan powers could take back with the left hand what they had given with the right.[1] Thus, in these cultural, diplomatic, and political relationships between European states and the new African states, a state of dependency has continued. Britain and France have sought not only to maintain many of the existing relationships with the new African states, but also to give them institutional form. The participation of African countries in these post-colonial associations has involved meetings of chiefs-of-state and governments or their designated ministers for such representation on both a regular and irregular basis.

African states have retained their colonial language as the *lingua franca* – the language of administration, commerce, business, communications and the classroom. Thus, in both Anglophone and Francophone Africa, the language of the colonizer became the language of compromise. Attempts to replace them with popular native languages have generally resulted in mass riots and bloodshed.

With the enormous expansion of educational institutions after independence and the equally great shortage of native teachers, the new African states have had to rely quite heavily on recruiting teachers from the former colonial powers. Similarly, the flow of African students to the institutions of higher learning of the former metropolitan powers has been kept open. The simple fact that a large number of African students are graduating from British and French universities has meant a continuing cultural link with the former colonizers. As a result, the stamp of the colonial cultural heritage is still strong and is perpetuated among the intellectuals by the continued flow of students to metropolitan universities. The colonial cultural heritage is also perpetuated by the channels of communications. For example, politicians and intellectuals in Francophone Africa read such popular French newspapers as *Le Monde, L'Express, France-Observateur*; and in Anglophone areas, their counterparts read the *Times*, the *Guardian*, the *New-Statesman and Nation*, and the *Economist*.

Although both Britain and France have tried to maintain cultural ties with their former African dependencies, they have, however, only achieved varying degrees of success. The French have been more successful in this area than their British counterparts. For example, the cultural ties between France and French-speaking Africa have been much more intimate than the cultural ties between Britain and English-speaking African states. Some analysts claim that the bond of friendship between Britain and Anglophone Africa has been based on mutual respect and not on cultural ties. They point out that the cultural relationships between Britain and her ex-colonies have not yet developed to the degree of intimacy existing between France and French-speaking African countries. It must be remembered that right from the colonial era France has emphasized her culture in dealings with her colonial subjects. The French believed in their civilizing mission in Africa. Thus, when they relinquished political control of their dependencies in Africa, they strengthened their cultural ties with the new states that emerged in the sixties. France did sign Cultural Conventions with the new states at the time of independence which were aimed at achieving cultural cooperation.

Britain's failure to establish intimate cultural ties with Anglophone Africa can be explained in terms of her attitude of racial arrogance in her dealings with the native populations. They maintained their social distance from the native Africans. In no way could they imagine their African subjects ever becoming part of the British nation; neither did they give them the least encouragement or even the incentive to try.[2]

The Francophone States and the French Community

The institution of the French Community as provided in the Constitution of the Fifth Republic, published on September 4, 1958, was designed to keep the new French-speaking African states within the French orbit and thus provide a continuity in terms of cultural, diplomatic, economic, and political relationships. The idea of the Community as it was originally conceived in the 1958 French Constitution did not provide immediate independence for the overseas dependencies. Instead, it gave them some sort of internal autonomy and linked them to France. The Community was granted special powers to control foreign policy, defense, currency, trade, strategic raw materials, higher education, transportation, and telecommunications.[3] The Constitution also provided for a consultative Executive Council and a Senate, presided over by the President of France, who was elected by all citizens[4] to serve as the President of the Community. It further provided that special agreements may establish other common spheres of competence or regulate the transfer of competences from the Community to one of its members.[5]

In practice, this meant that the dependencies would not be fully independent, but rather they would have some degree of self-government, with the Community exercising the most important functions of government. The proposed Constitution, however, did permit secession. It gave the African territories two choices. The first choice was to remain in the Community and the second was to opt for full and complete independence and thereby lose all benefits derived from close association with France.

The Community idea generated a great deal of hostility and opposition in Francophone Africa, with opinion sharply divided among the elite groups. Charges of neo-colonialist and neo-assimilationist aspirations of France were expressed in Francophone Africa. The new institution won strong support among the more conservative African leaders such as Felix Houphouet-Boigny of the Ivory Coast and was denounced by the more radical grops led by Sekou Touré of Guinea, who saw it only as a device to dominate the new states. President Charles de Gaulle made an extensive tour of Francophone Africa trying to sell the new plan. His proposal received enthusiastic welcome in all parts of Africa with the exception of Guinea. Sekou Touré was not prepared to join the political club. He was determined to take the opportunity which the Referendum offered him to remove Guinea from the French orbit. Thus, at his party's conference held on September 14, 1958, Sekou Touré explained his position on the matter when he made the following observation:

> It will fall to us to preserve for Guinea and for Africa the honour of the African man....We shall vote "no" to the Community which is merely the French Union rechristened – the old goods with new labels. We shall vote "no" to inequality. We shall vote "no" to irresponsibility. From the 29th of September, we shall be an independent country.[6]

The result of the de Gaulle Referendum was indeed an impressive victory for France. The French-speaking African states, with the exception of Guinea, voted overwhelmingly to remain in the French community. The "yes" votes in key selected African countries were as follows: the Ivory Coast, 99%; Dahomey, 97%; Mauritania, 87%; Upper Volta, 99%; Senegal, 97%; and Niger, 78%.

Sekou Touré carried Guinea with him. In Guinea, 95% of the electorate voted against the new constitution. Acting the part of the hurt parent, President de Gaulle immediately adopted punitive measures against Guinea. French financial assistance to Guinea, which amounted to about $17 million annually, was cut off immediately. French nationals who manned important administrative positions in Guinea were withdrawn. France began to make arrangements for the early return of French military units which constituted the territory's defense. The withdrawal of French support was indeed a serious blow to Guinea. Her goods would have no more free market in France, and therefore were to be subjected to the customs duties on goods coming from foreign countries. The severity of this punishment can be fully appreciated if one realizes that France in the past absorbed approximately 70-80 percent of Guinea's exports. France immediately ceased to buy Ginuea's bananas at subsidized prices. She removed or destroyed all equipment, including government records, maps, typewriters, medicines in hospitals, and even electric bulbs.[7] Guinea was isolated and left in the cold. To add to its misery, France pressured her allies to withhold recognition for the new state. Thus, Guinea's bold decision to opt for full independence proved to be a nightmare. By opting for such comprehensive punitive measures, France was able to isolate the center of opposition to its concept of community.[8]

At this hour of national crisis, aid managed to reach Guinea from other sources. For example, on November 23, 1958, Ghana and Guinea signed an agreement "to constitute their two states as the nucleus of a Union of West African states." The policies of both countries in such fields as defense, foreign affairs, and economic matters would be coordinated and pursued jointly. To its needy partner, Ghana gave a grant of £10 million (i.e., $28 million).

The dire economic plight of Guinea offered the Soviet Union and other socialist governments a golden opportunity to step into the vacuum created by French withdrawal of financial as well as technical assistance.

Thus, three days after the Republic of Guinea was proclaimed, it was very quickly granted diplomatic recognition by the Soviet Union and other Communist bloc nations. At this period, the Communist states served as the only source of trade and economic aid for the hard-pressed Guineans. By 1960, there were as many as 700 European Communist technicians working in Guinea on various projects, including the building of a powerful radio station and a big printing press. There were over 200 Guinean students in Eastern European universities. Towards the end of 1960, approximately 75% of Guinea's trade had been captured by the Communist bloc states. Guinea signed away its agricultural products in a series of barter agreements with the Soviet Union, East Germany, Poland, Hungary, and Czechoslovakia. Guinea asserted its independence by abruptly breaking away from the franc zone in 1960, and establishing its own currency.

Elsewhere in French-speaking Africa, the concept of Community was vigorously defended and justified. For example, Léopold Senghor of Senegal, was among the most active supporters of the Franco-African Community. He justified African participation in the following terms:

> The need for European-African cooperation derives from the fact that an underdeveloped country which has achieved nominal independence cannot acquire real independence if it remains underdeveloped. It must obtain external aid. The solution can be found in its entry into a larger ensemble, in the form of a confederacy. It is therefore in the interests of these countries, once their nominal independence is achieved, not to separate them from their former mother, but to achieve new ties based on liberty, equality, and cooperation. . . . Long-continued political and economic relations, and a common language of international character, have created links which it would be catastrophic to break. Africa and Europe are genuinely complementary, in terms of politics, economics, and culture.[9]

Shortly after these sentiments were expressed, Lépold-Sédar Senghor reaffirmed his earlier justification of African membership in the French Community in the following observation:

> The French Community, created by General de Gaulle in full agreement with Africa's true representatives, is one of the greatest achievements of our time....It enables the former mother country and its erstwhile colonies to form a friendly cultural and economic union and thus forge a lasting link between Western Europe and Africa.[10]

Other Leaders of Francophone Africa, such as Felix Houphouet-Boigny and Léon M'Ba of Gabon, echoed similar sentiments. For example, Léon M'Ba is quoted as having made the following statement:

> Without very substantial external aid, we cannot ensure our defense, the stability of our currency, the development of our country, and the improvement of our standard of living. These are the considerations that must guide us in our common attitude of loyalty vis-à-vis the Community, France, and General de Gaulle.[11]

The fact that Guinea survived after France had imposed sweeping economic sanctions against it encouraged other African states to seek complete independence, of course without paying the severe price of economic separation from France.[12] Thus, in 1960, the French yielded to pressures and amended their Constitution to permit members of the Community to opt for independence.[13] As a result of this amendment, all the African countries decided to achieve full and complete independence since they were now allowed to retain the benefits of the Community without sacrificing direct sovereignty.[14]

It is quite obvious that the character of the Community has changed following the achievement of independent status by its members. The French Government took steps to cope with the new situation. Thus, on May 18, 1961, it established new organs for handling the relations between France and Francophone Africa. The new post of Minister for Cooperation was created to deal specifically with the problem of technical assistance. Also, the powers exercised by the Community as laid down in Article 78 of the French Constitution were transferred to each member state on its attaining independence. Thus, competence of the Community has eroded. What is left of it is now mainly restricted to a coordination of foreign policy in very important matters and to cooperation in economic and cultural fields.

Although very few African countries have chosen to continue their membership in this association,[15] France has continued its support to all states in a liberal fashion whether or not they are still members.[16] However, she reserved the right to give priority in the allocation of aid funds to projects in states which have remained in the Community.[17] Arnold Rivkin suggested that France hoped by this liberal policy she would win back to the Community some of the states outside, particularly those among the Entente group.[18]

It must be pointed out that all Francophone African states, whether inside or outside the French Community, with the exception of Guinea and Mali, have continued intact the pre-existing ties with France. Thus, France has succeeded in establishing a much more intimate or close relationship with the French-speaking African states than exists between Britain and Anglophone Africa. This relationship has been so close, in fact, that African nationalist leaders outside the Community have frequently accused the African states within it of neo-colonial dependency.

In recent years, France has begun to seek a sort of rapprochement with Guinea. For example, in 1982, President Sekou Touré, once considered as the *enfant terrible*, went to Paris in order to settle the major disagreements between France and Guinea. While in Paris, President Touré had talks with President Mitterrand, Cooperation and Development Minister Jean-Pierre Cot and Foreign Minister Claude Cheyson. These talks were aimed at reconciling both countries and, thus, putting the final patches to the years of uneasy Guinea-France relations which began in 1958 when Guinea embarrassed France by deciding to break away from the French system rather than remaining in the French Community. This resulted in the mass exodus of French technicians, teachers, and experts. Since then, Franco-Guinean relationships have remained bitter and uneasy, with Guinea charging repeatedly that Paris was plotting to overthrow its government headed by President Sekou Touré. For example, in 1965, there was the "teachers' plot," in which President Sekou Touré accused Paris of masterminding the domestic disturbances. Then, in 1969, occurred the "Labe plot," in which thirteen people were sentenced to death and twenty-seven others were jailed.

Despite efforts to iron out the differences between Conakry and Paris, some problems remained. However, following his visit, Guinea released eighteen French prisoners who were jailed in Guinean prisons. France responded by banning the publication of the Guinean exile bulletin – the Guinee Perspectives Nouvelles, but declined the demand to extradite Guinean exiles so that they could be tried and punished for their crimes.

Diplomatic relations which were terminated at the time of the Guinean independence were restored between Conakry and Paris. The

French businessmen were once again reassured of their safety and friendship in Guinea.

A common bond between France and the new French-speaking African states has been in the fields of language and culture. Since granting political independence to her former African dependencies, France has reinforced her cultural ties with them. For example, it is estimated that the percentage of French aid spent on cultural and educational programs in Francophone Africa averaged over 20 percent of the French aid (FAC) budget for the period 1959-1969. Thus, although France has relinquished all overt political control in French Africa, still she continues to enjoy a considerable amount of influence and good will in the region. As indicated earlier in this discussion, France signed Cultural Conventions with each of the French-speaking African states, with the exception of Guinea, at the time of independence for purposes of cultural cooperation.

Franco-African cultural cooperation was influenced by two major factors. The first factor involved contacts which lasted for many years, coupled with the French policy of assimilation which was rigorously applied in overseas dependencies throughout most of the colonial period. Assimilation was based simply on the universality and validity of French civilization and institutions. In the field of culture, assimilation meant the absolute and universal superiority of the French culture and the belief that this culture could be transmitted through the process of education. Thus, in practice, cultural assimilation was aimed at the subversion or destruction of indigenous African institutions and traditions and their eventual replacement with French civilization. It was therefore directed to integrate the dependencies into a unitary French system economically, politically, and culturally.

The second factor involved the adoption of the French language as the medium or channel through which French cultural values, as well as technological knowledge, are transmitted. The French language has remained the *lingua franca* in a region where ethnic languages are indeed numerous.

Education has served as the main source of cultural contact between France and the new African states. In colonial days, it was designed to

150

produce a French-African elite whose loyalty to France would be assured. After the former dependencies had emerged as independent states, French presence in the area remained paramount. Thousands of French teachers, whose salaries are paid by the French Government, are working in African countries south of the Sahara. During the first two years of independence (1961-1962), for example, there were over 5,000 French teachers. A large number of these teachers were engaged in secondary schools, teacher-training colleges, technical schools, and other institutions for higher education. French teachers dominate the teaching staffs of universities in the region, such as the Universities of Dakar and Abidjan, and other high level institutions, such as the French Polytechnique, Centrale École des Mines, and École des Arts et Métiers. Even at the secondary school level, French teachers usually outnumber the native teachers.

Since the time of independence, the number of French nationals in African educational institutions has increased quite dramatically. The fact that these states are bent on expanding their educational programs has meant greater dependence on France for financial contributions and teaching personnel. This situation has placed France in a position to control education in general and higher education in particular in all Francophone states with the exception of Guinea.

French teachers handle all academic subjects, but generally concentrate on maintaining the purity of the French language. Their influence indeed permeates education and culture in the new states at all levels.[19] Similarly, French-speaking Africans have developed a taste for French education which they consider superior to any other system. This preference is reflected in the number of students from French-speaking African countries studying in France. The French governments have financed students from these areas in French universities as stipulated in the educational cooperation agreements. Similarly, France has carried out an elaborate program for training native administrators, technicians, and civil servants. Such institutes as the Institute des Hautes Études d'Outre-Mer (IHEOM), the Centre de Hautes Études Administratives sur l'Afrique at Asie Modernes (CHEAM), the Institute d'Études du Dévelopement Economique et Social (IEDES), and the Institute International de

Recherche et de Formation en Vue du Dévelopement Harmonisé (IRFED), are actively involved in training African civil servants, administrators, and technicians.[20]

The control of educational institutions in French-speaking African states is one strategy emphasized by France to ensure cultural dominance of the new states. Through her control of higher education in particular, France has indeed succeeded in influencing the values and attitudes of the emerging elite groups in order to build and preserve what Professor Spero has characterized as a Franco-African dominance-dependence system.[21] Professor Spero pointed out that the control of education in the region by France meant the control of a key area of public policy, since education is considered a crucial institution of socialization and politicization.[22]

Besides education, cultural appreciation and technical knowledge are being brought more and more into the daily life of the Africans through the various cultural and information media such as books, newspapers, cultural centers, libraries, lectures, art exhibitions, motion pictures, and the radio. All these media have helped to intensify cultural contacts and ties between France and her former dependencies.

Cultural contacts are also being maintained through "Cultural Exchange Programs." In 1960, for example, approximately 1,500 men and women from African and Malagasy states were invited under the aegis of the High Commission for Youth and Sports to attend information conferences in France and to stay at French centers and with French families. In the same manner, young French men and women have begun to develop the habit of spending the whole or part of their vacations in Africa under the exchange programs organized by various youth movements. These cultural contacts between young people from France and their African counterparts are designed to promote understanding and build bridges and lasting friendships among future leaders of their countries.

Art exhibitions also have played an important part in these cultural contacts. For example, in recent years, the sculptures of the Bingerville School in the Ivory Coast have become very popular with French tourists.

On the whole, one can very easily assert that, of all the types of post-independence relationships treated in this study, cultural relationships have been emphasized the most by France; hence, she has taken steps to expand and strengthen these ties as much as possible.

A major consequence of the continued French presence in French-speaking African countries has involved the slow progress of the program of Africanization of positions in the civil service in general, and educational institutions in particular. In both areas, French presence has remained very visible. French nationals have continued to dominate these structures. President Felix Houphouet-Boigny of the Ivory Coast has defended and even justified this situation. He emphatically rejected demands for immediate Africanization of positions at the top levels of the administrative hierarchy, as well as top positions in the universities, on the grounds that the development of his country, particularly, would be best served if jobs were held by competent French men and women rather than by incompetent Africans.[23] This is indeed a sharp contrast to Anglophone Africa, where the process of Africanization of the civil service progressed at a more rapid pace.

In the field of diplomatic relations, France has enjoyed the cooperation and friendship of the new African states. These diplomatic relationships provided France with solid support for her foreign policies. With the exception of the Congo Republic, Guinea, and Mali, it can be reasonably asserted that the foreign policies of French-speaking African states closely followed French policy and quite often served as agents of that policy.[24] At international organizations such as the United Nations and its numerous organs, France and her former African dependencies almost spoke with one voice. With France, they constituted a solid voting bloc at the United Nations and also at the Organization for African Unity (OAU). Although these new states professed neutrality and non-alignment as the cornerstones of their foreign policies, in reality, however, they stood behind France in important Cold War issues. They usually staged caucusing sessions with France at the UN at which time France made known to them her position and strategy. Unlike their British counterparts, which were ready to criticize and sometimes condemn and embarrass Britain over her unpopular policies involving controversial international questions such as the Rhodesian crisis generated by the unilateral declaration of independence by the white supremacists, or South Africa's illegal administration in Namibia, the leaders of Francophone Africa usually took the French position, or at least remained uncommitted and thus refrained from making the kind of public statements which France might consider unfriendly.

They also supported other "independent" French foreign policies such as, for example, the Algerian episode, the Bizerte crisis, or the tests of atomic weapons in the Sahara. In Africa, these policies were very unpopular and generated a lot of discussion and criticism. France was sharply condemned over these policies. Nevertheless, French Africa, with the exception of Guinea and Mali, remained silent at the time these issues were debated in international forums or arenas, while other African states were voicing their concern and indignation over these French policies.

The critics of the intimate cultural, diplomatic, and political relationships between France and Francophone Africa have wondered how long these relationships would last, considering the fact that they have involved very large French expenditures. Analysts of Franco-African relationships have nevertheless expressed the view that the general public in France supports cultural and technical assistance for the ex-French dependencies for reasons of national prestige and philanthropy. The ex-British dependencies have frequently accused France for being neo-colonialist. Such an accusation, whether valid or not, damages and even embarrasses any of the countries in the region which are indeed anxious and determined to demonstrate their genuine independence.

William Clark has raised an important question which has remained yet unanswered – namely, whether African cultural nationalism and "La Mission Civilistrice" of France are broad enough to embrace each other.[25]

It was the late President Charles de Gaulle who established the special relationship with Francophone Africa. The General was credited with the decolonization in Africa south of the Sahara. It was he who engineered the consolidation of a remarkable sphere of post-colonial influence in French-speaking Africa. His emotional ties with Africa can be traced to the forties when France turned to her African Empire for help during the Nazi occupation. Thus, one can appreciate the remarkable emotional links which existed between the General and the leaders of the new states of French-speaking Africa.

Presidents Giscard d'Estaing and Mitterrand continued that tradition. In 1978, for example, President Giscard d'Estaing visited French-speaking African countries to reassure them of continued French friendship and support. At Abidjan, the Ivory Coast, he stated that the visit bore testimony to the exceptional character of the relations between France and the Ivory Coast. Before he left for France, he announced to his audience that French companies had signed business contracts with the Ivory Coast worth 2.8 billion francs since January 1, 1976.[26] At a time when French policies in Africa were sharply criticized and condemned, particularly over the sale of nuclear reactors to South Africa, he labored hard to diffuse the uproar by demanding guarantees that the power stations to be built by Pretoria could not be used directly or indirectly for military purposes.

Similarly, the Socialist Government of President Mitterrand has vowed to continue the special relationship between France and Francophone Africa. Thus, during his state visit in Africa in 1982, two main themes, namely, security and development, were emphasized. Thus, he assured African leaders of continued French aid towards their development.

African States in the British Commonwealth

As Britain embarked on a rapid program of decolonization in Africa in the early sixties, its Empire was converted or transformed into a new multiracial Commonwealth. The idea of the British Commonwealth of Nations has been considered as an outgrowth of the imperial system. Nevertheless, the Commonwealth is an association of independent sovereign states all of which have been, at one time, British dependencies. Thus, any British territory, on attaining its independence, may seek membership in the Commonwealth; this is of course usually granted only by the unanimous consent of the members. The Statute of Westminster of 1931 offered all former colonies the undisputed right to secede from the Commonwealth if their national interests so dictated. However, the British governments usually urged this relationship upon these new states and quite frequently, as in the case of Kenya, acceptance of membership in the British Commonwealth hastened independence.[27]

Anglophone African states, after achieving political independence, have generally sought membership into this international multiracial association. However, not all former British dependencies have elected to remain within the British Commonwealth. The Sudan, for example, has severed this relationship, although it has remained within the pound sterling trading zone and continued close diplomatic and cultural links until the Rhodesian unilateral declaration of independence in 1965 and the Israeli-Arab crisis of 1967.[28] Like their French counterparts, Anglophone African states have shown genuine interest in maintaining ties with the ex-colonial power after independence was achieved to ensure a continuation of institutions and programs adapted and expanded to meet the new needs of their changed political status.[29] For example, during the early years of his rule in the new state of Ghana, the late President Kwame Nkrumah, in an overall assessment of the British Commonwealth, painted this glowing picture of the Commonwealth:

> It is the only organized world-wide association of people in which race, religion, nationality, and culture are all transcended by a common sense of fellowship. No policies are imposed on it from above. It does not even seek unity of policy....This is not a bloc. It is not a power grouping. It is a club or a family of friends who see their continuing friendship as a strand of peace in a troubled world.[30]

Many of the leaders in Anglophone African states shared the sentiments expressed by President Nkrumah in this passage. Membership in the Commonwealth provided the African states with a forum for voicing their opinions on important international questions–with a more responsive source of assistance for economic or educational programs, with the privilege of Commonwealth preference in matters of trade among Commonwealth members, and with a number of agencies for achieving cooperation in scientific research, civil aviation, and telecommunications. Membership has also provided the African countries additional leverage in pressuring Britain in matters relating to decolonization problems, particularly in Southern Africa where entrenched white supremacists denied the African majority their right to participate in the economic and political activities of their countries.

Nevertheless, in comparison with their counterparts in the French Community, the members of the British Commonwealth tended on the whole to pursue a more independent posture in their dealings with the ex-colonizer. Thus, after formal independence, they took steps such as the attainment of republican status, the cancellation of metropolitan defense arrangements, the withdrawal of colonial troops, the loosening of preferential market conditions, and the diversification of trade. Whatever ties of aid, culture, and sentiment remain, there is a widening of the material distance between the metropole and the ex-colony.[31] But Britain succeeded in converting an Empire into a Commonwealth and thus exchanged the old relationship of dominance for a special relationship of partnership with the new states.[32] This special relationship helped to salvage the prestige which was always considered a motive for empire,[33] and eventually softened the impact of the blow resulting from the loss of the colonies.

The composition of the Commonwealth has changed since Africans and Asians became members of it. The admission of Africans into the Commonwealth ended its former character as a white man's club. Thus, the "Kith and Kin" concept of the Commonwealth is now a thing of the past. As William Clark explained, the sudden expansion of the Commonwealth from a group of people with similar racial and political backgrounds and prospects has greatly weakened the old political and strategic motives for empire.[34] The new Commonwealth was compelled to make adjustments to accommodate the new members. In Commonwealth councils, the new African members have generally emphasized the importance of consultations and have also resisted Britain's efforts to dominate their organization. The equality of its members has been emphasized. Britain is simply considered the first among equals at Commonwealth conferences. Like other members, Britain has one vote, although meetings are usually held in Britain with the British Prime Minister serving as the host. Britain has remained the center, if not the formal capital, the clearinghouse, the organizer of agenda, and, of course, the tutor of aspiring members.[35]

Due to the fact that formal ties have dwindled in importance, increasing emphasis is now placed on the principle of consultation. In short, Commonwealth members try to avoid any prior commitment to a common policy. The decisions of the group are reached by general consensus instead of by majority votes. The association is no longer a closely knit family. Each member has other preoccupations which, at times, have priority over Commonwealth ties. The members very rarely speak with one voice on controversial international issues.[36]

The new Commonwealth is overwhelmingly anti-colonial and neutralist, and Britain's policies are supported when they fit that pattern[37] and vigorously condemned when they do not. The African Commonwealth members consider the British Commonwealth not just merely as an association for consultation, but an institution for cooperative assistance. To these new members the major function of the association is to provide aid to the poor members.

The Commonwealth has served a useful diplomatic function as well. All important questions of common interest to Commonwealth members are discussed at meetings of the Heads of Government of member states. A series of conferences are held annually involving economic, educational, medical, and scientific cooperation. For example, the Commonwealth Economic Committee provides economic and statistical data on questions related to Commonwealth productivity and trade. The Commonwealth Secretariat, established in London in July, 1965, is viewed as the visible symbol of the spirit of cooperation among members. The Secretariat has the responsibility for disseminating information on questions of common interest; for aiding the various Commonwealth Agencies, both official and unofficial, in promoting Commonwealth links in all fields; and for preparing and servicing the heads of governments and other ministerial meetings.[38]

At international forums, Commonwealth solidarity is strengthened by fairly frequent meetings of Finance Ministers before the World Bank annual meeting, and Foreign Ministers before the UN General Assembly sessions meet. In caucuses, Britain's position and policy are explained to Commonwealth members; nevertheless, each member reserves the right to disagree with Britain. Thus, African states were at odds with the policy of the British Government over the rebel regime of Prime Minister Ian Smith of Southern Rhodesia (Zimbabwe). In the sixties and seventies, consensus was strained by growing differences within the Commonwealth between the non-aligned and the aligned in the Cold War, and between anti-colonialists and imperialists. It is this diversity of attitudes which gives Commonwealth consultation its significance.

Cultural, economic, and diplomatic ties have continued to make the Commonwealth a viable association and a convenient vehicle for the exchange of goods as well as ideas among the member states. Commonwealth educators, jurists, prime ministers, finance ministers, and parliamentarians have maintained close contacts with one another. Recognizing the economic problems that beset the new states after independence, Britain tried to compensate for this to some extent by expanding the use of its Export Credit Scheme to finance British exports for development projects in these areas. Similarly, Britain expressed its willingness to consider requests from the new states for loans from the United Kingdom Treasury.[39] Britain participates very actively in the Special Commonwealth African Assistance Program (SCAAP) which was established in September, 1960, at the meeting of Commonwealth finance ministers. The purpose of this program is primarily to coordinate aid from the more wealthy Commonwealth members to African member states and the remaining British dependent territories in Africa.[40] Britain also extends some financial assistance to the new states through the Commonwealth Development Fund. The Department of Technical Cooperation was designated to provide technical assistance to the new Commonwealth countries. Its responsibilities include capital development assistance and the administration of the Overseas Civil Service Aid Scheme.

The Overseas Civil Service Aid Scheme was devised to allow all territories which achieved independence after September, 1960, to recruit and retain the services of experienced expatriate administrators and specialists before and after independence. Under this scheme, while the local government was responsible for local rates of salary, Britain paid the cost of inducement and educational allowances for overseas officials and contributed toward passage costs plus half of any compensation for loss of career. Through this medium, Britain has recruited highly qualified personnel for administrative, agricultural, educational, engineering, and medical appointments in Ghana, Kenya, Nigeria, Uganda, and Sierra Leone.

Regular arrangements for loan or securement of professional people also exist between Britain and the new African states. Recruitment on behalf of overseas Commonwealth countries is also undertaken by the British Council and the Crown Agents for Overseas Governments and Administrations. The British Council is directly responsible for recruiting the teaching staff of schools, universities, and training colleges in Commonwealth Africa.

Britain has also assisted these states in a number of other ways. One of these is by training scientists from these countries and by making the results of scientific research available to them. The Department of Technical Cooperation finances research bearing on the social and economic problems of these developing countries. Britain has remained the largest source of recruitment for university and technical college personnel in these lands. Commonwealth Scholarship and Fellowship Plan makes it possible for Ghanaians, Kenyans, Tanzanians, and Nigerians to pursue postgraduate and research programs in universities in Britain and other advanced members of the Commonwealth, such as Australia, Canada, and New Zealand, which are assisting Britain with the burden of aiding the new members of the Commonwealth.

The old imperial economic preference established in the thirties has been very beneficial to the trade of Commonwealth countries, although many African members have diversified their trade and have turned their attention to other aid donors and investors. Nevertheless, the sterling zone has generally promoted financial transactions among members. Britain's decision to join the European Common Market raised a political storm in the Commonwealth and was sharply criticized by those elements who benefitted from the Commonwealth preferences. Britain's entry into the EEC indeed demonstrated the desperate dependence on British markets and investments of the African members at the time. This explained why African Commonwealth Finance Ministers in Accra unanimously protested against Britain's determination to join the EEC. The African states were very suspicious of this European club which, they believed, was a device created by France and other imperialist groups to reimpose European dominance over African states. Their objections to the European Common Market at the time were influenced by political rather than economic considerations.

They viewed Britain's participation in the EEC not only as a major catastrophe for their economies, but also as an act of betrayal. They reached the conclusion that Britain had left them in the cold by preferring membership in the Common Market.

The cultural relationships between Britain and African Commonwealth countries are not as intimate as those between France and Francophone states. However, there has developed a very close contact in the educational field. Thus, Britain has remained the largest source for the recruitment of university, secondary school, and teacher-training teaching staffs. English-speaking African countries have continued to patronize the British educational system. For the academic year 1962-1963, there were 42,095 Commonwealth students in Britain, of which 11,705 came from West Africa alone – Gambia, 249; Ghana, 1,885; Nigeria, 8,954; and Sierra Leone, 617.[41] These were full-time students conducting research or studying in British universities and technical institutions, teacher-training colleges, hospitals or medical schools, commercial schools, or other professions.

In addition, Britain has provided advisory services through the system of securement in which British experts are posted to these countries to assist them with their educational programs. Besides advisory services, Commonwealth scholars from these countries are awarded postgraduate scholarships and fellowships to enable them to study in universities and technical colleges in both Great Britain and in other advanced countries of the Commonwealth, such as Australia, Canada, and New Zealand. Thus, during the academic year 1962-1963, there were 74 such scholars – Gambia, 4; Ghana, 22; Nigeria, 39; and Sierra Leone, 9.[42]

The English language has come to stay in this region plagued by a diversity of tongues and dialects. Like the French language in Francophone Africa, the English language has become the language of the classroom, of the courts, and of administration. It has also become the "language of compromise" in a region where many ethnic groups are proud of their own languages and dialects and, as a consequence, will resist any attempts to impose the languages of their rivals as the "national" language on them.

On the basis of Britain's support offered to Commonwealth countries, it can be asserted that the emergence of the new African states has affected the Commonwealth's conception of itself. The presence of African states in the association presented new problems for the organization and eventually led to new services for the new members. However, despite the several contributions Britain has made to assist Anglophone African states, it can be argued that Britain disengaged and departed from Africa faster and more completely than France except in East Africa, particularly Kenya, where British presence still remains paramount. In this area, the process of Africanization of the civil service has progressed very slowly.

Unlike their Francophone counterparts, Anglophone African states, since achieving independence, have been very critical of Britain's policies, which they have considered harmful to African interests. They have not hesitated to air their criticisms and grievances in the open in such forums as the Commonwealth meetings, the Organization of African Unity sessions, or at the United Nations conferences. The majority of the leaders of English-speaking states, with the exception of President Hastings K. Banda of Malawi, sharply criticized and quite vigorously opposed Britain's decolonization policies in Southern Africa.

Among the factors which have adversely affected the relationships between Britain and Commonwealth Africa are the following: (a) Britain's decision to enter the Common Market; (b) Britain's arms sale to South Africa; and (c) Britain's policy on Southern Rhodesia. Britain's expressed interest in seeking membership in the European Economic Community stirred up heated debate and bitter controversy in the British Commonwealth. At the initial stage of the negotiations to establish the Common Market, the six founding members[43] extended their invitation to Britain to join the Community. The British response was that the political aims of the EEC were unacceptable. She seemed to have a deep emotional commitment to the general notion of independent national sovereignty as opposed to internationalism which the founding members had emphasized. She also had an equally strong sentiment for the unique relationships of the Commonwealth.[44] Britain gave the founding members the impression that she was not interested in joining the European club if she could not negotiate favorable terms for the entry of Commonwealth products to the Common Market. Failing to secure assurances that the Commonwealth exports would be safeguarded, Britain dragged her feet for a while and thus refused to make any commitments concerning entry into the EEC. For the British, the Commonwealth, like the Empire before it, has provided opportunities for enterprise, prestige, and for the spirit of personal service.[45]

A combination of factors such as declining power status in the international community, price instability, balance of payments, crises, and economic stagnation, forced the British Government to make that historic change in policy when it applied in July, 1961, for membership in the Community. In making this move, Britain seemed to be seeking a new identity for herself. To this end, the Conservative Party saw a strong Europe, with British membership of the EEC as the bulwark of foreign policy.[46] Later on, the Labour Party adopted the Tory position of seeking membership in a "greater Europe" while agreeing to shed some Commonwealth ties and responsibilities. The Britons now believed that their destiny lay in the Common Market and not in the Commonwealth.

During the long protracted negotiations in Brussels that followed Britain's application for EEC membership, Britain still insisted that the economic interests of the Commonwealth must be protected. President de Gaulle, in a press conference on January 14, announced the French veto which ended abruptly the protracted negotiations between Britain and the European Economic Community and eventually denied Britain membership in the EEC. In his veto message, the French president acknowledged the fact that Britain had global economic and political interests which he believed would prevent the British from full acceptance and participation in the economic and political goals of the Community.

The discriminatory and oppressive policies of the white supremacist regimes in southern Africa were a source of antagonism between Britain and the African Commonwealth members. African states in general, and the radical ones in particular, were determined to complete the decolonization process on the African continent. Thus, they concentrated all their liberation efforts in those regions where pockets of colonialism existed, particularly in South Africa, and Rhodesia (Zimbabwe). It was African pressure that led to the ousting of South Africa from the British Commonwealth. Led by the late President Kwame Nkrumah of Ghana and President Julius Nyerere of

Tanzania, African members of the Commonwealth demanded the removal of Apartheid South Africa from the association of friends on the grounds that it had systematically excluded its African members who were in the majority from participating in the country's political process as well as economic activities. The African leaders noted that they were anxious to remain in the Commonwealth but only provided that it observed those principles of equality and justice for which it stood.[47]

They indicated that they would not continue their membership in any association of friends which included a state which was deliberately and ruthlessly pursuing a racialist policy.[48]

Britain's announcement of its intention to resume arms supply to the Republic of South Africa in 1970,[49] despite the United Nations arms embargo on that country, precipitated another round of controversy between Britain and Anglophone Africa. Presidents Kaunda and Nyerere led the opposition against British arms sale to South Africa. For example, President Nyerere contended that South Africa did not need the arms, but simply sought through such purchases a "certificate of respectability" from European nations and called upon Britain and France, in particular, to refrain from selling arms to South Africa.[50]

The anger and frustration generated by the arms deal consequently led to a joint delegation of the OAU and the non-aligned states protesting the British decision to Britain over this question.[51] Their protests fell on deaf ears. The issue was hotly debated during the January, 1971, Commonwealth Conference. African leaders argued that the sale of arms, no matter what restrictions might be placed on that sale, implied a declaration of support – an implied alliance of a kind. President Nyerere commented:

> You can trade with people you dislike; you can have diplomatic relations with governments you disapprove of; you can sit in conference with those nations whose policies you abhor. But you do not sell arms without saying in effect – in the light of the receiving country's known policies; friends and enemies, we will be on their side in the case of any conflict. We shall want them to defeat their enemies.[52]

Prime Minister Heath was not moved by criticisms leveled against Britain's proposed arms sale to South Africa. He made it clear that the

British Government would pursue its perception of Britain's interests regardless of the views and criticisms expressed by the Commonwealth members. Furthermore, he rationalized that support for South Africa's defense system did not imply an endorsement of its domestic policies. Thus, in February, 1971, his government announced that Britain would proceed as planned, to supply arms to South Africa in the midst of violent protests and anti-British indignation and moral condemnation all over Anglophone Africa.

The Rhodesian Crisis severely put a strain on British and Commonwealth African relations. In 1964, while anticipating an imminent seizure of independence by the white supremacists in Rhodesia, led by Ian Smith, the Commonwealth states from Africa demanded that Britain commit itself to the principle of summoning a constitutional conference to determine the political future of that dependency. They pressed this demand at the Commonwealth Prime Minister's Conference held in July, 1964. The question surfaced once again at the Commonwealth meeting held in London from 17-25 June 1965. At this Conference, the Heads of Government of the African Commonwealth states affirmed that they were irrevocably opposed to any unilateral declaration of independence and pressed Britain to take direct action to end the Smith rebellion.

Britain's refusal to commit herself to the principle of "No Independence Before Majority Rule" (NIBMAR) opened even wider the gap between Britain and the African members of the Commonwealth. The British strategy to end the rebellion was considered ineffectual and the British motives were suspect. The British were accused of secretly attempting to protect their "Kith and Kin" in Rhodesia and their policies were seriously questioned. At Accra, for example, the OAU member states passed a resolution which deplored "the refusal of Britain to meet with firmness and resolution the threat of a unilateral declaration of independence" and requested the convening of a constitutional conference and the release of all political prisoners. They requested all states to withhold recognition for the rebel state. Furthermore, they resolved to (a) reconsider all political, economic, diplomatic, and financial relations between African countries and the United Kingdom government in the event of this government's granting or tolerating Rhodesian independence under minority government; (b) use all possible means, including force, to oppose a unilateral declaration for independence; and (c) give immediate assistance to the people of Zimbabwe with a view to establishing a majority government in the country.[53]

Britain resisted African pressure and refused to use force to end the rebellion. All along, the British Government had contended that it could not intervene in Rhodesia because of its status as a self-governing territory since 1923 and, as a consequence, Britain did not have the power to interfere with its domestic affairs. This constitutional explanation was rejected by African states which argued that Britain had a moral obligation to see to it that the rights of the African majority were protected. Some analysts believed, however, that Britain feared the consequences to British economic interests in the region if force was used to bring the Smith regime to its knees. They pointed out that Britain tried as much as possible to avoid a showdown with South Africa. Moreover, there was very little public support in Great Britain for the use of force against Rhodesia,[54] and indeed, little concern was shown for African reactions. The official British position was that Rhodesia had been self-governing since 1923 and, thus, neither Britain nor the Commonwealth, nor even the United Nations had the right to intervene in Rhodesia's internal affairs.[55] Despite this British position, President Nyerere presented a special memorandum which called upon the Commonwealth members to impose economic and financial sanctions against Rhodesia immediately; prevent its admission to the United Nations; and, as a last resort, to create a joint Commonwealth military force to intervene and restore law and order in the territory in the event of Rhodesian rebellion.

The unilateral declaration of independence on November 11, 1965, by the Southern Rhodesian regime severely damaged the relations between Britain and Commonwealth Africa. Britain's refusal to use force to end the Rhodesian rebellion angered many African states which believed that Britain had a special responsibility to guarantee the rights of the African majority and, as such, should use military force to restore law and order in the area. While rejecting the use of force, Labour Prime Minister Harold Wilson preferred instead to use diplomatic and economic sanctions. The assumption was that these measures would pressure the Ian Smith regime to the negotiating table. Mr. Wilson's calculation was that the application of sanctions would directly threaten industry and agriculture in Rhodesia and force a return to legality. However, at this time, relations between Rhodesia and South Africa had become close enough to neutralize the impact of sanctions imposed against it. Britain's determination not to use force against the rebel state was overwhelmingly denounced by the African Commonwealth members which were convinced that Britain had at least a moral obligation which should transcend any constitutional limitations to protect the African majority from the white-dominated government of Southern Rhodesia.

Dissatisfied with the British handling of the Rhodesian question, many Commonwealth countries in Africa, including Ghana and Tanzania, broke off diplomatic relations on the 18th of December, 1965, in compliance with an OAU Council Resolution of December 3 recommending such action.[56]

African members of the Commonwealth embarrassed Britain at the United Nations General Assembly Emergency Session when they staged a walk-out protesting Prime Minister Harold Wilson's speech in which he defended Britain's policy over the Rhodesian question on December 16, 1965.

Malawi was the only African Commonwealth state that supported Britain's strategy to resolve the problem. When the Emergency Meeting of the OAU Council of Ministers resolved on December 3, 1965, that all members should sever diplomatic and economic relations with Britain unless she had crushed the Smith rebellion by December 15, Malawi abstained. Its president, Dr. Hastings Banda, explained in Parliament that Malawi had taken this position because he believed that Britain had taken effective steps to end the rebellion and because breaking diplomatic relations was an empty and idle gesture which would not help the Africans in Rhodesia in any way whatever.[57]

Malawi also abstained quite consistently on resolutions at the General Assembly calling on Britain to use force against the white supremacists in Southern Rhodesia. For example, with reference to a resolution passed by the OAU Council calling for withdrawal of African bank balances from Britain in retaliation for Britain's refusal to take decisive measures against the illegal regime, President Banda mockingly observed: Are they to withdraw their overdrafts?[58] Malawi thus became Britain's strongest supporter in terms of her Rhodesian policy.

By breaking diplomatic relations with Britain, Commonwealth Africa hoped to achieve effective exertion of African pressure on the British Government. They wanted to impress on Britain the importance of decolonization issues to them. However, when they broke diplomatic ties with Britain, they continued their participation in Commonwealth Affairs. President Nyerere explained that the Commonwealth was simply a multinational organization and was not a mere British institution.[59]

The Rhodesian crisis indeed created for the first time the existence of an African Commonwealth pressure group led by Presidents Kwame Nkrumah and Julius Nyerere. The African leaders warned the British Government that an expedient compromise with Rhodesia would be at the cost of a collapse of Britain's prestige in the African Commonwealth countries and possibly lead to a wholesale withdrawal from the Commonwealth itself.

By way of conclusion one can safely assert that both Britain and France have maintained cultural and political ties after the new states emerged as sovereign states. But, it must be pointed out that French cultural ties with French-speaking African states are more intimate than those between Britain and Commonwealth Africa. English-speaking African states have been much more outspoken in criticizing and sometimes challenging the former mother country than their French counterparts.

In the cultural field, the colonial legacy lingers on despite the fact that in their public or official policy statements, the leaders of the new states advocate a break away from their colonial past. Nevertheless, critics charge that calls for a cultural revival or renaissance seem to be lip-service pronouncements simply because those elements who make these calls are usually well steeped in European value systems. In the new African states, there have been heated discussions about the necessity of breaking the umbilical cord and thus terminating all dependency on the former metropolitan powers. The radical African states have stressed the point that political independence, to be real, must be accompanied by cultural decolonization as well.

The origins of cultural dependency can be traced to the colonial times when the imperial powers controlled the colonial peoples, forcing them to accept submission to their authority and institutions. This situation survived into the post-colonial period because of the fact that European values were strongly assimilated by those elements into whose hands the colonial regimes transferred power at independence. This assertion seems to be valid particularly in Francophone states where the new African elite embraced and identified with the French culture.

Analysts see the imposition of a culture of dependency upon the colonial subjects as fundamental to the establishment and survival of an imperial relationship. In other words, cultural dependency was imposed on African countries through a system of political education which, in essence, emphasized European superiority or supremacy and African inferiority. Critics point out that nothing short of a wholesale campaign of resocialization, including a rejection of many of the values the colonizers left behind and a massive overhaul of transplanted educational systems, will sever the links of cultural dominance by Europeans.

After handing over power to indigenous elite groups, the ex-metropolitan powers took concerted action to ensure the preservation of the cultural ties with the new African states. They were determined to preserve intact not only the economic and political institutions they left behind but also their educational systems. The attainment of political independence and sovereign status by African states made little or no difference at all. Thus, today, after over two decades of independence, many expatriate teachers, paid by either African governments or by their home governments, hold important positions in the educational systems of African states. These educators from the metropoles have labored hard to design systems of education for African countries based mainly on the educational systems in their home countries. The higher educational institutions in both Anglophone and Francophone Africa are modeled closely on those of Britain and France.

In the field of education, France has adopted a more ambitious development program. France has placed heavy emphasis on what she characterizes as the special mission of France in Africa. This is the so-called "civilizing mission." To this end, large sums of money and personnel are earmarked to implement this program. Thus, in French-speaking areas the universities are financed from French funds and the university staffs remain largely French expatriates.

It is evident that Britain did less in this field but it can be asserted that it too worked hard to preserve its language and culture in areas it once colonized. However, in English-speaking countries of Africa, the new leaders have demonstrated some degree of independence in terms of controlling their educational development. For example, in these areas efforts are being made to modify the curriculum to suit African development needs. Unlike their French counterparts Anglophone states do not show the same degree of cultural and sentimental attachments with the former imperial power.

The special relationship between African states and their former colonizers extends to the diplomatic and political areas. It can be argued that the metropolitan powers have managed to convert their African colonial empires into a Commonwealth and community respectively. They have succeeded in exchanging positions of power for ones of influence although they have claimed that the old relationship of dominance was being exchanged or transformed into a special relationship of partnership.

Like France, Britain has placed special emphasis on the cultural aspects of the relationship with English-speaking African states. For example, the Commonwealth Relations office has served as the cement that has brought the members of the Commonwealth together as they pursued common goals. This office usually sent out secret telegrams which explained Britain's position and policy regarding major international questions. Meetings of Commonwealth prime ministers, foreign ministers, and economic ministers have helped to strengthen the solidarity of the group.

In recent years however, the character of the membership has changed. What used to be predominantly a Caucasian political club is being dominated by Third World states whose interests differ quite considerably from those of the members of the old Dominions. The new Commonwealth is anti-colonial and its African members profess to be non-aligned in international power politics. Thus, Britain receives the support of the African bloc members when Britain's policies fit that pattern. The African members did not hesitate to criticize and even condemn Britain's foreign policies in Africa. In 1956 when Britain, France and Israel seized the Suez Canal in Egypt, African Commonwealth members led the attack against the British action at the United Nations General Assembly debates on the crisis of the Organization of African Unity. Similarly, Britain's policies involving South Africa's membership in the Commonwealth and the white supremacist regime in what used to be called Southern Rhodesia (Zimbabwe) nearly dissolved the Commonwealth.

France has similarly established a special relationship with Francophone Africa. Although she has relinquished political control of the region she still enjoys a large measure of influence and goodwill in Africa. It must be pointed out that Francophone states have relied very heavily on French assistance for their survival. However, the French culture and language serve as the glue that holds France and the Francophone states together.

A common problem which has plagued African states since the time of independence is the absence of unity in their dealings with one another. This problem stemmed from such factors as their cultural heritage, diverse languages and diverse interests. Efforts to achieve continental unity have failed. The effectiveness of the Organization of African Unity has been undermined due to the different political socialization they experienced during the colonial days. Anglophone and Francophone states do not see eye to eye on any given matter affecting the welfare of the continent as a whole. Regional groupings of African states are created on the basis of states with similar colonial heritage or background. The desire to establish common African institutions such as the Common Market as an alternative to the European Economic Community, and the African High Command, have been undermined or sabotaged because of disagreements among African states resulting from national interests and colonial heritage.

Endnotes Chapter 5

[1]   George W. Shepherd, Jr., *Non-aligned Black Africa* (Massachusetts: D. C. Heath and Co., 1970), p. 76.

[2]   Basil Davidson, *Let Freedom Come: Africa in Modern History* (Boston: Little, Brown & Company, 1978), p. 97.

[3]   Constitution du 4 October, 1958, Title XII, Article 78.

[4]   *Ibid.*, Article 82.

[5]   See, *Keesing's Research Report, Africa Independent: A Survey of Political Developments* (New York: Charles Scribner's Sons, 1972), p. 27.

[6]   Sekou Touré, Speech to the Territorial Conference of PDG, Conakry, 14th September 1958. Quoted in T. Hodgkin and R. Schachter, "French-speaking Africa in Transition," *International Conciliation* 528 (May 1960): 420.

[7]   See John Hughes, *The New Face of Africa South of the Sahara* (New York: Longmans, Green, 1961), pp. 37-38.

[8]   Shepherd, *Non-aligned Black Africa*, p. 80.

[9]   Lépold-Sédar Senghor, "A Community of Free and Equal Peoples with the Mother Country," *Western World* 18 (Brussels, 1958): 41-42; quoted from Arnold Rivkin, *Africa and the West: Elements of Free World Policy* (London: Thames and Hudson, 1962), p. 7.

[10]   Lépold-Sédar Senghor, "West Africa in Evolution," *Foreign Affairs* 39 (1961): 7.

[11]   Quoted in *Le Figaro* (Paris) February 27-28, 1960; see Rivkin, *Africa and the West*, p. 8.

[12]   Shepherd, *Non-aligned Black Africa*, p. 80.

[13]   Philip Neves, *French-Speaking West Africa* (London: Oxford University Press, 1962), p. 87.

[14]   Shepherd, *Non-aligned Black Africa*, p. 80.

[15]   Senegal and Mauritania and all four of the Equatorial members – Gabon, Congo, Chad, and the Central African Republic – have remained in the renovated Community.

16   The four West African Conseil de l'Entente states – Ivory Coast, Niger, Dahomey, and Upper Volta – have received the same treatment with respect to economic, technical, and other forms of assistance as the "Community States."

17   *New York Times*, 8 March 1961.

18   Rivkin, *Africa and the West*, p. 31.

19   Victor C. Ferkiss, *Africa's Search for Identity* (New York: George Braziller, 1966), p. 243.

20   See Brian G. Weinstein, *Training Programs in France for African Civil Servants* (Boston: Boston University African Studies Program Development Research Center, 1964).

21   Joan Edelman Spero, *Dominance-Dependence Relationships: The Case of France and Gabon* (Ph.D. diss., Columbia University, 1973), p. 285.

22   *Ibid.*

23   Ferkiss, *Africa's Search for Identity*, p. 243.

24   A good illustration of this point was the Nigerian-Biafran War (1967-1970). Gabon cooperated very closely with France in her pro-Biafran policy. Gabon indeed acted as an agent of French foreign policy by aiding Biafrans militarily, and by recognizing Biafra as a sovereign independent state. The Ivory Coast took a similar position following the French example. Thus, the Gabonese policy allowed France to be active while maintaining a very low profile.

25   William Clark, "New Europe and the New Nations," *Daedalus: Journal of American Academy of Arts and Sciences* 93, no. 1 (Winter 1964): 144.

26   *West Africa*, No. 3158, 23 January 1978, p. 137.

27   Shepherd, *Non-aligned Black Africa*, p. 78.

28   *Ibid.*

29   See Rivkin, *Africa and the West*, p. 110.

30   Kwame Nkrumah, *I Speak of Freedom* (London: Heinemann, 1961), p. 4. See also, *West Africa*, 25 July 1964, p. 825.

31   William Zartman, *International Relations in the New Africa* (New Jersey: Prentice-Hall, Inc., 1966), p. 163.

32   Clark, "New Europe and the New Nations," pp. 139-140.

33   *Ibid.*, p. 139.

34   *Ibid.*, p. 142.

35   See John Holmes, "The Impact of the Commonwealth on the Emergence of Africa," in *Africa and the World Order*, eds. Norman J. Padelford and Rupert Emerson (New York: Praeger, 1964), p. 24.

36   *Ibid.*, p. 49.

37   Clark, "New Europe and the New Nations," p. 141.

38   See Keesing's Research Report, *Africa Independent: A Survey of Political Developments* (New York: Charles Scribner's Sons, 1972), p. 24.

39   Rivkin, *Africa and the West*, p. 27.

40   *Ibid.*

41   *Britain and Education in the Commonwealth* (British Information Service), p. 46. (Year?)

42   *Ibid.*, p. 49.

43   The founding members were Belgium, Luxembourg, the Netherlands, France, West Germany, and Italy.

44   See Oliver Franks, "Britain and Europe," *Daedalus, Journal of the American Academy of Arts and Sciences* 93, no. 1 (Winter 1964), p. 67.

45   Francis O. Wilcox and H. Field Haviland, Jr., eds., *The Atlantic Community: Progress and Prospects* (New York: Frederick A. Praeger, 1964), p. 71.

46   Russell Warren Howe, *The African Revolution* (New York: Barnes and Nobles, Inc., 1969), p. 247.

47   John C. Hatch, *Two African Statesmen: Kaunda of Zambia and Nyerere of Tanzania* (Chicago: Henry Regnery Co., 1976), p. 142.

48   *The Observer* (London), 7 March 1961.

49   *The Guardian*, 3 September 1970.

50   Julius K. Nyerere, *Freedom and Development: A Selection from Writings and Speeches, 1968-1973* (London: Oxford University Press, 1973), p. 210.

51   *The Guardian*, 3 September 1970.

52   Nyerere, *Freedom and Development*, pp. 247-248.

53   OAU AHG/Res. 25/Rev. 1, 22 October 1965.

54   *Africa Confidential*, Supplement to no. 24, 9 December 1966. See also David Kay, "The UN and Decolonization," in *The United Nations, Past, Present, and Future*, ed. James Barros (New York: The Free Press, 1972), p. 155.

55   "Southern Rhodesia," *United Nations Review*, April 1964, pp. 16-17.

56   OAU Doc. ECM/Res. 13, VI. After UDI, a special session of the OAU Council of Ministers convened at Addis Ababa. They passed a resolution which, in effect, placed the responsibility for dealing with the rebellion upon Britain. To pressure Britain further, the African states unanimously agreed to break off diplomatic relations if Britain failed by December 15, 1965 to use force to put down the rebellion.

57   *Malawi Hansard*, 11 January 1966, p. 283.

58   *U.S. News and World Report*, 13 May 1968. See also Henry L. Bretton, *Power and Politics in Africa* (Chicago: Aldine Publishing Company, 1973), p. 90.

59   *The Observer* (London), 12 December 1964.

CHAPTER 6
SECURITY ARRANGEMENTS IN AFRICA

An important area of the post-colonial relationships between these two ex-imperial powers and the new African states has involved security arrangements. Thus, in many instances, security links have remained very strong. During the colonial period, African military forces were initially established, trained, and equipped by the former colonial powers. At the time independence was being negotiated, Britain and France discussed security arrangements with the elite groups in the former dependencies, which, in effect, promised protection for the new states from both internal and external aggression. Final agreements were reached during these negotiations which preceded the formal granting of independence in which plans were made to cope with any future internal or external violence that might affect the new states. In order to fulfill this commitment, both metropolitan powers demanded the right to operate military and naval bases in the African states, despite the fact that these states had attained the status of independent sovereign states. The two European powers were determined to link the defense of the metropole with that of the new states. The responses of African states varied quite considerably. For example, while Francophone states south of the Sahara, with the exception of Guinea and Mali, welcomed the idea of military cooperation with the former colonizer very enthusiastically, their Anglophone counterparts were rather skeptical, and right from the outset rejected the idea of linking military arrangements for the defense of the metropole with theirs.

The military establishments of the new African states are relatively weak and underdeveloped when compared with those of industrially developed states. Economic hardships have indeed limited their power to expand their military establishments. Their military budgets are rather small. Their level of military preparedness is low, in absolute as well as relative terms.[1] The ratio of military to civilian population is approximately 1:1131 compared to 15:1000 for the United States, 10:1000 for the United Kingdom,[2] and 1:780 for France.[3] Because of their relative military and economic weakness, these African states have depended very heavily on major powers in general, and the former colonizers in particular, for military assistance in the form of weapons and personnel. France, for example, has entered into military accords with the states of Francophone Africa in order to provide them with both internal and external security.

Since the post-independence period, the two ex-colonial powers have confined their military activity in Africa to (a) direct but temporary intervention by metropolitan security forces to protect their interests or to reinstate preferred friendly regimes; (b) stationing of forces on African soil or at convenient external bases; (c) provision of training facilities for the regular armed forces and police, either on African soil or abroad; and (d) provision of weapons and logistic support where and when needed.[4] British and French Governments have intervened to preserve friendly African governments as well as to protect other vital interests such as safety or security of nationals and their property. Thus, the French governments have reacted very swiftly to restore to power unpopular regimes ousted by radical revolutionary groups. Similarly, Britain did not hesitate to rush in aid to Tanzania in 1964 when President Nyerere requested British intervention. The two European powers will definitely present deaf ears to unfriendly regimes requesting military intervention. In fact, it would seem that the metropolitan powers would be relieved to see such unfrieindly regimes toppled with the hope that more friendly governments would replace them.

Interventions, though of relatively modest dimensions, have resulted in the restoration of regimes which were driven out by mass demonstrations and military coups. It must be pointed out, however, that the French governments were more involved than their British counterparts in this type of direct overt intervention. France has designated paratroopers in combat readiness to be called into action at a moment's notice on the African continent to protect friendly governments. She has sought special concessions such as permission to use naval bases and air fields, overflight privileges for military aircraft, and permission to emplace special military equipment.[5] The utilization of direct overt intervention in Africa by these former colonial powers has been a source of much embarrassment for all the parties involved, including the governments so aided.[6]

The influence of the ex-imperial powers has remained extremely high in the new states. For example, it has been pointed out that African military personnel trained in Britain and France are closer to their imperial counterparts than the elite in the other sectors of their society.[7] William F. Gutteridge explained that the simple fact that these military personnel lived as they did in closed communities caused their absorption rate of foreign traditions to be inevitably higher than for those outside.[8] British and French trained officers usually display a sense of loyalty to the countries where they received their military training. Thus, some critics have charged that Britain and France are usually behind the military coups which take place in Anglophone and Francophone African states respectively.

Since the early post-independence period African states have had military arrangements of various sorts with the former colonial powers. However, these relationships came increasingly under violent criticism, and were as such either abandoned or drastically modified. In support of their non-aligned stance, they have rejected formal alliances with their former colonizers, since it is assumed that in the case of outright aggression traditional friends would come to the aid of Commonwealth and Francophone African countries even without an alliance system.[9] Victor C. Ferkiss argued that alliances would add very little to the power available to defend African states and could make them the target of enemies who might not otherwise attack them.[10]

From the mid-sixties, the military arrangements between European powers and their former dependencies began to change quite drastically as Britain and France began active programs of disengagement brought about primarily by economic problems and, perhaps, declining interest in the affairs of their former dependencies. Nevertheless, it must be emphasized that Britain moved faster than France in its process of dissolving military links with its former colonies on the African continent. Following the controversial Anglo-Nigerian Defense Pact and the domestic disturbances that ensued, Britain showed reluctance to preserve its position with independent African states in any formal setting.[11] Since the Suez crisis of 1956, the British governments have reasoned that no part of Africa, with the exception of perhaps South Africa, was important to them strategically as a military base. Finally, Britain's determination to withdraw British forces east of Suez by 1971 further lessened the security ties of Britain on the African continent.

Like their British counterparts, the French governments adopted a systematic disengagement program. The objective was to achieve a sharp reduction of French troops in Africa. Thus, French troops in sub-Saharan Africa were reduced in 1964 to approximately 36,000 from 77,000 in 1960, the year when most of the Francophone states achieved their political independence. Responding to charges of neo-colonialism leveled at her, France made other significant changes in the French military presence in Black Africa. Thus, on September 29, 1964, the Minister of the Armed Forces, Pierre Messmer, announced that French troops in Black Africa would be drastically reduced from 27,800 to 6,600 by July 1965, and then in August 1965 the overseas commands were to be reorganized.[12] Following this drastic reduction of troops, French military bases were reduced to three; namely, Dakar, Fort Lamy, and Diego Suarez.[13] The troops that remained behind were spread out among the four chief strategic places in French–speaking Africa: namely, Dakar 2,500; Diego Suarez 2,500; Fort Lamy 1,000; and Abidjan 600. The political leaders in Francophone Africa expressed great concern over France's redeployment of French troops in the region.

To reassure them of continued French friendship and support, France, on numerous occasions, either in public official statements or communiques, expressed her commitment to honor the defense arrangements between herself and these new states. France tried to convince the leaders of French Africa that, to do this, she no longer needed to station large concentrations of French soldiers on the African soil. It is assumed that in an age of technological revolution, when long distance planes can easily be used to transport troops within a matter of hours, it would no longer be necessary to station troops abroad. For example, in France nowadays, there is a division of some 22,000 men arranged in three brigades, two of which are parachutists. This division is on the alert and ready for combat at a moment's notice.

French Security Commitments in Africa

Unlike Britain, France has featured quite prominently in African security arrangements. The French governments have generally regarded their military aid to Francophone states as crucial in maintaining the domestic political status quo. As a result of this situation, insecure African regimes have usually found out that French protection has worked to maintain the internal political balance.

The history of France's military involvement in Africa must be traced to the colonial period. France linked the defense of French Africa with the defense of metropolitan France itself. In the early 1900s, the French had recognized the fact that Africa served as a manpower reserve for the French Army. Thus, French military planners considered quite seriously the possibility of replacing French troops in North Africa and elsewhere with African soldiers. For example, on July 7, the French National Assembly passed a law which, in effect, established *Les troupes coloniales* for use in the colonies and, if necessary, in the defense of France at home and abroad.[14] The military planners in France appreciated the simple fact that African troops were cheaper to maintain and that, under the colonial system, could be subjected to longer terms of service than metropolitan troops. Thus, in 1913 the *troupes coloniales* were expanded from 20,000 to 225,000 during the 1914-1918 World War. It is estimated that approximately 25,000 colonial troops died in the defense of metropolitan France itself during that war.[15]

During World War II, French colonial territories made impressive military contributions toward the cause of the "Fighting French" under the leadership of the proud General Charles de Gaulle. The French authorities appreciated the war efforts of their African dependencies by speeding up the process of decolonization during the postwar years. When the war ended in 1945, African troops were used in the French colonial wars in Algeria and Indo-China in a vain effort to keep the Empire in one piece.[16]

The attainment of independence on the part of the former dependencies did not eliminate the possibility of using Black African bases and resources as part of a Franco-African strategic plan. Black Africans continued to serve in the French Army, while special clauses in the defense accords with many of the new states specified French military rights to bases, infrastructure and resources, transportation and communication faciliites, airspace, and the territorial sea.[17]

The absence of indigenous national armies in French-speaking African countries, as a direct consequence of France's assimilationist policies which characterized most of the colonial period, created a military vacuum of sorts in these new states. At the time of political independence, there were few experienced Africans in high military positions in the French Army. For example, in 1960 there were only ten experienced African staff officers in all of the French Community in Africa, which included four colonels and six chefs de bataillon, and 198 African officers, 157 of whom were lieutenants or sub-lieutenants.[18] Because of this military vacuum, and in conformity with her established policy of paternalism, France assumed full responsibility for providing both internal and external security for the new Francophone African states until such a time that they could take good care of themselves in terms of their own defense. Professor Spero has suggested that the Congo crisis of the early sixties, immediately following the attainment of independence by the former Belgian dependency, influenced France's determination to assume the role of protector of the new states. Thus, France accepted the full responsibility for coping with military and political weaknesses of the new states of Francophone Africa. It was not until 1968 or 1969 that the French-speaking states began developing their own national armies and thus began to assume a greater role in their own defense.

Before this time they were garrisoned by African troops in French military units. However, since the time of independence, France has withdrawn from most of the African bases but has retained ones of strategic value, such as the bases in Abidjan, Fort Lamy, and Madagascar.[19]

France has maintained a more visible military policy and presence in Africa than Britain. At the time of independence, France entered into bilateral agreements with the new states of Francophone Africa for purposes of mutual military cooperation. Under the defense accords France assumed responsibility for supplying the new states' armed forces with all the necessary military equipment including weapons, barracks, and buildings, as well as logistical support. The provisions of these defense agreements have been expanded in many instances to permit the use of French troops which are stationed within the area to prevent internal uprisings or revolutionary overthrow of friendly regimes. The mutual defense agreement between France and the Mali Federation, which might be taken as typical, stated that France and Mali would assist each other in defense matters. Thus, Mali would share with France in the defense of the Community and possibly of other African states. A Franco-Malian committee was set up to coordinate military activities of the parties. Mali would obtain military equipment exclusively from France and Malian nationals would be free to enlist in the French armed forces.

Similarly, the military accord with the Republic of Dahomey (Benin) contained almost identical provisions. Article 3 of that military agreement, signed in April 1961, provided that, in order to assure the standardization of its armory, the Republic of Dahomey would turn first to the French Republic to maintain and to renew the materials and the equipment for its armed forces. Thus, the supply of light weapons, materials for transport, and armored cars for the units of its land forces would be assured by France. Furthermore, France indicated that if supplies could not be given free of charge, the financial terms would be fixed by a mutual accord; and that if a particular supply could not be made by France, then the Republic of Dahomey reserved the right to accept the aid of other countries.

In the defense agreement between France, on the one hand, and the Ivory Coast, Dahomey, and Niger on the other, it provided that the three African countries would allow the French armed forces to stockpile primary materials and strategic goods. They would limit or prevent their exportation to other countries when the interests of defense demanded it. With regard to these materials and products the three West African states reserved the priority of their sale for defense needs to France.[20]

The defense accords with the Central African Republic, Chad, Gabon, and the Congo Republic, were modified in 1961 with special clauses added, providing also for assistance in the maintenance of internal security.

Since the time of political independence, some changes have taken place in terms of Franco-African military cooperation. For example, French troops have been evacuated from Guinea, Mali and Upper Volta at these states' requests. French troops were first withdrawn from Guinea at the time she broke away from the French political orbit in 1958. Mali followed Guinea's example after the breakup of the Mali Federation.[21] Earlier, Mali had ceded to France military bases mainly in the Southern Sahara and the Dakar-Thies region. Following the dissolution of the Federation with Senegal, Mali demanded that France withdraw from these military bases. However, unlike Britain, which withdrew from the African continent soon after decolonization, France remained very active militarily in the former French dependencies in a concerted effort to honor her post-colonial commitments.

Under the Technical Assistance Accords, France has instituted an extensive program of military aid to supply the material needs of the new Francophone states. Thus, apart from regular troops which are serving directly in the French army in various regions of French Africa, roughly 1400 French military personnel serve in several African states' national armies. France has remained the major source of military aid for these states, though in recent years states such as Mali, Cameroun, the Congo Republic, and Mauritania have begun to diversify their sources of military aid. These states are becoming more independent financially and thus have opened military ties with communist powers. Despite their efforts to seek military aid elsewhere, France still maintains a very extensive and costly military assistance support program for Francophone African countries. Thus, for all practical purposes, France continues to supply weapons, train personnel, and provide logistical support for the military establishments of the new states. Training in France or under French officers was a major provision of the military cooperations accords between France and the African states. In these agreements, France specifically demanded that other aid sources could not be sought or used without French consultation and approval. Cameroun, the Ivory Coast, Chad, and Senegal, among others, have been the principal recipients of this military assistance. This situation has made the states militarily dependent on France, a condition that has not altered very drastically after many years of political independence. One unique feature of this aid is the fact that in Francophone countries there is very little talk about France's neo-colonialist intentions as is generally heard in Anglophone states. Thus, with the exception of Guinea, there is no criticism or resistance of French aid to Francophone countries.

French Military Intervention in Africa

France's military intervention in French-speaking African countries during the post-independence period is indeed a common phenomenon. French military forces have been used on numerous occasions to protect friendly incumbent Francophone African regimes. Thus, there have been French interventions in Cameroun, Chad, Central African Republic, Congo-Brazzaville, Gabon, Mauritania, and Niger. In some instances, France intervened more than twice in the same country to provide internal security.

The military intervention by foreign forces in Africa can be explained in terms of the political instability and military weakness which have generally characterized the new states. This situation has thus created a real need for French military involvement in French Africa. At the time independence was granted to the former French colonies, France assumed full responsibility for both external and internal security in Francophone African countries. The arrangements to provide protection for the new states were formalized in a network of interlocking agreements which allowed France to place garrisons or training missions of different sizes in these countries. These accords authorized France to intervene in certain cases against external aggression or even domestic uprisings, and also provided the former mother-country with base facilities in some of these countries.[22] The result has been that for many years after they had achieved their political independence from France, detachments of French troops continued to be stationed in strategic areas for security considerations. As late as 1982, France had approximately 7,000 troops in sub-Saharan Africa.[23]

The French Eleventh Division, the so-called force d'intervention, stationed in metropolitan France and consisting of a total of betwen 10,000 to 12,000 men, stands ready to intervene in any part of Africa on short notice.[24] The Eleventh Airborne Division is made up of paratroop, marine, infantry, and artillery brigades. It has seaborne, amphibious, and armed elements in addition to some 220 supporting aircraft at its disposal. The importance of this elite corps lies in its deterrent effect. Potential challengers of the status quo in French Africa are fully aware of its existence; thus, they realize that France has the will and capacity to intervene swiftly during periods of emergency. With this force, France has intervened militarily in French Africa at least ten times in the 1960-1968 period.

In all these cases involving French intervention, France was able to preserve its vital interests by supporting friendly governments. In some instances, the French support autocratic and unpopular governments in Africa. French aid and technical assistance continued on a generous scale to all these states with few exceptions. The leaders of these states have shown their gratitude by maintaining cordial political and diplomatic relations with France.

France has not always responded favorably to every request for French intervention. For example, France refused aid to Abbé Fulbert Youlon's government in Congo Republic. She has claimed that it is her policy not to intervene against popular uprisings.[25] Thus, in defense of France's intervention in Gabon in 1964, French authorities pointed out that their decision to intervene militarily was simply based on the invitation made by the legitimate government for support against a handful of armed putschists.[26] Despite this French assertion, it is quite obvious that French intervention was directed precisely against popular uprisings in Gabon, Benin, and Cameroun.

French intervention in Gabon in 1964 on behalf of the deposed government of Leon M'Ba, who had been overthrown by an army-inspired coup d'état, was a classical example of French military intervention in the domestic affairs of a Francophone African state. That particular intervention aroused suspicions of French neo-colonialist intentions on the African continent. France intervened directly to restore the government of Leon M'Ba who was ousted in a military takeover masterminded by junior army officers on February 18, 1964. Upon seizing power, the army established a revolutionary committee to supervise the hastily formed temporary government under the leadership of Aubome. M'Ba was placed under arrest. The Vice President of the government, Yembit, requested French intervention. Within a matter of hours, French paratroopers landed in Gabon. French presence led to the arrest and trial of all the revolutionaries. The ring leaders of the coup drew prison sentences and peace was finally restored.

The French government explained and justified its intervention on the basis of the agreements on cooperation and defense between Gabon and France. It emphasized that M'Ba's government was the legal, and therefore the legitimate, one and that the uprising had not been a mass movement as such.

In addition to the justification of French military interventions on the basis of the legitimacy of the governments requesting such interventions, economic interests played an important part in influencing France's decision to intervene militarily. French businessmen and investors were convinced that if M'Ba was allowed to remain in power in Gabon, the economic climate would remain favorable to them; hence, they advocated French military intervention. In the past years, Gabon had provided French businessmen and investors with golden opportunities in terms of profits made from their economic transactions in the country. Thus, it is generally believed that of all France's former African dependencies, none was more French, nor any dearer to France, than Gabon. Gabon is rich in uranium which France needs for its force de frappe. The deposed Leon M'Ba was another factor that led to that intervention. He was a personal friend of the late French President General Charles de Gaulle who instructed his officers to restore Leon M'Ba to his position at all costs.

Another important explanation for France's intervention in Gabon in 1964 involved the events that took place in Africa during the previous year. The year 1963 was characterized by turbulence. The year began with the assassination of Sylvanus Olympio of Togo and the overthrow of his government. Fulbert Youlou's government in Brazzaville fell in August; in October, Hubert Maga's government was overthrown in Dahomey (Benin). The fact that all these were former French dependencies disturbed French authorities in Paris, and they eventually decided to draw the line and act decisively to prevent the fall of Leon M'Ba's government in Gabon.

The Republic of Chad has also witnessed several French interventions. Since the post-independence period, France has intervened thrice militarily in the desert country of Chad in order to assure domestic peace. The political crises in Chad have been precipitated by ethnic, geographic, and ideological, as well as religious, factors, which have threatened the territorial integrity of the country. The dictatorial government of Tombalbaye made many enemies for itself, including Sara intellectuals, civil servants, army officers, and student groups. But, his major enemies were the "northerners" and Muslims. The disturbances resulting from the challenge from these two last groups eventually led to the armed rebellion against his government. Mr. Tombalbaye antagonized northerners by perpetuating what his critics characterized as Sara or "southern" domination of the civil service and the armed forces as well. Virginia Thompson and Richard Adloff have pointed out that the root of the conflict was precipitated by ethnic and geographic imbalance in both the bureaucracy and the army, caused by the rapid promotion of unqualified and self-seeking southern officials and officers.[27] The northerners charged that Sara troops stationed in their territory behaved like armies of occupation, and consequently were treated as such. It was alleged that southern troops harassed northern populations and thus created discontent throughout the northern region. For example, in Tibesti, the region's "Derde" fled to Libya with roughly 1000 of his faithful followers as a way of protesting the policies of the Ndjamena Government in his region. Thus it can be asserted that the hostility of the Chadian army in Muslim areas derived from the abuses committed by the irregularly paid and poorly disciplined and equipped southern soldiers.[28]

The revolt of the Toubous which began with the attack of the Aozou garrison in March 1968 precipitated the crisis in Tibesti. The inability of government troops to suppress the rebel uprising forced Mr. Tombalbaye to request French support to end the rebellion. In August 1968 France responded by dispatching more than 3000 French troops, including a regiment of the Foreign Legion, to assist the government of François Tombalbaye in curbing the Muslim revolt. In the period 1969-1971, the French army was unable to defeat the rebel forces decisively or even cut off their arms supply; but it managed to check the Toubou revolt and temporarily forced the rebels to surrender.

The French expeditionary forces withdrew from the region in November and, soon after, the Toubous resumed their attacks on government troops with greater determination. Thus, by late 1969 the Ndjamena authorities had lost control over many settlements in the north except Fada, Faya, Bardai, and Ounianga.[29] By late 1971 the Tombalbaye government was seriously considering the possibility of writing off the far north simply as an economically unproductive region in favor of greater industrial development of the southern region.[30]

The continued military pressure from Frolinat rebels, combined with pressures from the civilian and military bureaucracy, led to the overthrow of Tombalbaye's government and thus paved the way for the domination of the south by the north. But, once again, French intervention halted the forward march of the rebel forces to the capital city of Ndjamena.

Colonel Khadafi's determination to annex the northern region of Chad (Tibesti) or possibly the entire country was not well received in Africa and France. On January 6, 1981, Goukouni, Colonel Khadafi's Chadian ally, announced that the governments of Chad and Libya would work together toward the goal of attaining complete political unity. Thus, Libya would guarantee Chad's security and train as well as equip its national army; and goods and individuals could move freely between the two countries. African states condemned what they characterized as Khadafi's aggression in Chad. In an emergency session, the OAU members collectively denounced the merger proposal and condemned Libya's violation of the territorial integrity of Chad.

France's immediate reaction to the Libya-Chad merger was to denounce quite strongly Khadafi's military intervention. France issued a stern warning to Libya to cease and desist from its aggressive ventures in Chad. Nevertheless, this warning came a few hours before Chad's capital, Ndjamena, fell to Goukouni and his Libyan allies. France dispatched troops to Chad in an effort to assist the shaky Chadian government in a life and death struggle with the northerners and their Libyan allies. She also offered weapons and troops to bolster the defenses of Chad's Francophone neighbors such as Niger, Cameroun and the Central African Republic. It was now obvious that France and Libya were actively supporting opposite sides in the Chadian civil war. Thus, while France aided what she termed "the legitimate government of Chad" led by Habré, Libya supported Goukouni, and the other Frolinat factions.

The presence of oil, uranium, and manganese are major incentives that led to the military interventions on the part of France and Libya. Both principal participants in the Chad civil war are looking forward to the economic exploitation of Chad at the end of the conflict. In this conflict, however, Libya's allies seem to be gaining the upper hand despite the French military presence. The French forces at best are simply holding their lines of operation and trying to salvage what is left in Southern Chad.

Thompson and Adloff have aptly summarized the main factors which influenced French intervention in Chad. These factors include: safeguarding France's economic and strategic interest in the area; the need or necessity for restoring French influence and prestige among leaders of French Africa; posing as Africa's protector or gendarme; forestalling Libya's annexation of the northern territory of Chad; preventing Nigeria from supplanting France as the most influential foreign arbiter of Chad's destiny; and finally, playing the role of the defender of Chad's legitimate governments.[31] France claimed that she was determined to restore the status quo in Chad, that is, supporting Chad's internationally recognized government against its internal enemies.

In conclusion, one can safely observe that after two decades of political independence, French military presence in French Africa has remained paramount. Military ties with the new states have remained very intimate despite charges of neo-colonialism leveled against France by African critics. The protection of these Francophone African states has continued to be a part of France's military planning. Both the de Gaulle and

Pompidou governments stressed France's commitment to the defense of these former colonies. For example, General Mitterand, addressing a group of distinguished defense experts, explained: "Our zone of privileged action remains . . . the Mediterranean, the Atlantic facade of Brest to Dakar, and Northern equatorial Africa."[32] France is linked to most of the French–speaking African countries in a series of bilateral military assistance accords. With the exception of Niger, the Congo Republic, and Mauritania, which indicated an interest in revising their relations with France, the network of economic and security ties with the Black African States remained essentially intact under the Pompidou government.[33]

There are many military assistance personnel groups operating in many parts of Africa and about seven thousand French troops stationed in various parts of Africa. A small, highly mobile force is ever ready for combat duty in Africa. Direct military intervention by France in Chad since August 1968, suggests the type of involvement that has characterized French policy in Africa since the early sixties. The Chadian intervention followed the Gabonese example of February 1964 when French paratroopers reinstated the deposed president of Gabon.

Analysts have theorized that French military strategy is oriented more toward responding swiftly and effectively to prevent the destruction of friendly governments than waging protracted warfare which in effect would sap France's limited conventional capability.

Britain and the Defense of Commonwealth Africa

Unlike France, which incorporated African elements within its own military forces, Britain set up at an early stage mature military and police forces commanded by African and European officers and NCOs.[34] Thus, by the time the British dependencies achieved their political independence, they already had their own national armies which were indeed quite independent from British forces. They were in a position to provide for their own internal security needs. Britain was not interested in making elaborate plans aimed at guaranteeing internal and external security needs of Commonwealth African states as France did in Francophone Africa. There were no formal pacts between Britain and the Anglophone states, with the exception of a short-lived Anglo-Nigerian Defense agreement, abandoned in 1962 as a result of widespread protests in Nigeria over the treaty. This military pact was signed in 1960 when Nigeria achieved her independence. By 1962 it had become very unpopular throughout the country. It became an incident that rallied together many Nigerian factions which opposed military ties with European metropolitan powers. Chief Obafemi Awolowo, Leader of the Opposition in the Nigerian House of Representatives, attacked the pact as an infringement on Nigeria's newly won sovereignty and resented what he characterized as an insult to the dignity of the leaders and people of a free nation. The Government of Sir Tafawa Balewa was nearly toppled following mass demonstrations organized by the Opposition Party which exploited the situation to create anti-British sentiments. Following this abortive defense pact between Britain and Nigeria, and the disturbances that ensued, Britain has shown great reluctance to preserve her position with independent Commonwealth African countries in any formal setting.[35]

The major continuing source of British military influence in Africa is through the training of personnel and, to a lesser degree, providing weapons for the new states. At the time of independence, all the African military establishments still maintained a contingent of British officers who were seconded to them from British Imperial Forces. Thus, in 1967, for example, Britain set aside £1.3 million to cover half the expenditure involved over British military personnel loaned to the new African states.[36] Chester Crocker indicated that in 1967 there were approximately 880 of these military personnel serving in Ghana, Kenya, Zambia, Malawi, Sierra Leone, and Sudan.[37]

The mere fact that these states, with a few exceptions, did not have military training academies of their own, has necessitated their reliance on British military academies at Sandhurst, Mons, and elsewhere in Britain for training their officer corps. Grants-in-aid and loans from Britain have made it possible for a number of Commonwealth states to buy military hardware and thus modernize their armies, navies, and air forces. British aid has included militarily-related grants-in-aid, such as funds to cover the costs of loaned and seconded military personnel and training teams which served in

African countries. In addition, Britain provided funds to cover tuition costs to African students attending British military academies.

A feature which has characterized Britain's military assistance to Commonwealth African states since the early sixties has involved the fact that the loan or secondment of British officers as instructors or trainers petered out gradually. Compared with the French, it must be pointed out that the British military withdrawal from Africa took place earlier, and, at present, is virtually complete. During the early stages of their independence, these African states retained a large number of British officers to man the top positions of their military establishments. These British nationals served in the capacity of military advisors. However, as the policy of Africanization progressed in the army and the civil service, the number of British personnel was drastically reduced. Ghana led the way in getting rid of British high-ranking officers in its national army. The late president Kwame Nkrumah adopted this policy mainly for security considerations as well as national pride. The dismissal of General Alexander, a British national, in 1960 by President Nkrumah caused a great uproar in Britain and eventually resulted in the straining of British-Ghanian relations for awhile. Other Commonwealth African states followed Ghana's example in adopting rapid programs of Africanization of their national armies.

The Anglophone African states have not depended very heavily on Britain for military support as their Francophone neighbors have depended on France in terms of their defense and their procurement of weapons. The former British dependencies have pursued active programs of diversification in terms of sources of military aid. Thus, Ghana under Nkrumah, Tanzania, Nigeria, and Sudan have been the quickest to introduce diversification and, as a result, to "decolonize" more rapidly the role of the former metropolitan power in their military establishments. Countries such as the United States, Canada, West Germany, the Soviet Union, and East European Communist states have all become donors of military aid to Commonwealth African countries. These powers have made more attractive training and arms aid offers which these professed ideologically non-aligned states have generally accepted in order to maintain the balance between the two hostile military camps in the Cold War.

With the exception of British military intervention in Tanzania in 1964, Britain has been very reluctant in pursuing a policy of direct military involvement in countries of Commonwealth Africa. This is a sharp contrast to France's resort to repeated military interventions to support friendly Francophone governments challenged by their internal enemies opposing the status quo. Britain's military intervention in Tanzania was indeed very unique. The Tanzanian government requested Britain's assistance to disarm mutinous soldiers who threatened domestic peace. The use of British security forces to restore internal peace was a source of much embarrassment to the Tanzanian government.

The army mutiny on January 30, 1964, involving the First Battalion of the Tanganyika Rifles stationed at Lugalo barracks, created a security crisis for the new state. The inability of the Tanzanian civilian authorities to cope with the internal disturbances led to the request for Britain's military intervention.

The major causes of the mutiny were attributed to slow Africanization of the Tanzanian army as well as poor wages for the soldiers. Prior to the disturbances, the officer corps of the army was dominated by British nationals who numbered some 26 officers and 16 NCOs. It was alleged that the highest rank held by Africans was that of captain. There was just one African captain, for that matter. Critics charged that there was no systematic program of Africanization of the Tanzanian army although the government had 10 African officer cadets at the British Military Academy at Sandhurst and 5 others at Mons. Thus, it seems that the motive force of the military disturbances was the desire to curb British domination of the officer corps and also the demand to make salary scales in the army much more attractive.

As the mutiny progressed, approximately 30 British officers and NCOs were placed under arrest and subsequently flown to Nairobi in the company of the British High Commissioner.[38] Brigadier Douglas, Commander of the Tanganyika army, was replaced by one Elijah Kavam, who was chosen by the mutineers as their leader.

In direct response to President Nyerere's request for British military intervention, 1,400 British marine commandos were immediately dispatched to the capital city of Dares-Salaam on January 24, 1964 from a British aircraft carrier in the Indian Ocean off the Tanzanian coastal waters. With little resistance from the mutineers, the British marines completed their assignment of disarming the mutinous soldiers and by January 30, 1964, domestic order had been restored in the Tanzanian army. However, British troops stayed in the country until early April when they were replaced by a contingent of Nigerian troops collaborating with the Ethiopian air force. The Nigerian troops left the country in September while the Ethiopians remained behind until December when they, too, left.

British intervention was a source of humiliation and embarrassment for the Tanzanian government. Thus, on January 28, 1964. President Julius Nyerere apologized to the Tanzanians for using British forces to end the rebellion. He indicated that the request for foreign colonialist troops was indeed a humiliation to the country but concluded, however, that there was no other alternative.[39] He had earlier dispatched a letter of gratitude to the British Prime Minister which was read in the House of Commons on January 27, 1964.

When domestic order was restored, Tanzania began to take measures to reduce her military dependence on Britain. She began to diversify her sources of military aid. To prevent future disturbances, efforts were made to promote loyal Tanzanians to the highest ranks available in the army, thus making it impossible for British officers to return to their former positions of dominance. Tanzania invited Canada and Sweden to supply military missions for the training of the new army. Tanzania also asked the Federal German Republic to take charge over the training of Tanzanian pilots and invited the People's Republic of China to provide military equipment and instructors.[40] The responses from these foreign governments were positive. Thus, West Germany agreed to supervise the training of Tanzanian airforce personnel and supply trainer aircraft, while Canada agreed to supply military training missions.[41] Finally, China and Tanzania entered into a military accord in June 1964 regarding Chinese military aid.

The Israelis were similarly asked to train Tanzanian soldiers. The Tanzanian government now embarked on a systematic policy of Africanization of the army on a large scale. The old army was disbanded and a new one created. To ensure confidence and build up national morale, a new recruitment program was instituted. From now on all new recruits must be members of the ruling party, the Tanganyika African National Union (TANU). Political education became a part of the curriculum for indoctrinating the new soldiers. Following the tradition of socialist and communist countries, political commissars were attached to every battalion to ensure party discipline and loyalty. The rapid systematic policy of Africanization made it possible for indigenous Tanzanians to occupy positions of authority in the army. Another major effect of the mutiny involved the fact that Tanzania decided to end her military dependence on Britain and thus diversify her military dependence.

In conclusion, four observations are in order. First, the influence of the two ex-imperial powers in what used to be their colonial preserve has remained paramount after two decades of political independence. However, of the two former metropolitan powers, France has maintained the more visible presence – stationing troops, controlling bases, and dispensing both military and economic assistance to Francophone African states. At the time of independence both powers, in different degrees, were committed to the defense of the new states from external aggression. Nevertheless, French commitment was more formal and comprehensive than the British. France negotiated bilateral defense agreements with French-speaking African countries in order to fulfill this obligation.

Both powers have trained African cadet officers in their military academies; have allowed their nationals to fill the top positions of the military establishments of African states until such a time that indigenous people can man those positions; and finally, the two powers have been the major sources of military hardware for the new states.

Second, the process of Africanization or indigenization of the army personnel has progressed much more rapidly in Anglophone areas than in Francophone areas. Africanization of the army has enabled African states to reduce their dependence on former colonial powers somewhat.

Third, France has intervened in French speaking African states much more often than Britain ever did in Commonwealth African countries. While Commonwealth African states have generally been very suspicious of British motives for providing military assistance to them, their Francophone counterparts, with a few exceptions, have accepted French military intervention in their countries without much criticism.

Finally, Commonwealth African states have tried hard to diversify their military dependence more so than their Francophone African neighbors, with the exception of Mali and Guinea. Their neutralist or non-aligned stance makes it possible for them to seek military aid from countries of the two major ideological blocs. In recent years, however, French-speaking countries such as the Congo Republic, Cameroun, and Mauritania have begun seeking military support from other sources to supplement what aid they received from France.

National security is another area of these post-colonial relationships where African states' dependence on the former colonizers has continued. Military weakness and the realization that African states must be protected against external and internal aggression have generally led their political leaders to seek outside sources of support. All African states, without exception, lack effective and well-equipped military establishments such as air forces, warships and tanks. Many of these states use the few weapons they have to maintain internal security but generally lack combat capability to mount effective military operations against other states. Since they lack munitions factories of their own, they must therefore rely very heavily on military assistance for their offensive and defensive weapons. These states, particularly the French-speaking countries, have maintained many links with the former metropolitan power which include, for example, defense agreements to secure the supply of arms, the permitting of air or naval bases on their soil, and the stationing of foreign troops and accords which permit direct military intervention. These arrangements have made it possible for the ex-colonial powers to make and break governments as they see fit.

The reliance on foreign military aid to provide security has been seen as one of the components of the crisis of independence. The presence of foreign military establishments in Africa is viewed as an eyesore. Radical African nationalists argue that states which allow foreign troops and bases on their soil compromise their independent and sovereign status. They stress that national security is a responsibility which no state should transfer to another and point out that the attainment of sovereignty is meaningless if the state lacks the capability to provide its own defense. The main point is that the capacity to govern must be drawn from the human and material resources of the state in question.

In recent times however, Britain and France have tried to reduce their physical presence in Africa. Foreign bases and the stationing of foreign troops have almost become irrelevant in the jet age when airborne troops can easily be transported to distant places on a moment's notice.

France's military presence in Africa in the post-independence period is very overwhelming. Compared with Britain, it must be said that France's military involvement in the defense of her former dependencies is by far much more elaborate. With a few exceptions, France signed agreements with Francophone states which provided for French military advice, arms supplies and training arrangements. France has base rights in such African states as Gabon, Djibouti, Ivory Coast, Senegal and Togo. A network of interlocking accords provide France with the authority to intervene directly in the region. Invoking the provisions of these agreements, France intervened in Gabon to restore President M'Ba to power after his government had been toppled. Similarly, in 1967 France dispatched a 2500-strong French expeditionary force to Chad where ethnic and religious rivals were engaged in a bloody civil war. Mauritania has also experienced French military intervention. Morocco and Mauritania had jointly annexed Western Sahara, a former Spanish colony. When the Polisario freedom fighters counterattacked, the territorial integrity of Mauritania was threatened, hence France rushed in to rescue her. Since 1975 France has been taking military action against the freedom fighters who have received Algeria's backing in their war to decolonize Western Sahara.

In all these interventions the French governments have claimed each time that they were there at the invitation of the friendly and legitimate African states whose regimes were threatened by their internal foes. Experience has shown however that France usually intervened to protect her own vital interests, such as valuable raw materials or minerals such as uranium. This explains why the French Governments have intervened more than once in a few selected states. The cases of Gabon and Chad will come to mind. Gabon, for example, produces urarium which France needs very badly for her independent nuclear power. Chad also has large deposits of uranium in the Aohzou strip in north Chad, which France and Libya are competing to control.

France's neo-colonialist stance in Africa annoys nationalist elements in Africa. Radicals resent the presence of some 10,000 French troops in Africa, including airmen, sailors, and infantry. In addition to these numbers, there is a highly trained, specialist force d'intervention available in southern France which serves at short notice as a mobile reserve. Its main function is to deal with emergency situations which may develop in Africa. The Eleventh Airborne Division is equipped with marine, artillery, paratroop and infantry brigades. It can strike anywhere in Africa at a moment's notice.

The creation of this force has a deterrent effect by simply impressing on potential revolutionary groups planning to overthrow their regimes, the futility of their actions. This force also conveys the message of France's determination and combat-readiness to respond swiftly to crisis situations in Africa.

Britain, unlike France, experienced difficulties as she tried to organize interlocking defense accords with Anglophone states of Africa. These states were more assertive of their non-aligned stance in East-West relations. They generally resisted British pressures to create military pacts. They denied Britain the right to establish naval and air bases on their soil. Nevertheless, Britain has training overflight supply arrangements with African Commonwealth countries short of full-scale agreements like those between France and French-speaking countries in Africa.

Endnotes Chapter 6

1   Kenneth W. Grundy, *Guerrilla Struggle in Africa: An Analysis and Preview* (New York: Grossman Publishers, 1971), p. 21.

2   *Ibid.*

3   Okwudiba Nnoli, *Self-Reliance and Foreign Policy in Tanzania: The Dynamics of the Diplomacy of a New State, 1961 to 1971* (New York: NOK Publishers, 1978), p. 146.

4   Henry L. Bretton, *Power and Politics in Africa* (Chicago: Aldine Publishing Company, 1973), p. 79.

5   *Ibid.*

6   *Ibid.*, pp. 79-80.

7   William F. Gutteridge, "Military and Police Forces in Colonial Africa," in Peter Duignan and L. H. Gann (eds.), *Colonialism in Africa 1870-1960, Vol. 2, The History and Politics of Colonialism, 1914-1960* (London: Cambridge University Press, 1970), p. 317.

8   *Ibid.*, pp. 317-318.

9   See Victor C. Ferkiss, *Africa's Search for Identity* (New York: George Braziller, 1966), p. 235.

10   *Ibid.*

11   Claude S. Phillips, *The Development of Nigerian Foreign Policy* (Evanston, IL: Northwestern University Press, 1964), p. 38.

12   *Anneé politique économique, sociale et diplomatique en France, 1964* (Paris: Presses Universitaires de France, 1964), p. 278.

13   *Ibid.*

14   See Chester A. Crocker, "France's Changing Military Interests," *West Africa*, June 1968, p. 16.

15   *Ibid.*, p. 17.

16   See Guy de Lusignan, *French-Speaking Africa Since Independence* (New York: Frederick A. Praeger, 1969), pp. 355-356.

17   Maurice Ligot, *Les Accords de Coopération entre La France et les états africaine et malgached'expression Française* (Paris: La Documentation Française, 1964), pp. 86-87.

18   J. M. Lee, *African Armies and Civil Order* (New York: Frederick A. Praeger, 1969), p. 39.

19   Ferkiss, *Africa's Search for Identity*, p. 244.

20   Dov Ronen, *Dahomey: Between Tradition and Modernity* (Ithaca, NY: Cornell University Press, 1975), p. 166.

21   The Mali Federation was a union between Soudan and Senegal. The break-up occurred because of ethnic and ideological differences between the leadership of the two French-speaking states. Besides, the two leaders, Lépold Senghor of Senegal and Modiko Keita of Mali were arch rivals.

22   See Arthur Gavshon, *Crisis in Africa: Battleground of East and West* (New York: Penguin Books, 1981), p. 172.

23   *West Africa*, no. 3382, 31 May 1982, p. 1437.

24   See Crocker, "France's Changing Military Interests," pp. 23-24.

25   See A. Mabileau and J. Meyriat, *Decolonisation et regimes politiques en Afrique noire* (Paris: Colin, 1967), p. 77.

26   Charles F. Darlington and Alice B. Darlington, *African Betrayal* (New York: McKay, 1968), pp. 138-139.

27   Virginia Thompson and Richard Adloff, *Conflict in Chad* (Berkeley: University of California, 1981), p. 39.

28   *Ibid.*, p. 47.

29   *Ibid.*

30   *Le Monde*, 29 January 1972.

31   Thompson and Adloff, *Conflict in Chad*, p. 130.

32   See Général J. Mitterrand, "La Place de l'action militaire entérieure dans la stratégie française," *Revue de defense nationale* 26 (June 1970): 901. Quotation from Edward A. Kolodzie, *French International Policy Under de Gaulle and Pompidou: The Politics of Grandeur* (Ithaca: Cornell University Press, 1974), p. 163.

33   *Le Monde*, 22 July 1972, p. 1.

34   See Lusignan, *French-Speaking Africa Since Independence*, p. 354.

35   See Phillips, *The Development of Nigerian Foreign Policy*, p. 38.

36 See Chester A. Crocker, External Military Assistance to Sub-Saharan Africa," *Africa Today*, April-May 1968.

37 *Ibid.*

38 Members of the British Commonwealth of Nations place High Commissioners instead of Ambassadors at each other's capital.

39 *Tanganyika Standard*, Dar-es-Salaam, 29 January 1964, p. 1.

40 *Observer* (London), 30 August 1964, p. 1.

41 *Ibid.*

CHAPTER 7

FROM BILATERAL RELATIONSHIPS
TO MULTILATERAL STRATEGY

In terms of the Eur-African relationships, the mid-seventies and early eighties witnessed a shift of strategy on the part of European states, from bilateral relationships with their former dependencies to multilateral arrangements. There was a realization on the part of these European states that the problems confronting Third World countries in general, and African states in particular, would be best tackled by multilateral rather than bilateral strategies. The proponents of the new approach argued that collective sharing of the burdens of development would serve the best interests of the developing countries. Thus, the different types of bilateral metropolitan relationships were gradually being replaced with multilateral arrangements which indeed extended beyond the former colonial zones of trade, currency and spheres of influence. In other words, links between Britain and Commonwealth Africa, and France and Francophone Africa became somewhat looser and more flexible. The new situation tended to lessen the bond between former dependencies and their individual mother countries.

This multilateral strategy was exemplified by the European Economic Community's decision to extend the benefits of association, which were formerly reserved for the enjoyment of African dependencies of the original founding EEC members, to developing countries of Africa, the Caribbean and the Pacific (ACP). The new direction has, in effect, reduced somewhat the dependence of the Anglophone and Francophone African countries on Britain and France respectively.

The EEC has provided African states new sources of markets, diversified trade, capital investment and high caliber personnel. The new relationships have encouraged or promoted industrialization, diversification and economic integration of the participating members, and are in tune with the demands of groups which advocate a New International Economic Order between the developed industrial powers and the developing states.

For Africans, the expansion and diversification of agricultural export products are considered essential development strategies which would enhance economic development programs. Greater access to European markets, capital and technology will improve the unfavorable balance of trade which has plagued Third World countries. Analysts consider this a viable option since it would yield foreign exchange revenue which is so badly needed for development projects.

The Lomé Conventions are good examples of the use of "multilateralism" in international negotiations and a vivid demonstration of the commercial and economic power of Europe.[1] These accords illustrated the economic dependence of the raw material-producing countries on the advanced industrial powers. The two conventions have been described as the Community's response to the demands of developing states for a New International Economic Order (NIEO). In these two conventions, the main thrust is "globalism" instead of "regionalism," which characterized earlier accords between EEC members and the African associates. This represented a reorientation of the Community's development policy on a global scale.[2]

Britain's EEC membership opened the doors for Commonwealth countries in Africa to establish formal relationships with the European Common Market countries. Earlier France had vigorously obstructed their bid to seek special relationships with the EEC. For example, France opposed the efforts of Nigeria and the three East-African countries – Kenya, Tanzania and Uganda which sought special agreements to protect their traditional markets in the community. British membership meant therefore that British would protect Commonwealth interests just as France had protected the interests of Francophone African countries. B. Vivekanandan shared this view when he suggested that until Britain joined the EEC, the Community did not have perception of a development strategy which took into account the problems of the developing countries all over the world; nor did it follow any universally applicable general principle. Instead, he contended that it followed a geographical pattern which was essentially Eur-African biased.[3] Similarly, W. Kenneth and J. Twitchett asserted that the globalization of ECC's commercial and aid policy was largely due to Britain's initiatives.[4]

Policymakers in Britain were fully aware of the fact that the preferential treatment which Commonwealth countries enjoyed in the British market would soon expire following Britain's EEC membership. Thus, alternative markets were being explored to absorb their major agricultural exports.

The negotiations which produced the Conventions were generally characterized by flexibility on both sides, although there were hurdles to be surmounted. To the ACP countries, the principle of recirpocity – the so-called reverse preferences which had characterized earlier agreements between the rich industrialized states and the poor developing countries – was unacceptable. Their opposition to the principle of reciprocity was that it prevented them from importing from the least cost suppliers, entailed losses in customs revenues, hindered their industrialization and led to discrimination against imports from other developing countries. On the other hand, Community negotiators stressed the economic interdependence between the developed and the developing world, arguing that it was necessary for all parties to reach a common analysis of the problems facing them and agreeing to work for mutually satisfactory solutions. Furthermore, they stated that there must be genuine progress toward a better and more balanced structure in international economic relations, a position which the developing states had adopted in past negotiations between the rich and the poor states at international conferences.

Compared with earlier North-South accords, Lomé I was indeed the most innovative convention which had addressed the various problems facing the developing countries. Its admirers have viewed it as a model of what

North-South economic relationships should be. Its provisions included more visible forms of financial, industrial, and technical cooperation and also provide a commodity income support system.

In the field of trade, its provisions were comprehensive and innovative. The accord provided duty-free, quota-free access for most African, Caribbean and Pacific (ACP) products to EEC markets[5] and thus discontinued the previous arrangements based on reciprocity. However, the Common Market members required the ACP states to apply the "most-favorable-nation clause" treatment of European exports to ACP states. Similarly, African states' manufactured goods and tropical agricultural commodities enjoyed an easy ride in the Common Market countries. But, as this stage, it must be stressed that duty-free access was not extended to all tropical products. Thus, competing ACP exports such as beef, sugar, oranges and vegetable oils were allowed duty-free quota but not unrestricted access.[6] ACP exports enjoyed a modest preference for coffee (7%) and cocoa (5%)).

The pattern of trade which has emerged since the ACP-EEC accord has revealed two major developments worth mentioning. The first development is that the ACP states have not yet succeeded in penetrating the EEC markets and, so far, are experiencing some difficulties in competing with other developing countries in the EEC markets. Thus, Brian Bayliss noted that even where ACP states have enjoyed a tariff advantage over other developing countries, such countries in Latin America and Asia have nevertheless often been able to outperform them.[7]

The second development had involved the fact that ACP exports to the EEC are concentrated in relatively few commodities and have generally originated from relatively few countries such as Nigeria, Ivory Coast, Kenya, Cameroun and Zairé.

The most radical provision of the first Lomé Convention was the STABEX Scheme – the object of which was to cope with the harmful effects of the instability of export earnings and therby enable the ACP states to achieve stability, profitability and sustained growth to the economies.[8] Thus, the scheme was created to even out the export earnings of a dozen[9] (subsequently expanded to 20 during the life of Lomé I Convention,[10]) commodities on which the ACP states depend quite heavily to finance their development programs. This scheme has been characterized as an export revenue stabilizer, a sort of insurance policy that paid off in bad economic times.

In order to qualify for STABEX compensation, the commodity covered must represent at least 7.5% of the total value of all goods exported. A special provision was made to accommodate the needs of the least-developed, landlocked and island ACP states. For these, LDC's exports of a commodity covered by STABEX need only represent 2.5% of total exports. The shortfalls in export earnings are usually based on a reference level which is the average earnings over the previous four years.

The STABEX Fund provides loans to the richer members of the ACP group, and these loans must be repaid when the export earning begin to show some appreciable improvement. For the LDC's it makes outright grants which are not refundable.

What has made the STABEX scheme very impressive in North-South relations is the simple fact that it has attempted to stabilize the price of commodities at the world market level and eventually provide ACP states an opportunity to improve their terms of trade. This enables countries involved in the scheme to achieve a better basis for planning their domestic economic development.[11] It must be pointed out that this is the first time a serious effort was made on the part of the producers of agricultural products. In the past, these countries shied away from discussions involving price stabilization of agricultural exports.

As provided in the Sugar Protocol, the STABEX Scheme moved a step further in the case of sugar, quaranteening a market for ACP exports. The EEC member countries agreed to import annually 1.4 million tons of cane sugar at the prices prevailing for European beet sugar. This is indeed a significant concession if one appreciates the fact that the price of sugar in Community markets is generally higher than that prevailing in other world markets.

African states were beneficiaries of liberal financial, technical and aid programs organized by the EEC members. A new emphasis was not placed on industrial and manpower development. The importance which the associated states placed on the aid program provided in the Lomé Accord was seen by Gordon Douglass as the strongest evidence yet of the determination of developing states to loosen their bilateral ties with former metropolitan powers and to multilateralize their international economic relations.[12]

The donors of this aid program claimed that the objective of the new emphasis on aid was to promote a better international division of labor on lines which the Community believed to be beneficial to ACP states. This strategy included the development of infrastructure projects linked to industrialization, assistance in setting up industries, training schemes and personnel development, technology transfers, and trade promotion.

A grand total of some 3.390 million EUA[13] was earmarked for the benefit of the ACP states. The European Development Fund (EDF) and the European Investment Bank (EIB) are the two major financial institutions for channeling Community financial and technical cooperation to those states with which the EEC is closely associated. The aid programs take three major forms: (a) grants which are not paid back by the recipients; (b) low-interest loans from the European Development Fund and the European Investment Bank; and (c) technical assistance involving training facilities for government officials and experts. These funds have generally financed specific infrastructures such as airfields, ports, roads, railways, engineering works and communication systems. Also, funds from EDF sources are spent for such purposes as increasing national revenues, encouraging ACP participation in international trade, diversifying and integrating economic structures in terms of sectors and geographical locations and helping regional cooperation schemes.[14]

The Convention allowed the participants greater latitude and aid management. These states were granted increased input in terms of planning the aid, preparing and appraising projects, making important financial decisions, as well as implementing the projects.

Lomé II continued the liberalizing tendencies of Lomé I. Indeed Lomé II was remarkably similar to its predecessor. The new accord retained many of the features of its predecessor with some modifications. Major changes in terms of emphasis appeared in such important areas as (a) the STABEX Schemes, (b) regional cooperation, (c) economic integration and

(d) the introduction of SYSMIN. The most significant changes involved the expansion of the STABEX product coverage from 34 to 44, thereby covering the main bulk of the agricultural exports which are crucial to the economies of ACP countries.

SYSMIN, which is simply the mineral production support scheme, was one of the most outstanding concessions the Community made in this new set of arrangements between itself and the ACP states. This scheme was established to assist mineral-producing countries which relied heavily on mineral exports but received little or no benefits from STABEX. Countries experiencing difficulties involving production and exporting qualify for direct assistance. The SYSMIN Scheme was to provide project and program aid to countries economically dependent on their mining sectors. The beneficiaries of this program include Zambia (copper and lead), Zairé (manganese, and tin), Togo (phosphate), Nigeria (tin), Botswana (manganese ore) and Ghana (manganese ore).

The series of complex commercial, aid, and industrial agreements between the EEC and the ACP states have inevitably benefited both parties. African and European exports are gaining easy access to each other's markets. There seems to have developed a clear division of labor in which African states have continued to export their agricultural commodities to Europe while purchasing their manufactured goods from that source. More favorable treatment for African states has provided them with many advantages over countries whose relationships with the EEC are covered by preferential trade and cooperation agreements only. The commercial and aid accords have stimulated trade between the ACP and the EEC states although the critics have charged that these programs would be counter-productive in the long run. These arrangements have reduced the dependence of African countries on their former mother countries for support. Thus, member states such as Germany and the Netherlands, which did not have colonies in Africa, have managed to penetrate the African market once dominated by Britain and France and also have begun to share the burdens of development on the African continent as a consequence.

208

Endnotes Chapter 7

1   Phillip Taylor, *When Europe Speaks With One Voice: The External Relations of the European Community* (Westport, Connecticut: Greenwood Press, 1979), p. 31.

2   B.   Vivekanandan , "Britain, the EEC, and The Third World," in *The EEC and The World*, eds. K. B. Lall and H. S. Chopra (Atlantic Highlands, NJ: Humanities Press 1981), p. 211.

3   *Ibid.*, p. 210.

4   W. Kenneth and J. Twitchett, *Europe and the Third World: The External Relations of the Common Market* (London, 1976), p. 23.

5   For full text of the Lomé Convention, see *Courier 31*, special issue (March 1975).

6   See Anthony J. C. Kerr, *The Common Market and How it Works*, 2nd ed. (New York: Pergamon Press, 1983), pp. 186-187.

7   Brian Bayuliss, "African, Caribbean and Pacific Countries" (ACP), p. 217.

8   Article 16, Lomé Convention.

9   The original 12 commodities were: (a) groundnut products, (b) cocoa, (c) coffee, (d) cotton, (e) coconut, (f) palm produce, (g) raw hides, (h) wood, (i) bananas, (j) tea, (k) sisial and (l) iron ores.

10   Products added during the life of Lomé I Convention were: (a) vanilla, (b) cloves, (c) wool, (d) mohair, (e) gum arabic, (f) pyrethrum, (g) essential oils and (h) sesame seed.

11   See C. G. Bamford and H. Robinson, *Geography of the EEC: A Systematic Economic Approach* (London: McDonald T. Evans, 1983), p. 42.

12   Douglass, Gordan K. and Steven Koblik, *The New Independence: The Eupopean Community and the United States* (Lexington, Massachusetts: D. C. Heath Company, 1979), p. 120.

13   European Unit of Account. In 1975, for example, a unit of account was approximately $1.24. The rate fluctuates.

14   Bailey, Richard, *The European Connection: Implications of EEC Membership* (New York: Pergamon Press, 1983), p. 180.

CHAPTER 8

CONCLUSION, ANALYISIS, OBSERVATIONS

This study has demonstrated that the post-colonial relationships between Britain and France on the one hand, and the new African states on the other, within the 1960-1985 period, have generally been characterized by dependence of the latter on the former. The first two decades of political independence really brought few major changes in the old colonial patterns of dependency. Thus, the new African states have continued to depend on the markets of the former colonizers for the sale of their agricultural produce and investment capital – for economic and technical assistance, and as sources of military personnel and material.

During the early years of independence, Britain and France offered generous financial, economic, and technical assistance to the new states. After the mid-1960s, the amount of aid decreased slightly as these aid donors were compelled to respond to the pressures of domestic needs. For example, financial difficulties forced Britain to institute austerity programs at home in order to strengthen the pound sterling and thus stimulate British trade. France, while maintaining a very high level of aid in Africa, tended to concentrate her own efforts mainly in friendly and more affluent Francophone states such as the Ivory Coast, Senegal, Gabon, and Upper Volta, or the mineral-rich countries such as Niger.

Aid to African states has taken many forms, such as loans, grants, capital investments, or commodities artificially fixed above world market prices. Nevertheless, the bulk of direct aid to African countries has taken the form of interest-bearing loans on both short-term and long-term bases. The main difficulty, as Robert July pointed out, involved the simple fact that these developing states are repaying old loans at a rate in excess of new borrowings. In short, he claimed that the flow of capital, as far as loans are concerned, has reversed itself from the poor to the rich nations.[1] Furthermore, Robert July contended that this situation has been compounded by other problems such as loans being tied to specific arrangements requiring that purchases be made in the creditor state usually at prices above the level set by international competition.[2] He argued that the real value of the loan is substantially reduced, although interest charges are based on its face value.[3] The mere fact that the prices of industrial goods are rising, while those of raw materials are declining steadily, has proven to be very burdensome to the new African states.

The experiences of the past twenty years have shown that the patterns of colonial trade have not been drastically altered. Thus, traditional suppliers have retained their markets. Raw materials have continued to flow steadily, not minding political independence. The franc zone has remained intact, with French ex-colonies in Africa purchasing the bulk of their goods from France. However, the fact that these French-speaking African states are associate members of the European Economic Community has made it possible for them to buy increasingly from France's EEC partners.

Similarly, Anglophone African states have generally conducted their trade mainly within the sterling zone. Despite policies of diversification, it is estimated that more than half the trade of all Commonwealth countries is conducted in the sterling area. The percentage is, however, steadily declining, simply because Britain is more and more interested in her trade with the rich developed states. Despite this trend, Britain remains an important trading partner of each of the African Commonwealth members. Thus, the commercial motive which was a dominant factor in the building of colonial empires has remained very strong in Europe's post-colonial relations with the new African states.

In the field of currencies and monetary systems, many Francophone African states, as recently as 1977, still were bound to the monetary systems and fiscal institutions they had inherited from the colonial era.[4] Their gradually towards greater autonomy. Thus, these Commonwealth African states established their own Central Banks with a reserve system allowing them to issue their own currency and to make their own clearing arrangements.[5] By contrast, nearly all the former French-speaking states, with the exception of Guinea and Mali, have remained within the franc zone and have maintained the monetary relationship with France which was begun during the colonial times. As Richard Hull explained, these states have maintained most of their foreign exchange reserves at the French Treasury in Paris. France usually guarantees their foreign exchange commitments by offering low-interest loans to those members which experience trade deficits.[6] These financial and monetary arrangements do make it easy for French nationals – businessmen and civil servants – to send their profits and earnings to France. They also serve as incentives which compel African states in the area to continue their close or intimate economic relations with France.

The two ex-imperial powers have not been indifferent to the needs of their ex-dependencies brought about by the process of decolonization. Each metropolitan power, in its own way, has developed programs and strategies to cope with the new political situation, particularly during the period of transition from colonial status to statehood. Having relinquished political authority over their former dependencies, the two European powers had exchanged positions of power for ones of influence. They claimed that the old relationships of dominance were being replaced by special relationships of partnership or interdependence. Thus, it can be pointed out that Britain and France have succeeded in transforming their African empires into the Commonwealth and the Community respectively. In different ways, Britain and France recognized and adjusted to the changing political situation in their former African dependencies.

The critics of British and French ties with African states have charged that these imperial powers have lured the new states into a neo-colonial situation. After examining the impact of foreign influence in general and the dominant presence of former colonizers in their former colonial preserves, one African intellectual protested:

> We are undergoing a second colonization: our present leaders are just like the old tribal chiefs who signed pacts with colonizers for a few beads. Friendship and military pacts are now penciled up in return for guns, aid or cash loans. Africa is up for grabs.[7]

These two European ex-imperial powers, Britain and France, have maintained physical presence in Africa many years after their dependencies achieved the status of independent sovereign states. However, of these two former colonizers, France has the more enviable position in terms of having established closer or more intimate relationships with countries of Francophone Africa and, thus, has enjoyed greater influence in the area. By contrast, British ties with Commonwealth African states are purely based on mutual respect and not on the basis of sentiment or admiration for British institutions.

Britain's imperial mission in Africa ended on April 18, 1980, when the British flag was hauled down in Salisbury, Zimbabwe. Having relinquished political authority in its dependencies in Africa, Britain did recognize its obligation to cope with the new problems which arose out of the decolonization process. For example, it instituted new programs to assist the newly independent states during their period of transition. The new programs included the creation of the Department of Technical Cooperation and the Special Commonwealth African Assistance Program. The Department of Technical Cooperation took over the British effort in the technical assistance field. Britain realized that chaos would result if the British colonial civil servants were removed immediately from the countries which had attained their sovereignty, since the new states lacked trained personnel to man their national civil service. Arrangements were made to loan the new state-experienced British civil servants who were considered as experts rather than administrators. In many instances, the British Government increased the salaries of many of these loaned officials by what they described as a "compensation-for-loss-of-career-arrangement," and, of course, charged the expenditure to the new government. Later, as the policy of Africanization of the national civil service progressed, Britain replaced its permanent corps of experts by technicians on short contracts and also by young people entering the civil service for the first time.

Upon achieving their political independence, English-speaking African states were admitted to the British Commonwealth of Nations – an association of countries which consider themselves members of the same family. In recent times, Commonwealth solidarity has been encouraged by regular meetings of heads of government, finance, and foreign ministers. At international conferences such as the United Nations, Commonwealth delegates usually hold secret caucuses in which they air their views and map out their strategy. It must be pointed out, however, that the new Commonwealth has lost its former character and composition. It used to be considered a club or family whose members were united by blood ties.[8] The new Commonwealth is, of course, anti-colonial and adopts a neutralist posture in cold war issues, and Britain receives support for its policies only when they fit that pattern.[9]

The changing character and composition of the Commonwealth has resulted in the declining British interest in the Commonwealth itself. William Clark has argued quite persuasively that the sudden expansion of the Commonwealth from a group of nations with similar political and racial backgrounds and outlook into a multiracial body with widely differing backgrounds and prospects has greatly weakened the old political and strategic motives for support in Britain itself for the association.[10] He cited the debates on Britain's entry into the European Economic Community and on the Commonwealth Immigration Bill,[11] as evidence of growing disenchantment with the new Commonwealth in Britain.

French assimilationist policies in colonial Africa resulted in the emergence of an elite group which regarded themselves as fully French in culture although they also considered themselves as African nationalists. Immediately following the war, France loosened slightly the bonds of union into a Community in which self-government, but not full independence, was the preferred objective. The upsurge of African nationalism which characterized the postwar era undermined France's declared objective of continuing political authority over her African subjects. Guinea led the way in terms of breaking away from the French orbit. She was followed by Mali later, and before long, many Francophone states decided to leave the Community but still maintained intimate ties with France.

The granting of full political independence to former French dependencies did not deter France from continuing her generous aid programs to these countries. French relations with the sixteen French-speaking republics of sub-Saharan Africa which were formerly known as French West Africa and French Equatorial Africa, have continued to be very intimate indeed. Having abandoned all overt political control over the new republics, France now places heavy emphasis on technical assistance and commercial and cultural ties. Thus, French teachers have continued to maintain a close cultural link between France and Francophone African states. Some analysts have noted that French culture and financial and technical assistance seem to be the main factors which have held France and French-speaking African countries together. There is a realization on the part of the African states that they are totally dependent on French financial and technical aid for their mere survival.

France intensified her aid programs to the new states after they had achieved their independence. Thus, the Frenchmen who had served as civil servants administering and developing French Africa remained on the French payroll as before, but became automatically "advisers" to the new indigenous civil service. Similarly, many of the school teachers were asked to stay behind while their salaries were paid from the French budget, although they were now serving the new states. In addition to French investments and aid in Francophone Africa, France's EEC partners are contributing funds towards the development of Francophone states which have enjoyed associate status in the European Economic Community since the ratification of the Treaty of Rome in 1957.

A major difference between pre-independence and post-independence relations between France and the new states, according to Dov Ronen, was that, prior to independence, French aid and support were an integral part of her institutionalized relations with her dependencies, whereas after independence the support became bilateral aid between two states, subject to formal agreements.[12] These Accords de Coopération, as they are usually known, and other bilateral agreements and treaties, replaced the old structure.[13]

The Franco-African accords covered political questions such as national defense, foreign policy, raw materials and products of strategic value, economic and financial relations, social and cultural matters, and technical cooperation. These agreements are mutual and express formal contractual relationships which could be terminated in just the same manner that other international agreements are terminated.

Since the scope of French aid is very comprehensive, many organizations have been created to implement and supervise its application. For example, there is the Secrétariat d'État aux Affaires d'Etrangeres Chargé de la Coopération in Paris, which is divided into two main departments, namely, Cultural and Technical cooperation, and Economic and Financial affairs. In addition to the offices at the French capital, there are two in each of the states receiving French aid. The aid mission is responsible to the French ambassador on the spot. The function of the permanent mission is to study the needs and the requests of the recipient state. Its members usually negotiate the terms of a particular aid project, its financing, and manner of implementation.

Other organizations were specifically created to handle new needs which emerged after independence. They include, for example, the following: The Caisse Centrale de Coopération Economique; Office de la Recherches Scientifiques et Techniques d'Outre-Mer and Institut de Recherches Agronomiques Tropicales et de Culture, Viviéres. These last two organizations deal with scientific research. As indicated earlier in this discussion, the financing of French aid and cooperation is conducted through the Fonds d'Aide et de Coopération (FAC) which transfers funds through the Caisse Centrale de Coopération Economique. FAC makes sure that the financing of both monetary aid and French investments as well as technical assistance are effectively implemented.

The number of French advisers in Africa since the post-independence period has remained very high indeed. For example, some 300,000 French nationals now live and work in Africa, more than twice the number that did so during the colonial period.[14] In the Ivory Coast, which enjoys a special relationship with France, there were about 45,000 French nationals in the country in 1978. This figure was over four times as many as at the time of independence. About 3,500 of these were classified as technical assistants. During his five-day state visit to Abidjan, the Ivory Coast, President Giscard d'Estaing asserted that the visit bore testimony to the exceptional character of the relationship between France and the Ivory Coast. Before he left for France, he announced that French companies had signed contracts with the Ivory Coast worth 2.8 billion francs since January 1, 1972.[15]

In all of Francophone Africa, with the exception of Guinea and Mali, French nationals have continued to dominate entire departments and even subdivisions of the civil service. In 1969, for example, French nationals in the Ivory Coast occupied important decision-making positions: there were 68 technical assistants in the department of economic and financial affairs; 25 in Justice; 21 in the Interior; 22 in Public Functions; 59 in Agriculture; 37 in Transport and Public Works; and 109 in Public Health.[16] The heavy reliance on French experts to man the top ranks of the bureaucracy has slowed down the process of Africanization of the civil service in French-speaking areas.

Trade relations between France and the new Francophone states in the post-colonial period have been very intimate. Nevertheless, the trade of Francophone states has been characterized by chronic deficits, high costs of both imports and exports, and monopolies held by French firms.[17] In general, France has enjoyed a favorable balance of trade with each of the states of Francophone Africa. For example, in 1979, France exported goods worth approximately $4.6 billion to French-speaking African countries and imported roughly $3.1 billion from them in return. The huge French trading firms have continued their exploitation of French-speaking areas in Africa in the name of "African development." For example, the Compagnie Française de l'Afrique Occidentale is still in the business of purchasing and selling anything from coffee to Caravelle airliners.

The French have regarded their presence in Africa not merely as exploitation, as their critics have often charged, but see it simply as a way of assisting the poorest countries of the world as they struggle to achieve economic development. But the French have failed to admit the fact that their national interests are involved in their decision to aid these countries. Africa's oil, manganese, diamonds, uranium, cobalt, phosphates, and other useful scarce minerals are indeed of immeasurable significance to France's industrial and military power.[18] It has been pointed out by some analysts that, without access to Africa's uranium, there would have been no credible French independent nuclear deterrence.

In the post-colonial era, successive French governments made many commercial concessions to African countries simply by enlarging import quotas, subsidies, and guaranteed prices. In so doing, France bought African produce at prices slightly above those of the world market and indeed guaranteed Francophone states an important commercial outlet.

The result of this arrangement has been that Africans have restricted themselves to the purchasing of French goods at prices far above those prevailing in other foreign markets. Thus, the critics of French African policy have pointed out that the excessive level of French prices has been responsible for high production costs in Francophone African countries which, in effect, has wiped out any benefits they hoped to derive from the entry of their exports into the French market.

Francophone states are members of the franc zone. Their currency system, known as the Communauté des Francs Africains (CFA), is managed by the Bank of France. These countries hold their reserves in French francs and conduct their monetary transactions in the Paris money market. Their currency is linked with the French franc at a fixed rate of exchange. The main objective in setting up this arrangement was to preserve old arrangements under which Africa's raw materials or primary products could be extracted for profitable development in France while French manufactured goods could in turn be marketed in Africa.

France has been of much help to the French-speaking African countries in many different ways. It has assisted African states in balancing their national budgets. Thus, between 1960 and 1969, Benin, then Dahomey, was constantly in deficit. This deficit reached 7.3 billion CFA francs despite French contributions of 6.8 billion CFA francs over the same period. In 1970, it experienced a surplus of 400 million CFA francs after French budgetary aid of 600 million CFA francs; and in 1971, it registered a surplus of 600 million with French aid of 450 million.[19]

French governments have generally intervened politically and militarily in Africa to support those regimes which were pro-French. French presidents have made many state visits to French Africa to demonstrate the solidarity of the French-African association. For example, President Giscard d'Estaing, during his presidency from 1974 to 1981, made over fifteen well-publicized official visits to various French-speaking African states. His immediate successor, President Mitterrand, upon assuming power in France, visited French Africa in order to reassure these states of continued French support and friendship.

French relations with countries such as Guinea and Mali have not been as close as its relations with others such as Gabon, the Ivory Coast, and Senegal. The former tried hard to assert their independence by breaking away from the French political and economic orbit. These states were generally denied French aid. Thus, Guinea's determination to stay outside the French Community in 1958, following the de Gaulle Referendum, led to the removal of France's financial aid, trade preferences, subsidies, and technical assistance. These punitive measures undermined Guinea's efforts to achieve economic development.

Mali followed Guinea's example. After breaking the federation with Senegal, it left the Community, and the franc zone as well, in 1962, and established its own currency. But growing foreign debts and the need for a hard currency led to protracted negotiations with France in 1967 for returning Mali to the franc zone. This objective was achieved in 1968 when Mali officially returned to the franc zone.

The membership of Francophone African states in the European Common Market has slightly altered France's post-colonial relationships with these states. At the time the original Treaty of Rome was being negotiated, France persuaded her other EEC partners to realize her Eur-African concept. She succeeded in getting for the dependencies "associate" status in the EEC and thus shared with her European partners the burden of providing support to these African states. As a result, bilateral aid was transformed to multilateral aid. It meant therefore, that French industries now shared the African market with other European countries. Africans were indeed beneficiaries. Not only did their development funds substantially increase, but the opening up to their inhabitants of low-priced and well-stocked foreign markets did, in a way, offset the elimination of

French price-supports for their produce in the French market. Progressively, the old colonial tariff structures, which favored French exports, were modified to give France's partners in the EEC equal access to African markets. The European Development Fund provided these new states with a new source of multilateral aid.

European dominance of the economies of African states, which began during the colonial period, continued after independence. All African countries, without exception, had in common varying degrees of dependence on their former colonizers and other advanced industrial powers of the world. African countries could not compete very effectively with developed countries' superior technology, managerial skill, and access to capital. Thus, the attainment of economic independence has been a major concern of both Anglophone and Francophone African states since independence. These states are struggling not only for political independence but also for economic freedom; they fully realize that the former is a meaningless accomplishment without the latter.

African states inherited economic systems in which foreign interests were dominant. For example, during the early stages of independence, the marketing and export of such cash crops as cocoa, palm produce, peanuts, cotton, coffee, and tea were monopolized by British and French companies. African states' import, export, and wholesale trade was dominated by Europeans, while the retail trade in countries such as Ghana and Nigeria was in the hands of Lebanese and Syrian merchants. Ghana's gold mines were British-owned, while the exploitation and marketing of diamonds were controlled by foreign interests. In Sierra Leone, another British dependency, the situation was very similar. The country's mineral resources such as diamonds, iron ore, and gold were exploited by foreign companies which had exclusive rights to mine, prospect for, and export all minerals. Similarly, foreign firms controlled about 98 percent of export-import trade while two British-owned banks dominated commercial banking in British Africa. Leone. Thus, the simple fact that foreign interests owned and controlled the major assets in the various African countries gave cause to the desire and perhaps the determination on the part of African states to achieve economic autonomy.

Since the time of political independence, African states in general, and Anglophone states in particular, have adopted various measures and strategies to decolonize their national economies. These measures were designed to strengthen their African economies. They included greater government intervention in economic life; nationalization of foreign-owned business enterprises; and the rapid replacement of foreign labor by the process of Africanization. The process of Africanization or indigenization is a way or means whereby African states have attempted to reduce their dependence on former colonial powers. By this process, African states take over foreign-owned businesses and encourage local entrepreneurs to become actively involved in business ventures. The governments usually protect these native businessmen against foreign competition. Nigerian leadership in this area is worth mentioning. In 1972, it announced the Nigerian Enterprises Promotion Decree which, in effect specified that twenty-two categories of businesses must be reserved exclusively for Nigerian citizens.[20] The Government of President Idi Amin followed a similar program in Uganda in 1972. The government decreed that all foreign-owned businesses must be placed in the hands of deserving Ugandans. This meant that Asians would be the victims. Their businesses were seized and handed over to indigenous black Ugandans. The government itself controlled the larger Asian business interests such as large hotels, factories, and garages.

At the United Nations, African states, in collaboration with other Third World countries, demanded full and permanent sovereignty of every state over its own natural resources as well as all forms of economic activities. They advocated policies which the capitalist states considered very radical. These included, for example, tighter control of foreign aid and capital investments in the developing countries of the world and unrestricted right to nationalize foreign-owned property and pay compensation as prescribed by national law, not minding international law provisions governing such business transactions. African states have welcomed foreign aid and capital investments in their respective countries, and some African states have created tax and other incentives to attract foreign investors. However, foreign investors in Africa are beginning to express their concern about the policies of nationalization and Africanization pursued by African states. These foreign investors usually expect a favorable investment climate in which to invest their capital. In both Anglophone and Francophone Africa, there is the expressed suspicion that international companies and foreign investors only enter the African market with the intention of having quick profits and thus are not prepared to accumulate large reserves within the host countries to be used for further local investment. African critics have condemned the large drain of money and resources leaving their countries. They have demanded that profits should be retained in the African countries for purposes of domestic development. Even prosperous Francophone states such as the Ivory Coast, Senegal, and Gabon have followed the footsteps of their English-speaking neighbors in formulating a framework within which foreign investment can operate in their respective countries. After overcoming tenacious French opposition, several of the new Francophone states are beginning to create openings for competitors from the outside by directly inviting non-French investors and bankers.

Trade is another area where the new African states are making concerted efforts to decolonize. These states are fully aware of the fact that there exists an unfavorable balance in terms of trade. After independence, African countries continued to depend heavily on a few cash crops or minerals for as much as 80 percent to 90 percent of their total export earnings. Thus, the post-independence period was characterized by hardships resulting from the declining terms of trade for these agricultural products. While there was general decline in the prices of coffee, cotton, peanuts, and sisal on the world market, African imports continued to rise quite sharply.

Diversification is seen as the solution to combat this problem. This would prevent the dependence on one primary commodity as the main source of foreign exchange earnings.

A way suggested by radical African states to move away from a state of dependency on former colonizers has involved the creation of an African Common Market. Nevertheless, critics have pointed out that African countries' economies are competitive rather than complementary. The proponents of the African Common Market idea suggest that since African countries cannot adequately compete in world markets in terms of exporting their manufactured products, they should consider the other alternative which involves exporting their manufactures to each other. The Economic Commission for Africa supports this approach. This UN organization has indeed provided the African states with an invaluable forum for the discussion of problems and issues which affect the economic and political interests of African states. The ECA has stressed collective efforts or cooperative ventures as effective strategies which can enhance the economic independence of African states. It tended to discard the former notion which asserted that each country was primarily responsible for its own development according to its own means. The question of economic cooperation on a continental scale has not been very successful owing to such problems as geography, communications, and transportation difficulties; the existence of different currency zones; fiscal policies of the various African governments; and the membership of some African states in the European Common Market. Other discouraging factors to the African Common Market concept include the fact that most African markets are very limited, partly as a result of the small population of many African countries and partly because of the low income per capita. Analysts indicate that many industries cannot hope to be successful without a sizeable market owing to the influence of economics of scale.

This study has demonstrated that connections which were established in the colonial period between Africa and Europe cannot easily be disrupted. The post-independence relationships between European powers and the new African states have, on the whole, remained very friendly and, in most cases, very intimate. Trade has maintained its colonial character although concerted efforts have been made to diversify trade relations on the part of African states. Economic, military, and cultural ties have remained strong. Aid has continued to flow generously to Francophone states after independence. The proponents of the Eur-African concept have indicated that Africans and Europeans need each other. They argue that Europe needs the untapped resources of Africa, while the Africans need economic aid and technical assistance from Europe.

With the exception of a few instances involving the worsening of relationships, such as the breaking of diplomatic relations between Britain and the radical Commonwealth states over the Rhodesian question, or Guinea's break with France in 1958, these post-colonial relationships have been very satisfactory to both sides and have not been what the Conservative elements and the imperialist forces in Britain and France had earlier predicted.

In the final analysis, this author outlines measures or strategies which might reduce the dependence of African states on European powers and eventually help them to achieve greater autonomy.

First, there should be concerted efforts to break the umbilical cord which has tied the new states very closely to the metropolitan powers and substitute it with aggressive diversification programs in terms of trade partners, sources of aid, investment capital, technology and military procurement. Concentrated dependence on the former colonizers for markets, capital, technology and high-level manpower, has substantially limited freedom in selecting economic policies and strategies. Thus, decolonization has not ended economic exploitation in Africa. The dominant position which the colonial powers enjoyed in Africa during the colonial times has continued to the present time. For example, the bulk of exports of African states continue to go to former metropolitan powers and other industrial powers in Western Europe and North America. In Francophone Africa the attachments between the former colonizer and the new states are so intimate and so intense that it has been frequently charged that these nations are victims of the dependency syndrome. Thus, two decades after political independence, France has continued to provide high-level personnel to staff the army in Chad, run the banks in the Ivory Coast and assist in the administration of rural development projects in places such as Niger, Gabon and Upper Volta. France has continued to be the major source of investment capital. She continues to buy more products from and sell more products to former French dependencies than does any other foreign industrial power.

Their continued association with France has broadened their economic opportunities, since their associate membership status in the European Common Market granted them under the Treaty of Rome (1957), the Yaoundé Conventions 1963 and 1969, and finally, the Lomé Conventions.

These arrangements provided these African states short-term benefits such as access to investment funds and markets within the West European area. But in the long-run these arrangements might place African participants in an unenviable position as suppliers of raw materials in the international division of labor, and thus, prolong underdevelopment in these countries. These short-term benefits which are enjoyed by African associate members of the European Economic Community are denied to non-members of this predominantly European economic club. This means that other Third World states are discriminated against as a result of the preferential treatment which associate members have received from the EEC.

Critics of the Eur-African cooperation exemplified by EEC-Associate status have argued that it would not give African participants the significant control over export prices, the access to markets or even the guarantees of investment flows which they need very badly for developmental purposes. Instead, they point out that these benefits simply retard structural change and national planning.

Diversification, in terms of trade, aid, investment and technology, is a sure way to lessen dependence on former metropolitan powers. Nevertheless, little effort has been made to increase trade with socialist states; similarly, most of the states covered in this study have shown reluctance in opening up trade with these communist powers or even seeking financial as well as technological aid from this source. This author is convinced that African states' interests would be best served if they begin to take drastic steps to diversify contacts with countries of both ideological blocs and, thus, avoid putting all their eggs into one basket. These contacts are indeed necessary if African states' claim to positive neutrality is to be credible.

Second, economic development is one way to reduce African dependence on European powers in general and the former colonizers in particular. The narrowness of the resource base in African economies has contributed to their dependence on foreign countries. In order to combat this phenomenon, African economic integration must be sought or pursued as a desirable objective. African leaders in both Anglophone and Francophone states have now realized the urgent need to adopt radical economic changes in the structure of production as well as changes in international economic relations. The colonial structures of African economies should be liberated. It is argued that very little can be achieved by way of development within economic units as small as the present states, hence the appeal for African political unity. Thus, economic unity on a continental scale or even a regional basis would enhance the possibility of achieving rapid economic growth and development. An integrated economic system could create a significantly more natural resource base than the sum of resources divided among separate states. Investments could be concentrated on efficient large-scale plants resulting in rapid increases in productivity at reduced costs. It has been pointed out also that an economic unit encompassing all African countries would be in a position to exert significant bargaining power on the world market. There is also the impressive argument that comprehensive economic planning would be much more practicable on a continental or regional basis than for individual African states. In this integrated system, production, markets, and investments could be better planned and implemented on a consolidated basis. All over Africa nowadays, there is general consensus about the need for economic integration in terms of policy, planning and coordination in such fields as production, trade, technology, transportation and communications. The coordination of individual state plans will definitely promote intra-African trade and enhance development.

Third, the idea of collective self-help is another strategy to reduce African states' dependence on foreign countries. Regional cooperation exemplified by river-basin projects discussed earlier in this study are good illustrations of cooperative ventures in mind.

The OAU's Special Economic Summit which met in Lagos, Nigeria in 1980 addressed itself to this general theme of collective self-reliance. Emphasis was placed on such terms as economic integration, promotion of greater intra-African trade, an African Energy policy, self-sufficiency in food production, improved transport and communication systems and the creation of an African Monetary Fund.

Regional groupings, such as the Economic Organization of West African States, ECOWAS;[21] the Organization Commune Africaine et

Mauricience, OCAM;[22] and the Communante Economique de l'Afrique de l'Ouest, CEAO,[23] should be encouraged and others like them created.

Some critics are indeed very pessimistic about the success of these regional organizations. This author believes that these regional organizations will serve as steppingstones on which continental unity can be later built.

Endnotes Chapter 8

1   Robert W. July, *A History of the African People* (New York: Charles Scribner's Sons, 1974), p. 653.

2   *Ibid.*

3   *Ibid.*

4   Richard W. Hull, *Modern Africa: Change and Continuity* (Englewood Cliffs, NJ: Prentice-Hall, 1980), p. 215.

5   *Ibid.*

6   *Ibid.*, p. 216.

7   *Time*, 16 January 1984, p. 28.

8   The Old Dominions which made up the British Commonwealth included Canada, Australia, New Zealand, and South Africa. During the postwar period, India, Ceylon, and Malaysia joined the club. Ghana became the first African state to join the organization, in 1975.

9   William Clark, "New Europe and New Nations," *Daedalus: Journal of American Academy of Arts and Sciences* 93 (Winter 1964), p. 141.

10   *Ibid.*, p. 142.

11   The Commonwealth Immigration Bill limited the freedom of Commonwealth citizens to enter Britain. The bill was sharply criticized and condemned by Commonwealth members.

12   Dov Ronen, *Dahomey: Between Tradition and Modernity* (Ithaca, NY: Cornell University Press, 1975), p. 164.

13   France, Secrétariat Général du Gouvernment, Notes et études documentaires, no. 3330, October 25, 1966, "La Coopération entre la France, l'Afrique Noire d'Expression Française et Madagascar."

14   *Time*, 16 January 1984, p. 28.

15   *West Africa*, No. 3158, 23 January 1978, p. 137.

16   See Henry L. Bretton, *Power and Politics in Africa* (Chicago: Aldine Publishing Company, 1973), p. 189.

17   Virginia Thompson and Richard Adloff, *Conflict in Chad* (Berkeley: University of California Institute of International Studies, No. 45, 1981), p. 19.

18   Gabon, Niger, Chad, and the Central African Republic feature prominently in the production of these strategic raw materials.

19   See Ronen, *Dahomey*, p. 169.

20   *Schedule 1*: Categories of Enterprises Reserved for Nigerians. These included (1) advertising agencies and public relations business; (2) all aspects of pool betting business and lotteries; (3) assembly of radios, radiograms, record changers, televisions sets, tape recorders, and other electric domestic appliances not combined with manufacture of components; (4) blending and bottling of alcoholic drinks; (5) blocks, bricks, and ordinary tiles manufactured for building and construction works; (6) bread and cake making; (7) candle manufacture; (8) casinos and gaming centers; (9) cinemas and other places of entertainment; (10) clearing and forwarding agencies; (11) hairdressing; (12) haulage of goods by road; (13) laundry and dry cleaning; (14) manufacture of jewelry and related articles; (15) newspaper publishing and printing; (16) ordinary garment manufacture not combined with production of textile materials; (17) municipal bus services and taxis; (18) radio and television broadcasting; (19) retail trade (except by or within the departmental stores and supermarkets); (20) rice milling; (21) singlet manufacture; and (22) tire retreading.

21   The membership includes both Anglophone and Francophone African States.

22   The members are as follows: Benin, Central African Republic, Gabon, Ivory Coast, Mauritius, Niger, Rwanda, Senegal, Togo and Upper Volta.

23   The membership includes: Ivory Coast, Mali, Mauritania, Niger, Senegal and Upper Volta.

BIBLIOGRAPHY

Abbai, Belai. "Some Aspects of Trade and Development." In *Africa and the World.* Edited by Robert K. A. Gardiner, M. J. Anstee, and C. L. Patterson. Addis Ababa: Oxford University Press, 1970.

Adloff, Richard. *West Africa: The French Speaking Nations.* New York: Holt-Rinehart and Winston, 1964.

Ajayi, J. F. A. "Colonialism: An Episode in African History." In *Colonialism in Africa 1870-1960, Vol. 1, The History and Politics of Colonialism 1870-1914.* London: Cambridge University Press, 1969.

Ajayi, J. F. A., and Webster, J. B. "The Emergence of a New Elite in Africa." In *Africa in the Nineteenth and Twentieth-Centuries.* Edited by Joseph C. Anene and Geofrey N. Brown. London: Ibadan University Press, 1966.

Albert, Paul. *Partnership or Confrontation: Poor Lands and Rich.* New York: The Free Press, 1973.

Albertini, Rudolf von. *Decolonization: The Administration and Future of the Colonies, 1919-1960.* New York: Doubleday, 1971.

Bagchi, Amiya Kumar. *The Political Economy of Underdevelopment.* New York: Cambridge University Press, 1982.

Baumgart, Winfried. *Imperialism: The Idea and Reality of British and French Colonial Expansion 1880-1914.* London: Oxford University Press, 1982.

Beachey, R. W. "The Arms Trade in East Africa." *Journal of African History,* 3, No. 3 (1962): 451-467.

Berry, Sara S. "Economic Change in Contemporary Africa." In *Africa.* Edited by Phyllis M. Martin and Patrick O'Meara. Bloomington: Indiana University Press, 1977.

Bert, Elliot J. "The Economic Basis of Political Choice in French West Africa." In *Independent Black Africa: The Politics of Freedom.* Edited by William John Hanna. Chicago: Rand McNally & Company, 1964.

Bhagwati, Jagdish N., ed. *The Typing of Aid.* New Delhi: United National Conference on Trade and Development, 1968, 2nd Session.

Boateng, E. A. *A Political Geography of Africa.* London: Cambridge University Press, 1978.

230

Bodenheimer, Susanne. "Dependency and Imperialism: The Roots of Latin American Underdevelopment." In *Readings in U.S. Imperialism*. Edited by K. T. Fann and Donald C. Hodges. Boston: Porter Sargent, 1971.

Brett, E. A. *Colonialism and Underdevelopment in East Africa: The Politics of Economic Change, 1919-1939*. New York: NOK Publishers, Ltd., 1973.

Bretton, Henry L. *Power and Politics in Africa*. Chicago: Aldine Publishing Company, 1973.

Brunschwig, Henri. *French Colonialism 1871-1914: Myths and Realities*. Translated by William Granville Brown. New York: Praeger, 1966.

Buell, Raymond Leslie. *The Native Problem in Africa*. Vol. 11. New York: Macmillan, 1928.

Bywater, Marion. *The Lomé Convention*. European Community, March 1975.

Cairncross, Alexander K. *Home and Foreign Investment 1870-1913: Studies in Capital Accumulation*. Cambridge: Cambridge University Press, 1953.

Carter, Gwendolyn. *Transition in Africa: Studies in Political Adaptation*. Boston: Boston University Press, 1958.

Chidzero, B. T. G. "Constructive Disengagement." In *Africa and the World*. Edited by Robert K. A. Gardiner, M. J. Anstee, and C. L. Patterson. Addis Ababa: Oxford University Press, 1970.

Clark, William. "New Europe and the New Nations. *Daedalus* 93, No. 1 (Winter 1964): 134-152.

Collins, P. *The African Review: A Journal of African Politics, Development and International Affairs*, 4. No. 2. Department of Political Science, University of Dar-es-Salaam, 1974.

Crocker, Chester A. "External Military Assistance to Sub-Saharan Africa." *Africa Today*, April-May 1968.

Crow, Duncan. *Investment in Progress: British Contribution to Overseas Development*. London: Fosh and Cross, Ltd., 1958.

Crowder, Michael. *West Africa under Colonial Rule*. Evanston, IL: Northwestern University Press, 1968.

Curtin, Philip; Feieman, Steven; Thompson, Leonard; and Vansina, Jan. *African History*. Boston: Little, Brown and Co., 1978.

Darlington, Charles F., and Darlington, Alice B. *African Betrayal.* New York: McKay, 1968.

Davidson, Basil. *Let Freedom Come: Africa in Modern History.* Boston: Little, Brown and Company, 1978.

Delorme, Nicole. *The Association of Africa and Malagasy States and the European Economic Community.* General Library of Law and Jurisprudence, 1972.

Duignan, Peter, and Gann, L. H., eds. *Colonialism in Africa, 1870-1960, Vol. 4, The Economics of Colonialism.* London: Cambridge University Press, 1975.

Emerson, Rupert. *From Empire to Nation: The Rise to Self-Assertion of Asians and Africans.* Boston: Beacon Press, 1960.

Erb, Guy F., and Kallab, Valeriana. *Beyond Dependency: The Developing World Speaks Out.* Washington, D.C.: Overseas Development Council, 1975.

Ewing, Arthur F. "Industrial Development in Africa: The Respective Roles of African Countries and External Assistance." In *Africa and the World.* Edited by Robert K. A. Gardiner, M. J. Anstee, and C. L. Patterson. Addis Ababa: Oxford University Press, 1970.

Ferkiss, Victor C. *Africa's Search for Identity.* New York: George Braziller, 1966.

Fieldhouse, David K. "The Economic Exploitation of Africa: Some British and French Comparisons." In *France and Britain in Africa: Imperial Rivalry and Colonial Rule.* Edited by Prosser Gifford and William Roger Louis. New Haven: Yale University Press, 1971.

_____. *Economics and Empire 1830-1914.* London: Oxford University Press, 1973.

Flynn, J. K. "Ghana-Asante" (Ashanti). In *West African Resistance: The Military Response to Colonial Occupation.* Edited by Michael Crowder. New York: Africana Publishing Corporation, 1972.

Frankel, Herbert. *Capital Investment in Africa.* London: Oxford University Press, 1938.

Franks, Oliver. "Britain and Europe." *Daedalus, Journal of the American Academy of Arts and Sciences.* 93. No. 1 (Winter 1964): 67-82.

Friedmann, Wolfgang G.; Lissitzyn, Oliver J.; and Pugh, Richard Crawford. *Cases and Materials on International Law.* St. Paul, MN: West Publishing Co., 1969.

232

Galbraith, John S. "The Turbulent Frontier as a Factor in British Expansionism." *Comparative Studies in Society and History* 2. No. 2 (January 1960): 150-168.

Gardiner, Robert K. A. "Africa and the World." In *Africa and the World*. Edited by Robert K. A. Gardiner, M. J. Anstee, and C. L. Patterson. Addis Ababa: Oxford University Press, 1970.

Gavshon, Arthur. *Crisis in Africa: Battleground of East and West*. New York: Penguin Books, 1981.

Gellar, Sheldon. "The Colonial Era." In *Africa*. Edited by Phyllis M. Martin and Patrick O'Meara. Bloomington: Indiana University Press, 1977.

Gifford, Prosser, and Louis, William Roger, eds. *France and Britain in Africa: Imperial Rivalry and Colonial Rule*. New Haven: Yale University Press, 1971.

Gray, L. *Imperialism, Colonialism and After*. New York: Columbia University Library, 1966. Unpublished.

Griffin, K. B. "Foreign Capital, Domestic Savings and Economic Development." *Bulletin* 32. No. 2 (May 1970):

Griffin, K. B., and Enos, J. L. "Foreign Assistance: Objectives and Consequences." *Economic Development and Cultural Change*, 18. No. 3 (March 1970):

Gruhn, Isebill V. "The Lomé Convention: Inching Toward Interdependence." *International Organization* 30. No. 2 (Spring, 1976): 241-262.

Grundy, Kenneth W. *Guerrilla Struggle in Africa: An Analysis and Preview*. New York: Grossman Publishers, 1971.

Gutteridge, William F. "Military and Police Forces in Colonial Africa." In *Colonialism in Africa 1870-1960, Vol. 2, The History and Politics of Colonialism, 1914-1960*. Edited by Peter Duignan and L. H. Gann. London: Cambridge University Press, 1970.

Hailey, Lord. *An African Survey*. London: Oxford University Press, 1938.

Hallett, Robin. *Africa Since 1875: A Modern History*. Ann Arbor: The University of Michigan Press, 1974.

Hanrieder, Wolfram F., and Auton, Graeme P. *The Foreign Policies of West Germany, France and Britain*. Englewood Cliffs, New Jersey: Prentice Hall, Inc., 1980.

Hatch, John C. *Two African Statesmen: Kaunda of Zambia and Nyerere of Tanzania*. Chicago: Henry Regnery Co., 1976.

Hayter, Teresa. *French Aid*. London: Overseas Development Institute, 1966.

Hazlewood, Arthur, and Holtham, Gerald. *Aid and Inequality in Kenya: British Development Assistance to Kenya*. London: Croom Helm in association with the Overseas Development Institute, 1976.

Headrick, Daniel R. *The Tools of Empire: Technology and European Imperialism in the Nineteenth- Century*. New York: Oxford University Press, 1981.

Hobson, J. A. *Imperialism: A Study*. London: G. Allen & Unwin, 1938.

Hodder, B. W. *Africa Today: A Short Introduction to African Affairs*. New York: Africana Publishing Company, Inc., 1978.

Hodder, B. W., and Harris, D. R., eds. *Africa in Transition: Geographical Essays*. London: Methuen and Co. Ltd., 1967.

Hodgkin, Thomas. *Nationalism in Colonial Africa*. New York: New York University Press, 1957.

Hodgkin, T., and Schrachter, R. "French-speaking Africa in Transition." *International Conciliation* 528 (May 1960): 375-436.

Holmes, John. "The Impact of the Commonwealth on the Emergence of Africa." In *Africa and the World Order*. Edited by Norman J. Padelford and Rupert Emerson. New York: Praeger, 1964.

Houphouet-Boigny, Felix. "Black Africa and the French Union." *Foreign Affairs* 35. No. 4 (July 1957): 593-599.

Howe, Russell Warren. *The African Revolution*. New York: Barnes and Nobles, Inc., 1969.

Hughes, John. *The New Face of Africa South of the Sahara*. New York: Longmans, Green, 1961.

Hull, Richard W. *Modern Africa: Change and Continuity*. Englewood Cliffs, NJ: Prentice-Hall, 1980.

Ibingira, Grace Steward. *African Upheavals Since Independence*. Boulder, CO: Westview Press, Inc., 1980.

Jaleé, Pierre. *Le Pillage du tiers monde*. Paris: Maspero, 1970.

Jeffries, Charles J. *The Colonial Empire and its Civil Service*. Cambridge: Cambridge University Press, 1938.

_____. *Transfer of Power: The Problem of the Passage to Self-Government*. London: Pall Mall Press, 1960.

234

Johnson, Dale L. "Dependence and the International System." In *Dependence and Underdevelopment: Latin American Political Economy*. Edited by James D. Cockcroff, André Gunder Frank, and Dale L. Johnson. New York: Doubleday & Co., Inc., 1972.

Johnson, Harry G. *Economic Policies Toward Less Developed Countries*. Washington: Brookings Institution, 1967.

July, Robert W. *A History of the African People*. New York: Charles Scribner's Sons, 1974.

Kaplinsky, Raphael, ed. *Readings of the Multinational Corporation in Kenya*. New York: Oxford University Press, 1978.

Kay, David. "The UN and Decolonization." In *The United Nations: Past, Present, and Future*. Edited by James Barros. New York: The Free Press, 1972.

Keegan, John. "The Ashanti Campaign 1873-1874." In *Victorian Military Campaigns*. Edited by Brian Bond. London: Hutchinson, 1967.

_____. *Keesing's Research Report, Africa Independent: A Survey of Political Developments*. New York: Charles Scribner's Sons, 1972.

Kendle, John E. *The Colonial and Imperial Conferences 1887-1911: A Study in Imperial Organization*. London: Longmans, 1967.

King, R. B. M. "The Planning of The British Aid Programme." *Journal of Administration Overseas*. January 1972.

Kiwanuka, Semakula. *From Colonialism to Independence*. Nairobi: East African Literature Bureau, 1973.

Kolodzie, Edward A. *French International Policy Under De Gaulle and Pompidou: The Politics of Grandeur*. Ithaca: Cornell University Press, 1974.

Landes, David S. "Some Thoughts on the Nature of Economic Imperialism." *Journal of Economic History* 21 (1961): 510-551.

Lee, J. M. *African Armies and Civil Order*. New York: Frederick A. Praeger, 1969.

Legum, Colin, ed. *Africa, A Handbook to the Continent*. New York: Praeger Inc., 1962.

Leroy-Beaulieu, Pierre Paul. *De la colonisation chez les peuples modernes*. 2nd ed. Paris: Presses Universitaires de France, 1882.

235

Ligot, Maurice. *Les Accords de Coopération entre La France et les états africaine et malgache d'expression Française.* Paris: La Documentation Française, 1964.

Lugard, F. J. D. *The Dual Mandate in British Tropical Africa.* London: Blackwood and Sons, 1922.

Lusignan, Guy de. *French-Speaking Africa Since Independence.* New York: Frederick A. Praeger, 1969.

Mabileau, A., and Meyriat, J. *Decolonisation et regimes politiques en Afrique noire.* Paris: D'étude d'Afrique noir de l'Université de Bordeaux, 1967.

Mair, L. P. *Native Policies in Africa.* New York: Negro Universities Press, 1969.

Mallamud, Jonathan. "Legal Safeguards for Foreign Investment." In *Financing African Development.* Edited by Tom J. Farer. Cambridge, MA: M.I.T. Press, 1965.

Markovitz, Irving Leonard. *Power and Class in Africa: An Introduction to Change and Conflict in African Politics.* Englewood Cliffs, NJ: Prentice-Hall, Inc., 1972.

Martin, Phyllis M., and O'Meara, Patrick, eds. *AFRICA.* Bloomington: Indiana University Press, 1977.

McKay, Vernon. *Africa in World Politics.* New York: Harper and Row, 1963.

Mende, T. *From Aid to Re-Colonization: Lessons of a Failure.* New York: Pantheon Books, 1973.

Mitterrand, Général J. "La Place de l'action militaire extérieure dans la stratégie française." *Revue de defense nationale* 26 (June 1970).

Mittleman, James H. "Collective Decolonization and the UN Committee of 24." *Journal of Modern African Studies* 14 (1976): 41-64.

Mohammed, Duri. "Notes on the Common Market and Africa." In *Africa and the World.* Edited by Robert K. A. Gardiner, M. J. Anstee, and C. L. Patterson. Addis Ababa: Oxford University Press, 1970.

Morris, Colin. *Nationalism in Africa.* London: Edinburgh House Press, 1963.

Neves, Philip. *French-Speaking West Africa.* London: Oxford University Press, 1962.

236

Ngoue-Ngabissie, N. "Finances zone franc: les africains sont satisfaits." *Jeune Afrique* 509 (October 7, 1970).

Nielsen, Waldemar. *The Great Powers and Africa*. New York: Praeger Publishers, 1969.

Nkrumah, Kwame. *I Speak of Freedom*. London: Heinemann, 1961.

Nyerere, Julius K. *Freedom and Development: A Selection from Writings and Speeches, 1968-1973*. London: Oxford University Press, 1973.

Okumu, John. "Kenya's Foreign Policy." In *The Foreign Policies of African States*. Edited by Olajide Aluko. London: Hodder & Stoughton, 1977.

Okwudiba, Nnoli. *Self-Reliance and Foreign Policy in Tanzania: The Dynamics of the Diplomacy of a New State, 1961 to 1971*. New York: NOK Publishers, 1978.

Oliver R., and Fage, J. D. *A Short History of Africa*. Harmondsworth: Penguin Books, 1962.

Oloruntimehim, B. Lolatunji. "Senegambia-Mahmadou Lamine." In *West African Resistance*. Edited by Michael Crowder. New York: Africana Publishing Corporation, 1971.

Ormsby-Gore, W. G. M. (later Lord Harlech). *Developments and Opportunities in the Colonial Empire*. London: n.p., 1929.

Padelford, Norman J., and Emerson, Rupert. *Africa and the World Order*. New York: Praeger, 1964.

Phillips, Claude S. *The Development of Nigerian Foreign Policy*. Evanston, IL: Northwestern University Press, 1964.

Rivkin, Arnold. *Africa and the West: Elements of Free World Policy*. London: Thames and Hudson, 1962.

_____. *Africa and the European Common Market: A Perspective*. Denver: The University of Denver Press, 1963.

Roberts, Stephen H. *The History of French Colonial Policy, 1870-1925*. Hamden, Connecticut: Archon Books, 1963.

Robinson, Ronald, and Gallagher, John. *Africa and the Victorians: The Climax of Imperialism*. Garden City, NY: Doubleday and Company, Inc., 1968.

Ronen, Dov. *Dahomey: Between Tradition and Modernity*. Ithaca, NY: Cornell University Press, 1975.

Sarraut, Albert. *La Mise en valeur des colonies françaises*. Paris: Colin, 1923.

Senghor, Lépold-Sédar. "A Community of Free and Equal Peoples with the Mother Country." *Western World* 18 (Brussels: 1958).

Senghor, Lépold-Sédar. "West Africa in Evolution." *Foreign Affairs* 39. No. 2 (January 1961): 240-246.

Shepherd, George W., Jr. *Non-aligned Black Africa*. Massachusetts: D. C. Heath and Co., 1979.

_____. "Southern Rhodesia." *United Nations Review* (April 1964): 16-17.

Spero, Joan Edelman. *Dominance-Dependence Relationships: The Case of France and Gabon*. Ph.D. Dissertation, Columbia University, 1973.

Spero, Joan Edelman. *The Politics of International Economic Relations*. New York: St. Martin's Press, 1977.

Suret-Canale, Jean. *French Colonialism in Tropical Africa 1900-1945*. Translated by Till Gottheimer. New York: Pica Press, 1971.

Symonds, R. *The British and Their Successors*. London: Faber and Faber, 1966.

Thompson, Leonard. *France and Britain in Africa: Imperial Rivalry and Colonial Rule*. London: Yale University Press, 1971.

Thompson, Virginia, and Adloff, Richard. "French Economic Policy in Tropical Africa." In *Colonialism in Africa 1870-1960, Vol. 4, The Economics of Colonialism*. Edited by Peter Duignan and L. H. Gann. London: Cambridge University Press, 1975.

Thompson, Virginia, and Adloff, Richard. *Conflict in Chad*. Berkeley: University of California, 1981.

Wallerstein, Immanuel. *Africa: The Politics of Independence*. New York: Random House, 1971.

Wasserman, Gary. *Politics of Decolonization: Kenya, Europeans and the Land Issue*. London: Cambridge University Press, 1976.

Weinstein, Brian G. *Training Programs in France for African Civil Servants*. Boston: Boston University African Studies Program Development Research Center, 1964.

White, John. *The Politics of Foreign Aid*. New York: St. Martin's Press, 1974.

Whiteman, Kaye. "Pompidou and Africa: Gaullism and De Gaulle." *The World Today* 26. No. 6 (June 1970): 241-249.

Wilcox, Francis O., and Haviland, H. Field, Jr., eds. *The Atlantic Community: Progress and Prospects*. New York: Frederick A. Praeger, 1964.

Winslow, E. M. *The Pattern of Imperialism*. New York: Columbia University Press, 1948.

Zartman, William. *International Relations in the New Africa*. New Jersey: Prentice-Hall, Inc., 1966.

NEWSPAPERS AND PERIODICALS

Africa Confidential, Supplement to No. 24, 9 December 1966.

The Courier, 31 March 1975.

Le Figaro (Paris), 27-28 February 1960.

The Guardian, 3 September 1970.

Malawi Hansard, 11 January 1966.

Le Monde, 19 January 1967.

Le Monde, 16 December 1970.

Le Monde, 29 January 1972.

Le Monde, 22 July 1972.

New York Times, 8 March 1961.

The Observer (London), 7 March 1961.

The Observer (London), 30 August 1964.

The Observer (London), 12 December 1964.

Tanganyika Standard, dar-es-Salaam, 29 January 1964.

Time, 16 January 1984.

U.S. News and World Report, 13 May 1968.

Washington Post, 7 January 1973.

Washington Post, 6 January 1966.

West Africa, 25 July 1964.

West Africa, 2-8 January 1971.

West Africa, 16 April 1971.

West Africa, 21 April 1972.

West Africa, 23 January 1978.

West Africa, 22 November 1979.

West Africa, 1 May 1982.

West Africa, 31 May 1982.

West Africa, 27 June 1983.

OTHER SOURCES

Address on Togoland and Black Africa, Speeches and Press Conferences No. 85, New York: Ambassade de France, Service de Presse et d'Information, January 1957.

Anneé politique économique, sociale et diplomatique en France, 1964. Paris: Presses Universitaires de France, 1964.

Britain and Education in the Commonwealth. British Information Service, 1964.

La documentation Française, La Politique de Coopération avec les pays en voie de developpement. Paris, November 1964.

Europe, Common Market No. 2173, July 10, 1965, p. 3.

France, Aid and Cooperation, December 1962.

France, Constitution du 4 October, 1958, Title XII, Article 78.

France, Secrétariat Général du Gouvernment, Notes et études documentaires, no. 3330, October 25, 1966, La Coopération entre la France, l'Afrique Noire d'Expression Française et Madagascar.

French Economic Assistance in West and Equatorial Africa, "A Decade of Progress, 1948-1958."

Journal officiel de la République Française Textes d'Interét Général Communanté Accords Franco-Gabonais, November 1960, no. 60, 278S.OAU AHG/Res. 25/Rev. 1, 22 October 1965.

OAU AHG/Res. 25/Rev. 1, 22 October 1965.

OAU Doc. ECM/Res. 13, VI.

Overseas Development Institute. *British Aid*, vol. 2, *Government Finance*. London, 1964.

Overseas Development Institute. *British Aid*, vol. 5, *Colonial Development*. London, 1964.

Proceedings of UCTAD, Feb.-March 1968, Second Session, vol. 4, *Problems and Policies and Financing*.

Report of the Commission on Closer Union of the Dependencies in Eastern and Central Africa, Cmd. 3234 g 1949.

Speech on World Trade in Commodities, delivered by Prime Minister Harold Wilson to the Commonwealth Heads of Government Meeting in Kingston, Jamaica, May 1, 1975. British Information Service, Policy and Reference Division, 33/75.

The Yaoundé Convention, Articles 1-6.

Index

Houphouet-Boigny, Felix 17, 95,
110, 122, 132, 144, 146, 152.
Hull, Richard 4, 55, 60, 212.
Humanitarianism 7, 9.

I

Imperial economic preference 3,
7-8.
Imperialism defined 3.
Imperialism rationalize 3-4.
Import-export companies 44.
International Monetary Fund
(IMF) 125.
Intra-African Trade 57, 67, 226.
Investment Fund for Economic &
Social Development (FIDES)
83-5.
Investment incentive or
encouragement programs 88.
Ivory Coast 8, 17, 56, 60, 62, 65-6,
81, 84, 87, 95, 110, 111, 114,
119, 123, 130, 132, 144,
151-2, 154, 173, 182, 184,
197, 205, 210, 216-17, 219,
222, 224, 229.

J

July, Robert 11, 211.

K

Kenya 7, 8, 19, 22-3, 25, 79, 80, 87,
89, 92, 94, 111-12, 119, 125,
127-31, 154, 159, 161, 191,
203, 205.
Kenyatta, Jomo 19.
Khadafi, Muamar 188.
L

Lamine Mahmadon 6.
Landes, David S. 3.
Libya 187-88, 198.
Lomé Conventions 53, 100, 119,
203, 224.
Lugard, Lord, Frederick - The
Dual Mandate 8.

M

Mali 30, 49, 58, 63-6, 87, 90, 95,
98, 102, 114, 117, 119,
121-22, 135, 148, 152-53,
176, 182-83, 196, 212, 214,
217, 219.
Marx, Karl 7.
Menelik, Emperor 6.
Mittelman, James H. 20
Mitterrand Francois 148, 154, 219.
Monetary control 44, 47.
Morocco 57 (see note 53), 121,
197.
Multinational corporations 86.

N

Nationalization programs 87, 89,
94-5, 221.
Neo-colonialism 1, 28, 57, 65,
109-10, 122, 179, 189.
New International Economic
Order (NIEO) 132-33, 203.
(NIEO) 133, 203.
Niger River Basin Commission 31,
132.
Nigeria 19, 25, 31, 49, 50, 56, 59,
64, 66, 78, 87, 92-4, 107,
112, 116, 125,-27, 135,
159-60, 179, 191-92. 194,
203, 205, 208, 220, 226.
Nigerian Association Agreement
50.u
Nigeria's Enterprise Promotion
Decree 94.
Nkrumah, Kwame 17, 19, 21, 51,
64, 88, 110, 155, 163, 167,
192.
Nyerere, Julius 21 (see note 97),
163, 165, 167, 177, 193-94.

O

Organization of African Unity
(OAU) 152, 161, 170.
Organization Commune Africaine
Mauricienne (OCAM) 132,
226.

STUDIES IN AFRICAN ECONOMIC AND SOCIAL DEVELOPMENT

1. Richard Vengroff and Alan Johnston, **Decentralization and the Implementation of Rural Development in Senegal**

2. Olayiwola Abegunrin, **Economic Dependence and Regional Cooperation in Southern Africa: SADCC and South Africa in Confrontation**

3. Charles O. Chikeka, **Britain, France, and the New African States: A Study of Post-Independence Relationships, 1960-1985**

4. Daniel Teferra, **The Making and Economy of Ethiopia**

5. Santosh Saha, **A History of Agriculture in Liberia, 1822- 1970: Transference of American Values**

6. Santosh Saha, **A History of Agriculture in West Africa: A Guide to Information Sources**